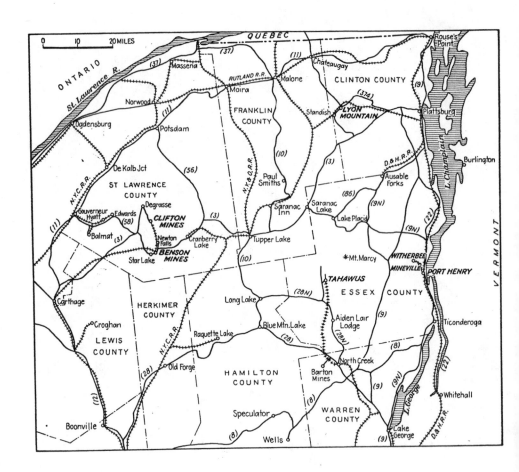

THROUGH THE LIGHT HOLE

LIGHT HOLE

A Saga of Adirondack Mines and Men

by

Patrick F. Farrell

North Country Books
Utica, New York

THROUGH THE LIGHT HOLE
A Saga of Adirondack Mines and Men

ISBN 0-952168-55-6
Printed in the United States of America

Library of Congress Cataloging-In-Publication Data

Farrell, Patrick F., 1918 - 1996
  Through the light hole : a saga of Adirondack mines and
men / by Patrick F. Farrell.
    p. cm.
  ISBN 0-925168-55-6 (alk. paper)
    1. Iron industry and trade—New York (State)—Adirondack
Mountains—History. 2. Steel industry and trade—New York
(State)—Adirondack Mountains—History. 3. Iron mines and
mining—New York (State)—Adirondack Mountains— His-
tory. 4. Adirondack Mountains (N.Y.)—Economic conditions.
5. Adirondack Mountains (N.Y.)—Social conditions. 6.
Adirondack Mountains (N.Y.)—History. I. Title.
HD9517.N54F37 1995
338.2'73'097475—dc20   94-38137
                                                   CIP

Cover Photo:
Joker Shaft steel headframe in 1908.
In later years it was called "Joker Light Hole."

Published by
NORTH COUNTRY BOOKS, INC.
311 Turner Street
Utica, New York 13501

This book is respectfully dedicated to

THE ADIRONDACK MINERS

To the Northern Wilderness Valley of Champlain,
For a new life and home, their forebears came,
From Mines of Cornwall, the Saar and Ukraine;
And Freiberg and Russia, and Ireland and Spain.
They were the vanguard who would train their sons,
When minerals were located and mines were won.

They ascended escarpments and examined outcrops;
The limestone, the gneisses, the gabbro and black rocks.
With hammers and picks they extracted lodestones.
As diggings flourished, they built their homes.
For decades to follow their discoveries expanded.
As the Nation's need grew, more ore was demanded.

The mines gained fame as their output grew,
And more exploration found veins that were new.
Cheever was first, but others were legion;
And mines named hamlets throughout the region.
There were Irondale, Hammondville, Palmer Hill Mountain;
Arnold Hill, Tahawus, Pilfershire and Lyon Mountain.

Mines of Mineville, six miles by Plank Road,
Overlooked the lake and valley below.
Here were Sanford, Twenty-One, Miller and Old Bed;
Joker, Bonanza, Lovers Hole and New Bed;
Fisher Hill, Sherman, O'Neil and Smith;
Humbug, Cook Shaft, Swamp and Cliff.

From cavernous pits by sledge, drill and blast,
They mined crude ore so iron could be cast;
By light of the wick lamp they toiled in the depths,
And fashioned pillars, drove drifts and the rest.
Their ore was raised with horse and whim,
By cable and skip over timber track to bin.

With forge fire and anvil they sharpened drill bits
That were made from ore they raised from the pits.
Timber for shoring, track and pump beams
Were cut from hills near the ore seams.
With ingenuity and skill they got work done,
And thus set a pattern for years to come.

For the hundreds who toiled in dark mine workings,
A common bond linked them to avoid danger lurking.
The ping of drills when struck by the sledge,
Had a tinkling sound heard far from the ledge.
The ore-laden skips made a rumbling noise,
And viewed from above seemed as mere toys.

With holes all drilled and loaded for blast
All men left, but the powderman last;
When fuses had burned, the blast erupted with a roar,
And another day's production lay on the mine floor.
With the skill of work, pride showed in their eyes,
As they came through the Light Hole and gazed at the sky.

The glow from furnace fires painted the heavens,
And showed them the worth of their mining endeavors.
As years became decades and then became scores,
They taught their sons skills as well as mine chores;
And their footsteps would follow for a century and more,
For this was the legacy of men who mined ore.

— P. F. F.

Contents

"I ride the open end of the ore skip near the bail. I hear the clatter of wheels on rail joints and the whine of track rolls spun by the fast moving cable. Ahead, beyond the range of my cap lamp, there is only blackness. Finally a small speck that is the Light Hole appears, increasing in size as the skip rushes upward and passes through to surface and the full light of day."

P. F. F.

Preface

Through a half century working in the Adirondack iron mining industry I have from the beginning felt the strong sense of history and achievement that sustained Adirondack iron mining for one hundred and fifty years. For every successful venture there were many failures. For each fortune made, many were lost. However, this has been the pattern throughout the growth of the American free enterprise system.

Furnace and forge ruins; cave-like mine openings with rock dumps sprouting birch trees; building foundations, some by abandoned dirt roads and nearly covered by vegetation; all give evidence of a vigorous industrial activity that once contributed to the economy of northern New York State. Few artifacts remain to portray the struggle and hardships endured by the early pioneers in wresting a livelihood and rearing their families in this then remote area with its severe Adirondack winters. With little capital and meager knowledge or experience to guide them, these men labored against terrific odds and, by trial and error, created an iron industry, solved problems and devised mining and iron making methods down through the years that would be accepted and applied in other mining districts throughout the world.

For more than a hundred years following the War of Independence, there was a steady flow of immigrants to the Champlain Valley and Adirondacks. They were from many nations and of diverse tongue, but shared a common bond in seeking a better life. They came from France, Italy, Poland, Lithuania, Russia, Rumania, Hungary, Ireland, Wales and Spain. They found new customs in this land and many were handicapped by the language barrier. Most were poor and uneducated. By their labors land was cleared, crops were planted, roads were built, ore was mined and they made the developing nation grow. The Adirondack iron mining industry was a melting pot of these nationalities. They became skilled miners, millmen and furnacemen. And, by their hard labors they made the mining ventures successful.

My grandfather, James Farrell, came from Ireland in the 1870's and found employment in the mines at Fisher Hill. He sent for Mary Ryan Farrell and two small sons whom he had left in Ireland. She arrived in New York with her children, including a third son born aboard ship off

vii

Newfoundland. How strange the New World must have seemed to her with no one to meet her. With the characteristic determination of those immigrants, she found her way to the Champlain Valley and lived her life in Mineville, bearing four more sons and four daughters. My father was her youngest son.

This book is not a history in the truest sense of the word, nor is it a technical treatise. Rather, it is a response to many queries I have received over the years from students, teachers, engineers, geologists, museum personnel, historians, former miners and their families. Therefore it was necessary to describe the operations in some detail without being too technical, and at the same time include a glimpse of demographic and social conditions of the times.

I was fortunate to be in a position to collect information over many years that would be useful for my purpose. In addition, during those years I worked for and with managers, engineers, superintendents, foremen and miners. Conversations with them and some elder acquaintances over the years furnished some of the "painted peg" in the text.

To maintain the continuity of the story I wish to tell, some lengthy detailed descriptions of what, why and how certain things were done or occurred are given in the proper appendix noted throughout the text.

Through the Light Hole covers a span of 230 years from the initial discovery of iron ore in the region to the end of mining and plant dismantlement in the Town of Moriah. During that period ore from the mines of Moriah contributed to America's part in all conflicts from the capture of Fort Ticonderoga and the Naval Battle of Valcour on Lake Champlain through the Vietnam War. Mineville ore was used in the stainless steel on the nose cone of the first vehicle America put into space.

I researched the early history of the region at the Carnegie Library in Boise, Idaho and at the Crandall Library in Glens Falls, New York. I perused the writings of Frank S. Witherbee. I drew upon articles published in *The American Railroad Journal*; publications by the Delaware and Hudson Railroad Company; *The Engineering and Mining Journal; The Explosives Engineer* magazine; *Mining Engineering Magazine*; technical papers of the American Institute of Mining Engineers; publications of the U. S. Bureau of Mines; *The History of Essex County, New York* by Watson in 1869 and by Smith in 1885. My personal files furnished data collected by me over the years on production and operations of Port Henry Iron Ore Company, Witherbee Sherman and Company and Republic Steel Corporation.

Throughout the narrative the cyclical nature of the iron ore industry, and the impact of foreign ore and steel dumped into the American market will be apparent. These economic forces have continued from pre-

Revolutionary War days to the present time.

My own experience and knowledge gained has been primarily in the Mineville Iron District plus visits to mine and plant operations in several states, Canada and Sweden. This book will reflect those experiences and occasionally touch on other areas that may be interlocked with the story I believe should be told. Mostly, however, this book is an attempt to clearly portray the character and continuity of this industry as I studied it, and as I lived it, with a glimpse of some of the men who made its success possible, and thus shaped the times.

—P. F. F.

Following page:
Erecting ladders in an open stope at Old Bed Mine, 1950's.

1

The Adirondack Mountain region of northern New York State is bounded on the east by the Champlain Valley, with steeply rising foothills inland to the High Peaks area. To the north and west the mountains recede to rolling plains approaching the Canadian border and the St. Lawrence Valley. To the south the slope is toward the Mohawk Valley and the cities of Glens Falls, Johnstown, Utica and Rome. This mountain region embraces nearly ten thousand square miles with many rugged peaks, including forty-six over four thousand feet above sea level. There are more than two hundred clear lakes fed by rushing mountain streams, and all of these features offer scenic vistas unmatched on the North American continent.

My own appreciation of the Adirondack region and its wilderness area goes back more than a half century to those youthful years when my companions and I hunted, fished and climbed mountain peaks in that primitive forest land. One of my best memories of that era was a ten-day hiking trip into a high mountain range. I recall it vividly, not for the miles we hiked nor the mountains we climbed, but for the forest itself; my sudden realization in those surroundings, was the insignificance of any single being in the overall scheme of human events and time.

During three days of incessant rain and fog we had camped at a leanto located in a notch between two high peaks, and our main activity had been gathering and drying wood over a continuous fire for warmth during the bitter cold nights. On the morning of the fourth day rain ceased and the fog lifted, exposing the broad valley far below that stretched to the north. The pinnacle of the highest peak was still shrouded in fog as we shouldered our packs and began the steep ascent.

Above the timberline a muddy trail through scrub growth ended on slippery barren rock, and we carefully picked our way to the summit. We rested there, watching the fog drift and disperse into scattered clouds. After a time the sun burst through, burning off the remaining haze. We could see mountain peaks, lakes and forested valleys as far as forty miles in any direction. It was then, sitting on that high mountaintop, that I suddenly became fully conscious of the consummate beauty of God's great ageless panorama that stretched before me. And the

1

vision from that lofty summit is as clear to me today as it was those long years ago.

Historically, the geologic formation of the Adirondack area embraces a period of from one to possibly three billion years, with nature's forces ever continuing to record minute changes with the passing centuries. During the long eras of geologic time, eruptive, receding, eroding, chemical, metamorphic and glacial processes on and within the earth's crust formed the mountain region as it appears today with an abundance of mineral wealth locked within. Of commercial value there are vast ore reserves of iron, talc, zinc, ilmenite, vanadium, wollastonite, graphite, garnet, and rare earths plus an inestimable supply of rocks suited to the building trades.

The eastern area and along both shores of Lake Champlain was a land of conflict for two hundred years following Champlain's discovery in 1609. Indian tribes, French, English and finally the American colonists fought to control the lake as an avenue of military movement and commerce. The valley has often been called "The Warpath of Nations."

Along both sides of the Champlain Valley the great forests of pine, hemlock, spruce and hardwoods touched the shores of the lake and the earliest settlements appeared near the vantage points and fortresses which controlled the valley during the French and Indian Wars and the American War of Independence.

It is impossible to document the initial discovery and use of iron ore in the Champlain Valley but reference has been made to "iron sand" in the writings of Peter Kalm, a Swedish naturalist who visited Fort St. Frederic at Crown Point in 1749. Kalm had been sent to North America by the Swedish Academy of Science to obtain seed material for new herbs and trees hardy enough to thrive in Swedish soil. He arrived in Philadelphia in 1748 and explored Pennsylvania, New Jersey and New York, collecting and shipping the seeds back to Sweden. In 1749 he headed north to French controlled Lake Champlain and Canada. On July 2 he arrived at Fort St. Frederic where he was welcomed by the French governor; he remained a guest at the fortress until July 19.

Kalm's work was not confined to horticulture. His interests included architecture, animal life, minerals and ore deposits, American history and antiquity, Indian dialects, fortresses and even the health of the American people. He carefully studied all aspects of the fortress and its environs including the lake shore. He found some black sand along the lake shore which was attracted by a magnet and commented, "I cannot determine the origin of the black or steel-colored sand, for it was not known here whether there were mines in the neighborhood or not. But I am rather inclined to believe they may be found in these parts, as they are common in different parts of Canada, and as this sand is found on the shores of almost all the lakes and rivers in Canada, though not in equal quantities." At the time Kalm made this observation, the only known ironworks in the French controlled region was near Three Rivers in Quebec.

Kalm also reported crossing the lake by canoe to the west shore and climbing one of the high mountains, noting that there were some much higher at a greater distance inland. Returning to the shore he found the lake too rough to cross by canoe, and walked along the shore around the bay about "seven English miles" to the fortress, again noting the black iron sand.

I find it worth speculation to consider that the mountain Kalm climbed was Cheney Mountain east of Bartlett Brook. Looking from the Crown Point fortress area to the northwest, Cheney Mountain and Bald Peak offer the best unobstructed views of the surrounding area for many miles. The elevation of Cheney Mountain is 1,364 feet above sea level and four miles straight-line distant from St. Frederic. The summit is about a mile and one half hike from the lake shore, and that lake shore starting point is about seven miles walking distance along the shoreline around the bay to Fort St. Frederic. Bald Peak, although several hundred feet higher than Cheney Mountain, is six miles straight-line distant from St. Frederic, a two and one half mile hike from the lake shore, and a comparable shoreline walking distance of about nine miles to the fortress.

If indeed Kalm was on Cheney Mountain on July 16, 1749, little did he realize future iron mines were close at hand. Two and one half miles northwest lay the great Sanford and Twenty-One ore beds that would be discovered seventy-five years hence, and still later the Pilfershire ore bed that lay beneath him at the foot of the western slope of Cheney Mountain near Bartlett Brook. Although Kalm came close to the great iron ore deposits which would later be mined, his published notation of the possibility of iron mines not too distant from Fort St. Frederic no doubt foreshadowed the discovery of iron ore near the western shore of Lake Champlain.

Fort St. Frederic, built by the French in 1731, was a strategic bastion for control of the Champlain Valley. In 1755-56 the French position was enhanced by the construction of Fort Carillon at Ticonderoga. It was here in 1758 that British General James Abercrombie, with a force of 15,000 men, was defeated by a French force of 4,000 under command of Marquis Louis de Montcalm. The following year, on July 31, 1759, as the British under command of General Jeffrey Amherst advanced from

Lake George, the French, acting on instructions from French Governor Marquis de Vaudreuil, abandoned Forts Carillon and St. Frederic, blowing up the latter fortress as they retreated to Canada.

On the heels of the departing French, Amherst occupied the fortresses at Ticonderoga and Crown Point. Rather than rebuild St. Frederic he decided to build a new and larger fortress at Crown Point. The labors of three thousand men and ten million dollars were expended on the project and it was never really completed. Its major strategic importance lessened when hostilities with the French ended following British victories in Canada.

With the end of one hundred fifty years of French domination in the region and the onset of British control, settlements began along the Champlain Valley. Philip Skene established Skenesborough (now Whitehall) in 1761. Benjamin Porter settled and built a lumber mill at Porter's Mills (now Port Henry) in 1766. Other settlements began along both east and west shores of the lake.

South of French-controlled Lake Champlain and New France, the early American colonies under the British had not been allowed to manufacture many products. The British government adopted this policy so that the colonies would provide a ready market for British goods. British manufacturers approved smelting of iron ore in the colonies as a source of iron, but laws were passed to prevent colonial production of hollowware and other finished products. The colonies were thus limited to producing raw iron for refinement by British manufacturers. These laws also applied to textiles and other goods. In 1774, the year before the American Revolution, Britain forbade the importation of tools to the colonies that could be used for producing finished goods. These laws were not effective as the colonies were sparsely populated and goods of necessity were produced for local markets.

It was known that there was abundant iron ore in the American colonies before they were actually settled. The ore and contiguous fuel were developed because of the lack of necessities such as hollowware and tools rather than as a profit-making business venture. Early iron mining was principally in the bog ores of eastern Massachusetts, along the New Jersey coast and in the rock ores which supplied furnaces from the Connecticut River in a circle to the lower Hudson River, through northern New Jersey and eastern Pennsylvania southward. In 1653 both bog ores and rock ores were used at Lynn, Massachusetts. Successful iron manufacture in that colony was enhanced by the availability of water transportation.

The colonial white English population was estimated at 25,000 by 1640; tripled to 75,000 by 1660; increased to 200,000 by 1688 and to

250,000 by 1700. This number doubled by 1730 and reached 1,000,000 by 1745. By 1775 the colonial white American population was two and one quarter million plus one half million black slaves. This rapid population growth increased the demand for tools and implements for clearing land in settling this vast new country, and gave impetus to a rapid growth in the native iron manufacturing capability.

The approaching war with England forced the colonies to manufacture arms and munitions for their own defense. Saltpeter works were developed in Rhode Island, a gunlock factory in Maryland and Virginia produced salt and other war supplies. The furnaces of New Jersey and Massachusetts supplied armament for Washington's Continental Army.

At Skenesborough, Philip Skene built the first ironworks on Lake Champlain consisting of a forge with four fires and two hammers. He secured ore from sources near his settlement and from a 600-acre patent granted to him in 1761 by the Crown in the Cheever area north of Port Henry. Here, ore outcropped close to the margin of the lake and Skene built boats for transporting the ore to his forge. It was one of these ore boats heading up the lake that Ethan Allen commandeered for crossing from Vermont to capture Fort Ticonderoga from the British on May 10, 1775. During this same period, colonial forces also captured Crown Point and Skenesborough.

Following capture of the fortresses, Benedict Arnold was placed in command at Crown Point. His regimental book recorded that on June 13, 1775 he sent Skene's Negroes by boat to dig ore, and on the sixteenth sent to Raymond's Mills for them and for timber and provisions. Raymond's Mills was at Cole's Bay, south of Westport, and Skene's Negroes were no doubt digging ore at Skene's Patent in the Cheever area.

Concurrent with Arnold's action, by letters in June 1775, General Schuyler reported available boats, lumber and milling capacity along the lake with specific mention of Porter's and Carr's Mills. These logistics were in preparation for defensive and offensive operations for control of the Champlain Valley, the gateway to the heart of the American colonies. For that purpose forces were hurriedly marshalled to build a fleet of ships at Skenesborough, to be outfitted at Ticonderoga for rendezvous at Crown Point. Skene's ironworks, utilizing iron ore from the Cheever area, produced the necessary fittings.

This is the first record of mining in the Town of Moriah. Although slave labor was used, Skene is reported to have freed his slaves after the war and settled them at Black Point in Ticonderoga.

By August 18, 1776, the new American Fleet was ready to contest the British for control of the lake and access to the colonies. The fleet consisted of the sloop *Enterprise*; schooners *Liberty*, *Royal Savage* and *Revenge*; row galleys *Congress*, *Washington*, *Trumbull*, *Gates* and *Lee*; gondolas *Philadelphia*, *New York*, *Jersey*, *Providence*, *New Haven*, *Spit-fire*, *Boston* and *Connecticut*. Thirteen of the vessels had been constructed and one remodeled at Skenesborough, the *Revenge* was built at Ticonderoga, and the *Enterprise* and *Royal Savage* had been captured earlier from the British.

Arnold, chosen by General Gates to command, set sail from Crown Point on August 20 and patrolled the lake northward. His force consisted of one sloop, three schooners and five gunboats carrying fifty-five guns, seventy swivels and a complement of three hundred ninety-five men. On September 23 he anchored in the channel between Valcour Island and the mainland. Here he was joined by additional galleys, building his fleet to fifteen vessels. This placed all but two ships of the small American navy at Valcour.

On October 10 the British Fleet of thirty-one vessels, heavily armed and manned by seven hundred veteran seamen and a corps of artillery under command of General Carleton, sailed south toward Crown Point, the supposed location of Arnold. As the fleet passed Valcour Island on the main lake, Arnold's concealed ships were observed, and on October 11 the battle was joined.

Arnold fought desperately and, with his ships severely damaged, inflicted heavy loss and damage on the British. His schooner *Royal Savage* was grounded and burned. He transferred his flag to the *Congress*, continuing to lead the colonial attack. At dusk the British withdrew and, in darkness, Arnold's remaining ships managed to slip by the British and head for Crown Point. They were overtaken and the battle was resumed on October 13. Outgunned and outmanned, Arnold grounded and burned his heavily damaged ships on the Vermont shore and, according to legend, was the last man to drop from the bowsprit of his burning vessel. Having recovered small arms from the ships, he led his party overland through the woods to Crown Point. Here he found three of his less damaged ships that had managed to escape from the British fleet. Thus ended the first American naval battle, the Battle of Lake Champlain; it was in this conflict that iron from the mines of Moriah first went to war.

Although Arnold's fleet was virtually destroyed, damage to the British delayed their timetable for conquest of the Champlain Valley route through the colonies. The colonials retreated from Crown Point to Ticonderoga and Carleton occupied Crown Point on October 14. He lacked the strength to attack Ticonderoga and withdrew to Canada in November before the onset of winter.

Porter's Mills was destroyed, probably during Carleton's withdrawal or during the following years of British-American conflict. After the war, Porter and Robert Lewis of Albany rebuilt and operated the mills. In 1824 the Porter and Lewis property, including the mills and 4,000 acres of land, was acquired by Major James Dalliba and John D. Dickerson of Troy.

2

Development of settlements and commerce moved forward rapidly in the Champlain Valley following the War of Independence. In 1788 a new county was formed in northern New York called Clinton, and included the present Essex, Clinton and the eastern part of Franklin counties. This new county was divided into four towns; Champlain, Plattsburgh, Willsboro and Crown Point. The village of Plattsburgh, with a population of 250, was the county seat and it was necessary for many residents to travel seventy miles to transact business or attend court. The Town of Crown Point included the present towns of Minerva, Newcomb, Ticonderoga, Schroon, Crown Point, Moriah, North Hudson, Elizabethtown and a part of Keene. This one town embraced an area of approximately nine hundred square miles.

The present bounds of Essex County were established in 1789 with the county seat located in the village of Essex. County court and other business was conducted in a blockhouse that had been erected two years earlier for protection against Indian uprisings. The population of the county at the time of the subdivision was eighty-five hundred including fifty-eight slaves. In 1811 the county seat was transferred to Elizabeth-town with business transacted in temporary quarters on about the site of the present county buildings. In 1824 the first part of the present brick county government complex was built.

Clinton County, adjoining the northern border of Essex, bounded on the east by Lake Champlain and stretching north to Canada, shared a concurrent early development with Essex County. In 1798, Zephaniah Platt and associates, who had founded Plattsburgh, erected and operated an iron forge at the mouth of the Saranac River. They secured ore from Skene's ore bed under terms of a concession granted them by the State of New York in 1785.

During the final decade before 1800 several forges were built along both sides of the lake, including four in Addison and two in Chittenden counties in Vermont. Most of the ore used in these forges was obtained from the Skene Ore Bed. Noah Tomlinson, Levi and Samuel Cole, and Liberty Newton operated forges at Ticonderoga during this period uti-lizing the water power of the upper and lower falls of the LeChute River.

The forge, with its origin in antiquity, is the oldest facility used in the manufacture of iron. It is probable that the first iron brought to a metallic state resulted by contact of the glowing coals of a primitive savage's fire with the heavy stones containing iron ore, causing the iron to deoxidize. This would differ from any object he had previously seen and he would determine that it resulted from the burning action of wood on certain heavy stones. He found he could pound the iron into many useful shapes. It only followed naturally that he would improve his fire by putting it and these stones on the weather side of some bank with an opening toward the prevailing wind.

The coals which deoxidized the iron ore in the primitive forge fire would contain some lumps carburized so far as to turn them into cast iron, and some only hard enough to convert them into steel, strong and very useful in its unhardened state. Thus it is almost certain that much of the earliest iron was in fact steel. How soon after man learned he could beat cold iron and steel into useful shapes, that he learned to forge it while hot, is hard to conjecture. Because iron would have been so easily made by prehistoric and even primeval man, and would be useful to him, it is not surprising that Tubal Cain, the sixth in descent from Adam (Genesis 4:22) was "an artificer of brass and iron in every form." I consider him to be the first Ironmaster of record.

The Iron Age was the third period of prehistoric times, following the Stone and Bronze Ages. In some portions of the world, such as islands of the South Pacific, interior of Africa and parts of North and South America, civilization passed directly from the Stone to the Iron Age. In Egypt, Chaldea, Assyria and China the Iron Age reaches back perhaps 4,000 years before the Christian Era. Iron was in general use in Northern Europe long before the invasion of Caesar. For convenience we can classify the history of iron manufacture into three periods; wrought iron, cast iron and molten steel; recognizing that in the second and third periods the earlier processes continued in use. The first period began in extremely remote times, the second in the fourteenth century, and the third with the invention of the Bessemer Process in 1856.

Iron manufacturing in the Town of Moriah was, from the beginning, based on blast furnace operations, and the only notable forge of record was located at Forge Hollow, near the Sherman race track. Iron manufacturing in other areas of the Champlain Valley, following discovery and development of ore deposits, utilized the forge. The mines of Crown Point and Lyon Mountain became large early producers of forge or bloomery iron but in subsequent years converted to blast furnace operations. The mines in the AuSable district produced forge iron in large tonnages until their final shutdown in the late 1800's. Ore from the mines of Moriah was shipped to many of the early forges such as those in Skenesborough, Ticonderoga and Vermont during early development of the iron industry. Reflecting on the lack of productive forges in the Town of Moriah in favor of blast furnaces in those early times, Frank Witherbee speculated that the lack of abundant water power may have been a contributing factor. However, these two basic methods of iron manufacture—the forge and the blast furnace—spurred development and growth of the iron industry along Lake Champlain, extending westward to the Lyon Mountain and AuSable iron districts of Clinton County and to the Sanford Lake region in the Essex County wilderness.

Early forges in the Champlain Valley were patterned after those long previously developed in Catalonia, Spain. Some were built not only to supply the immediate area, but to make bar iron for the outside market. In general this was the type built at Roth's Forge in North Hudson, the Split Rock Forge at Elizabethtown, the Kingdom Forge on Black Brook, the forge at Forge Hollow in Moriah, the more refined forges at Ticonderoga and Crown Point, and much later at the larger and more productive forges at Arnold Hill and at Belmont on the outlet of Chateaugay Lake.

The typical Catalan forge furnace, in which iron was made direct from ore, was an open hearth about two and one-half feet by three feet, with a stack about twenty feet high to carry off the gas. A bellows or a trompe, in which water falling some twenty-five feet induced an air current, furnished the blast. To a charcoal fire, stimulated by the blast, ore and charcoal were added alternately in small quantities until a batch of iron called a "loupe," weighing about three hundred pounds, was made. This usually took about three hours and was a very expensive process.

The "loupe," in a pasty state, was pried loose, then lifted from the furnace with great tongs and taken to a trip hammer where it was forged into a "bloom," or billet, about five inches square and from two to six feet long, depending on market requirements. Because the heat of the fire could not be kept constant, billets produced from forges were not uniform, even when made by the same workmen.

The blast furnace was an outgrowth of the forge. As the size of the early forge was increased for greater capacity, the length of the stack increased, and with more blowing capacity provided by the use of water power, greater contact occurred between the ore and fuel, carburizing the metal and turning it into cast iron. It became so fusible that it melted and, running together in a single molten mass, freed itself mechanically from the "gangue," as the minerals mixed with ore are called. This improvement in freeing the iron from the gangue and permitting iron to be poured in a molten state, led to the casting of iron into useful shapes. By this method ornamental iron castings were made in England in the fourteenth century, and in the sixteenth century cannons weighing three tons each were cast.

Early blast furnaces were constructed of stone and brick, shaped like a truncated pyramid, and usually located at the foot of a hillside so that a bridge could be easily built from the hillside to the top of the furnace to facilitate dumping the fuel, ore and flux to charge the furnace. This type of construction can still be observed at the ruins of the Colburn furnace west of Moriah Center, the Fletcherville furnace on the west side of the road leading from Mineville to North Pond and the more preserved Adirondack Iron Company furnace at Tahawus.

As settlers flocked to the Champlain Valley, timber and forest industries thrived. Great rafts of logs and lumber were floated through the lake north to Canada for shipment to England and Europe. The abundant hardwoods were harvested for conversion to charcoal for the burgeoning iron industry and as land became cleared, agriculture thrived. With the opening of the Champlain Canal in 1823 water traffic began to move through Whitehall to the Albany, Troy and New York City markets. Shipbuilding became an important industry at Ticonderoga where barges were built for transporting ore and lumber to these new markets.

A tract of land was granted to John Williams in 1788, adjoining the south bounds of the Skene Ore Bed Patent. This Williams Patent was sometimes called the Rogers Ore Bed and embraces the Cheever mine workings. The close proximity to Skene's Patent suggests that early mining by Skene and others could have removed ore from the Williams Patent. Historical accounts state that ore was known to have been taken from that location in 1804, and known to exist prior to that time as it outcropped and was clearly visible. In 1820 Charles Fisher leased the property, and a few years later it came into the hands of John Coates who owed funds to Dr. Abijah Cheever, guardian for some minor children. Either in payment of the loan or as security, Coates transferred title to Dr. Cheever and the property became known thereafter as Cheever. Ore had been produced in a small way with some shipments through the newly completed barge canal to a new U.S. Government arsenal at West Troy. Here quality of the ore attracted the attention of Major James Dalliba, an ordnance officer attached to the arsenal.

As a young man, James Dalliba was appointed to the newly formed United States Military Academy at West Point and became the 61st graduate of the Academy in 1811. He served during the War of 1812, seeing action at Brownstown near Detroit and in the battles of Erie and Lyon's Creek. He became a prisoner of war and was exchanged in 1813. He then served at various military posts on ordnance duty, the last being the new West Troy, New York Arsenal. He attained the rank of Major.

Major Dalliba resigned from the army in 1824 and in that year formed a partnership with John D. Dickerson of Troy. Having been impressed with the Cheever ore used in ordnance manufacture at Troy, they thought it would be more efficient to build a furnace near the source of ore and ship the pig iron rather than the bulkier ore to market. To achieve their goals they purchased the Porter and Lewis property, including the settlement called Lewis Mills on the west shore of Lake Champlain.

Major Dalliba had married Susan Huntington in 1815 and they lived with their three small children at the Barnes Home at Chimney Point (on the Vermont side of the present Crown Point Champlain Bridge) while he travelled by canoe back and forth across the lake to supervise the building of the furnace and his home, Dalliba House. When they moved

Dalliba House, built in 1824-25 by Major James Dalliba when he built the first blast furnace at Port Henry on the west shore of Lake Champlain.

into their new home in 1825, Major Dalliba changed the name of Lewis Mills to Port Henry, in honor of his wife's uncle, Henry Huntington, with whom he had formed a lasting friendship.

The Dalliba furnace was small, capable of producing fifteen to eighteen tons of pig iron per week for shipment to Troy. Ore for the furnace was secured from the Cheever mine and from the Dalliba, or Lee mine as it was later known. This latter mine was about three quarters of a mile from the furnace and just east of the present Stone Street on the outskirts

Colburn Furnace built in 1848. Early 1900's photo.

Fletcherville Furnace built in 1865 and operated through 1874. Photo in 1973 of the furnace ruins.

of Port Henry Village. In 1827 the Dalliba furnace became a stove and hollowware plant. This was in response to the growing demand for stoves to replace fireplaces for home heating and cooking. A furnace for that same purpose was built in Ticonderoga in 1840 by John Porter.

Major Dalliba died at his home in Port Henry on October 9, 1832 at 46 years of age. Although he spent only eight years initiating the iron industry in Moriah, his activities as its first ironmaster blazed a trail for others to follow who would build successive furnaces that would redden the night skies over the valley for more than a hundred years.

Following the death of James Dalliba the furnace was acquired by Stephen Keyes who then conveyed it to Lansing, Powell and Tarbell in 1834. In 1836 Tarbell sold his interest to Lansing and Powell who rebuilt or replaced the Dalliba furnace and resumed production of pig iron. George Goff bought the furnace in 1838 and in that same year conveyed it to Horace Gray who had also, in 1838, purchased the Cheever property from Dr. Cheever for $5,000. This transaction led to the formation in May 1840 of the Port Henry Iron Company "for the purpose of manufacturing iron in all its branches in the County of Essex." Horace Gray, George W. Goff, Francis H. Jackson, James Jackson and Ralph W. Crooker constituted the corporate body.

The capital stock of the Port Henry Iron Company was seventy thousand dollars with authority to increase it to one hundred and fifty thousand dollars. Horace Gray was chosen president and George W. Goff was named superintendent. Mr. Gray transferred his interest in the furnace and Cheever ore bed to the newly formed furnace company. F. H. Jackson, named clerk and treasurer, was also appointed with Horace Gray and Ralph Crooker to a committee of directors to manage the corporation. With these organizational matters completed, the capital stock of seventy thousand dollars was subscribed at one hundred dollars per share by October 1840.

At the annual meeting of stockholders of the Port Henry Iron Company in 1843, S. H. Witherbee was elected a director, replacing George Goff. Others who served as directors during the following four years included Robert Hooper, William Coffin, William Bullard and Nathaniel Francis. Most of those named became involved during ensuing years with other Adirondack furnace and mining properties.

In April 1845 the Port Henry Iron Company leased the furnace and Cheever ore bed to Horace Gray. In 1847 Mr. Gray built and put into production another furnace with an eight to ten ton daily output. Also added to one of the casting houses was a four-ton cupola furnace. Later that same year Mr. Gray encountered financial difficulties and his business ventures failed.

3

By 1800 the American Frontier had advanced from the Atlantic Coast States beyond the Alleghenies, and the westward movement was on. During the next three decades the frontier was extended to Louisiana and along the Mississippi north to the Great Lakes. It was an agricultural migration, preceded only by trappers and traders. In the course of this advance, lumbering and mining were established where timber and minerals were found.

Farm implements, wagons and utensils, necessary requirements for the westward moving pioneers, gave impetus to the iron industry in the Champlain Valley. With transportation greatly improved by completion of the barge canal system, the number of forges and furnaces increased as mines were developed to furnish ore. The rugged mountain terrain west of Lake Champlain in Essex County was a vast unmapped wilderness area and only the river valleys and mountain passes offered access to the interior.

By order of Simon DeWitt, Surveyor General of New York, a tract of unappropriated land in Essex County, later called the Iron Ore Tract, in the present towns of Moriah, Elizabethtown, Westport and Lewis, was surveyed and laid out into 234 lots during the years 1810 and 1811 by Silas D. Kellogg, Deputy Surveyor. The completed report was filed by the surveyor general on March 11, 1812. This became known as the Kellogg Survey.

During the course of the survey the compass was affected rather strongly on certain lots to the extent that Kellogg recorded in his field notes the presence of iron ore. In remarks on the description of bounds for Lot 21 he wrote: "This is a middling good lot, well watered. A road runs through it. Timber beech, maple, birch, hemlock. Many places on this lot have the appearance of iron ore. Price per acre $1.50." He also noted on Lot 23: "This lot descends southeast, is not very well watered, soil light and sandy. Timber short, consists of maple, birch, hemlock and spruce. In the west end of this lot I think there is iron ore in abundance. Price per acre $1.10." These lots were about six miles distant and eleven hundred feet above Lake Champlain in an unsettled area remote from transportation.

In the spring of 1824 on Lot 25 of the Iron Ore Tract, owned by D. E. Sanford, and adjoining Lots 21 and 23, a plow turning a furrow exposed iron ore and the discovery caused great interest that summer. Harry Sherman and Elijah Bishop proposed to join Mr. Sanford in exploring Lot 25, and each paid him one hundred dollars for which each received an undivided one quarter interest. They immediately started operations near the northeast corner, and ore was discovered one foot below the surface. Other places nearby were explored with the same results. As their efforts continued they soon learned they had discovered the outcrop of a large ore vein but they had no concept of its magnitude. This discovery, later referred to as the Sanford or Old Bed Deposit, proved to be the outcrop of the major ore structure that would be mined for a century and a half.

Jeramiah Cook, owner of Lot 23, noting the development underway in 1824 on Lot 25 by Sanford, Sherman and Bishop, began searching for ore near his boundary line with Lot 25. He sold a one-half interest to Solomon and Hiram Everest for $200. An excavation was started and shares in the venture as small as one-sixteenth were sold for $250. The ore on Lot 23 was the eastern continuation of the Sanford or Old Bed ore discovered on Lot 25.

Jonas Reed and Elias Smith of Moriah, and Allan Smith of Addison, Vermont had purchased Lot 21 of the Iron Ore Tract from the original owners for a nominal sum, and in 1829 ore was discovered by digging a shaft about twelve feet deep. A one-half interest in the property was sold by Allan Smith, and Sanford, Bishop and Sherman acquired a substantial portion to curb competition with their holdings on Lot 25, giving in consideration 500 tons of Old Bed ore in the ground. This equaled about $250.

In the earliest stages of development on Lots 23 and 25 some Old Bed ore was shipped to bloomery forges in Ticonderoga. In 1834 this ore was tried in the blast furnace at Port Henry but for some unknown reason in the furnace operation it did not produce satisfactory iron. I suspect that the changes in ownership and management of the furnace at that time were contributing factors in the failure to produce good iron.

Francis H. Jackson had purchased the Sisco Farm in Westport and in 1845 applied his experience gained at Port Henry in building a furnace at Westport. The furnace became known as the Sisco or Jackson furnace. Ores from within Westport were mixed with hematite from Vermont and Cheever ore from Moriah. Ore from the Goff mine, part of the Skene Patent north of Cheever mine, was also reportedly used. In 1847 Mr. Jackson purchased 20,000 tons of Sanford Old Bed ore. This was the largest single order for Old Bed ore to that time and high quality iron was produced, proving the worth of Old Bed ore.

While transactions affecting blast furnace ownership and iron manufacturing were underway, the search for and development of iron ore in the town of Moriah continued in anticipation of a growing demand. Harry Sherman, D. E. Sanford and Elijah Bishop had operated the Sanford pit with small production. In 1846 they sold the Sanford pit to John A. Lee, Eliphalet Hall and George Sherman who formed the firm of Lee, Hall and Sherman. Sanford had also discovered the New Bed deposit in the southwest corner of Lot 24 in 1844, and this was included in the 1846 sale to Lee, Hall and Sherman.

In the fall of 1845 Nathaniel Storrs, who operated a mercantile establishment in Moriah, became interested in the possibilities of iron ore in Lot 21. He observed the holes the owners had dug and the extent of ore that had been taken out that past summer. He dug some prospect holes and spent considerable time studying the magnetic attraction with a compass. He became satisfied there was a substantial amount of ore on Lot 21. As ownership of Lot 21 was widely held, Storrs negotiated with the various owners: John W. Wood, the sons of Jonas Reed, Jeramiah Cook and D. E. Sanford. He determined he could acquire the whole interest for about $1,200 but was unable to commit his own funds without jeopardizing his business in Moriah. He therefore decided to approach an old friend and backer for many years, Mr. A. J. Rousseau, a grocery merchant in Troy.

Storrs travelled to Troy and discussed with Rousseau the prospect for developing an ore bed. He related his own personal investigations of the property and the probable purchase price. He proposed, and Rousseau accepted, that Rousseau furnish the necessary funds to acquire the property and he, Storrs, would arrange the purchase and develop the property, charging nothing for his efforts. All deeds would be conveyed to Storrs and Rousseau as joint owners. Rousseau would be reimbursed for funds advanced out of the proceeds of the mine operation.

Upon his return from Troy, Storrs began to purchase the various interests in Lot 21. He acquired the one-half interest from Wood and the interest of Jonas and Levi Reed. These interests were conveyed to Storrs and Rousseau jointly and paid for with funds advanced by Rousseau. Storrs was unable to deal with Sanford and Cook for their interests in Lot 21 as he was not on friendly terms with Sanford. Rousseau obtained the Sanford and Cook interests and Storrs assumed the deeds were to he and Rousseau jointly. He learned in later years that the conveyances were to Rousseau only. In his difficulty with Sanford, Storrs assumed that although he had no personal problem with Cook, the latter was a neighbor of Sanford and they attended the same Presbyterian Church while Storrs belonged to the Baptist Church in the same village.

Storrs and Rousseau's ore bed company consisted of all of Lot 21 except for a share held by Charles Miller. Storrs negotiated with Miller on several occasions but Miller kept raising the price and it was not until 1853 that Storrs was able to purchase Miller's share for $1,000. Storrs reported that, from funds drawn by him on Rousseau, on one occasion he paid $300 or $400 to David Sanford for land conveyed by Sanford to Rousseau individually and which was not a part of Lot 21. Rousseau also acquired the majority of shares in Lot 23 which had been sold by Jeramiah Cook after he began operations on the eastern end of the Sanford pit on that lot in 1824.

It is noteworthy how well Storrs had convinced Rousseau of the investment possibilities in the iron ore venture. In addition to being a successful grocery merchant, Rousseau had the vision and the capital to seize an investment opportunity. In 1846 he purchased for himself the Hall interest in Lots 24 and 25 owned by Lee, Hall and Sherman. This included the western end of the Sanford mine and the New Bed workings in the southwest corner of Lot 24. In 1849 Mr. Rousseau sold his interest in Lot 24, and in 1851 his interest in Lot 25 to Silas H. Witherbee and his nephew Jonathan G. Witherbee. This resulted in the formation of the firm of Lee, Sherman and Witherbees.

During the period of land acquisition in connection with the ore prospect on Lot 21, Storrs proceeded to develop the property to produce ore. He resumed operations in the shaft which was started in 1829, and after sinking it thirty feet reached the main ore body. He purchased a two-acre lot and erected a separator for pulverizing the ore. This was located on the west side of the brook on the south side of what is now called Joyce Road. Storrs and Rousseau with their Ore Bed Company managed to produce about one thousand tons of ore, and in so doing developed enough of the property to prove a valuable ore deposit. For all his efforts, Storrs received no compensation other than his share of any profit which would result from the sale of ore.

Old Bed ore in the Sanford and 21 mines is crystalline magnetite and the many facets of the crystals favor crushing and separating. Associated with this ore, and mechanically dispersed throughout the ore mass and adjacent rock contacts, are an abundance of phosphate rock crystals called apatite. These are rice-shaped grains that were referred to locally as "red sand." Heavy concentrations of this material in the ore were avoided in mining as the phosphate content was detrimental to iron production.

Dr. Ebenezer Emmons, a geologist associated with the early surveys in New York State, became interested in phosphate rock to be used for agricultural purposes. About 1850, in association with Silas M. Still-well, he arranged to mine about six thousand tons of a green chloritic phosphate rock a short distance south of the village of Crown Point near Lake Champlain. The material was not satisfactory and mining was stopped. In the meantime Dr. Emmons became aware of the "red sand" spread through the Sanford ore bed.

In the fall of 1851, John and Charles Hammond of Crown Point and Dr. Emmons managed to acquire from Storrs, Rousseau, Lee and Sher-man the rights to the "red sand," or apatite rock, in the Sanford and 21 ore beds. The Moriah Phosphate Company was formed to produce phos-phate for fertilizing purposes. The phosphate company, under terms of the agreement, was required to transport to its separator, at its own expense, the ore which had been raised by the grantors. After recovery of the apatite, the separated or cleaned ore was to be returned to the grantors.

This arrangement was particularly beneficial to the mine owners. The agreement also specified that if the mine owners found it not prof-itable to raise the ore, the phosphate company would either pay for the ore to be raised or mine it under the direction of the grantors. In either case the separated iron ore would belong to the grantors.

The proprietors of the Moriah Phosphate Company, aware of the uncertainties they faced, prepared to push the project forward to produce phosphate, hoping to sell the company at a handsome profit or realize some profit from their operation. In August 1852 they granted a one-eighth interest in the phosphate company to William P. Blake of New York, for which Mr. Blake would act as consultant and superintendent of the phosphate operation. He had previously been associated with Dr. Emmons in the Crown Point venture.

Mr. Blake, in a paper entitled "Contributions To The Early History Of The Industry Of Phosphate Lime In The United States," presented at a meeting of the American Institute of Mining Engineers at Baltimore in February 1892, referred to their 1850 association in part as follows:

> "The attention of Dr. Emmons and myself had in the meantime been attracted to the granular red mineral, known locally as "red sand," spread in layers through a large portion of the old Sanford Ore Bed at Moriah, west of Port Henry. This mineral we found to be ap-atite in small hexagonal crystals, and in such abundance and so closely associated and mingled with the grains of magnetite that large portions of the ore bed were avoided as too lean in iron for profitable working. There were also large quantities of lean ore in piles at the sides of the cart roads and paths in and from the various pits and openings in that enormous mass of iron ore. Acquiring some of the lots into which the ore bed was divided, and taking leases on

others, we prepared to separate the iron ore from the apatite or "red sand," by means of a magnetic separator constructed for us in Vermont. . . ."

In June 1892 at the Lake Champlain-Plattsburgh meeting of the American Institute of Mining Engineers, Mr. Blake discussed in more detail the operation of the magnetic separator in a paper entitled "Note Of The Magnetic Separation Of Iron Ore At The Sanford Ore Bed, Moriah, Essex County, In 1852":

"In my short 'Contribution To The Early History Of The Industry Of Phosphate Of Lime In The United States,' mention is made of the erection by Dr. Emmons and myself of a magnetic machine for the removal of iron ore from the so-called "red sand," a granular form of apatite. At the time of writing it was not possible to refer to my diary and notes, and the general statements were made from recollection. The subject seems to have special interest at this time, by reason of the many forms of machines now being introduced and patented for similar purposes; and having received letters of inquiry for further details, I have availed myself of the opportunity, when recently at home, to refer to the original notes and records made by me in 1852, when living at Crown Point and Moriah on Lake Champlain.

"The machine mentioned in my former communication was purchased of Ransom Cook of Vermont. It arrived and was unloaded from the boat and taken part way up to the mine on October 18, 1852. The weight was 1,400 pounds and the cost $1,200. It was constructed, not with permanent magnets but with electro-magnets. It was set up and first turned by hand on October 28th, using twelve battery-cups or cells, the connections being made with wires in small cups of quicksilver. The magnets were not sufficiently strong, and the machine did not work well. More batteries were sent for, and the machine was started with steam power on November 6th.

"The ore was dried in kilns, then put through a coffee-mill crusher or grinder, and then fed upon the leather belt which carried it under the magnets. Many experimental runs were made, and some difficulties were overcome, before December 21st, when the record states that the machine was working pretty well, using 24 cells and giving a product of from three to five tons a day of granular phosphate. The original material contained about twenty percent of iron ore. In this work we sought to use the lowest grade of iron ore containing the highest percentage of phosphate.

"At one time 36 battery cells were used. The strength of the magnets was unequal, and the connections did not appear to be good. The belt was uneven in its tension and had to be kept up against the magnets by a roller at one side of the line of magnets and a fixed straight ridge of wood on the other. Both the belt and the magnets showed rapid wear. A brush was necessary to secure complete delivery of the iron. The dust was oppressive and no provision seems to have been made for its removal, though one was devised and drawn. The agitation of the mixed ore was found to be important as the separation was much more thorough when the charge was stirred.

"Although the operation of this machine could only be reported as partially successful, the proprietors of the ore bed were desirous of contracting with the works for 5,000 tons of cleaned iron ore."

In December 1852 the Hammonds conveyed all their interest in the ore beds and the Moriah Phosphate Company to Chauncy Watson of Albany who acted as agent for Silas Stillwell of New York City. They received four thousand dollars for their "red sand" interest and thirty-seven hundred dollars for buildings, equipment and other expenditures they had made for the phosphate venture.

In 1852 Nathaniel Storrs, encumbered by debts to Rousseau and others, began negotiations for the sale of his share of the Ore Bed Company. Silas Stillwell and John Trotter acquired both the Storrs and Rousseau interests in 1853. This acquisition and the Hammond "red sand" purchase, embracing the Lee and Sherman Sanford Ore Bed, consolidated the rights for production of apatite with one group. They formed the American Mineral Company in which the Patroon Henry VanRensselaer was associated. This company also acquired the Storrs and Rousseau ore separator and lot.

The American Mineral Company produced apatite as their primary product and shipped it to England for fertilizer. The separated iron ore was considered a by-product and was sold to S. H. and J. G. Witherbee. The separating process for apatite was not successful on a productive scale and in December 1857 the company leased its holdings for forty years to a group which formed the Port Henry Iron Ore Company of Lake Champlain. Silas Stillwell and Richard Remington were among the principals and officers, with Henry VanRensselaer as president.

By the end of 1858, mining on Lots 21, 23, 24 and 25 of the Iron Ore Tract was under the direction of two concerns, Lee, Sherman and Witherbees and the Port Henry Iron Ore Company. The Sanford bed, called the Old Bed, was opened on both Lots 23 and 25. Lee, Sherman and Witherbees mined the west end of the pit on Lot 25, and the Port Henry Iron Ore Company mined the east end on Lot 23. A cable was suspended north-south across the pit to denote the line between Lots 23 and 25. Lacking agreement as to the exact location of this line, both companies engaged D. M. Arnold to correctly establish by survey the boundary lines of these lots. For both companies the Sanford was referred to as the main pit.

John A. Lee

George Sherman

S. H. Witherbee

J. G. Witherbee

The firm of Lee, Sherman and Witherbees was formed in 1851. The principals were George Sherman of Moriah, John A. Lee, S. H. Witherbee and J. G. Witherbee of Port Henry. In 1862 the Lee interest was acquired by the Witherbees.

In 1862 S. H. and J. G. Witherbee purchased the Lee interest for $50,000 in what was considered an amicable settlement. It was reported that following completion of the sale documents, and during a friendly toast, Silas Witherbee remarked that they had been prepared to pay John Lee $100,000. This remark infuriated Lee so much that he disposed of his remaining property in Port Henry and moved to Saratoga. The name of the firm was changed to Witherbees Sherman and Company.

In 1900 the firm was incorporated as Witherbee Sherman and Company, Incorporated with Frank S. Witherbee named president. In that same year the Sherman interest was sold to the Lackawanna Steel Company of Buffalo.

The Port Henry Iron Ore Company was organized under the laws of New York State in December 1858 with capital of $200,000. The company paid $40,000 at the time the lease was given, and as a further consideration agreed to pay twenty-five cents for every ton mined. In addition the company gave its bonds for $85,000 secured by a mortgage of the lease. The premises covered by the lease were found not to include full and complete title to all of the ore, and the property was encumbered by mortages and liens against the whole property or portions thereof in the amount of $206,000. It is unquestionably true that the parties who were interested in the property at the commencement of the enterprise believed they had acquired a good title to the property covered by the lease, and were not aware of the encumbrance. No one evaluating these factors would consider that the Port Henry Iron Ore Company was launched into existence under favorable circumstances.

The first five years of the existence of the company was spent in a struggle for survival. Development of the property called for large outlays of money; questions of title to various portions were constantly arising; the holders of the encumbrance were pressing for their money and receipts from the production of the mines were required for improvements and development, and the stockholders, either from lack of funds or desire, failed to come forward to the relief of the company. And yet the struggle was a successful one, and that success was due only to the intrinsic and productive value of the property.

During those five years, ownership of the stock changed hands from time to time until in 1864 it had all passed into new hands and the newly elected board of trustees included Edward S. Beck, James B. Brinsmade and Albert Tower of the Poughkeepsie Furnaces, John A. Griswold and later Erastus Corning of the Troy Steel Works. The Burden Iron Company of Troy and Witherbees Sherman and Company were involved with the early development of the company. John A. Griswold, a member of the Thirty-eighth U.S. Congress and former mayor of Troy, served as treasurer. In 1864 Mr. Griswold, in association with Erastus Corning, A. L. Holley, John Winslow and Erastus Corning, Jr. secured control of the Bessemer patents in America. His firm, known after 1868 as John A. Griswold and Company, exerted a profound influence upon development of the iron and steel industry in the United States.

It is of great historical interest that Mr. Griswold with John Winslow and C. S. Bushnell showed the U.S. Naval Board a model of John Ericsson's *Monitor* and, gaining the interest of President Lincoln, agreed to construct and deliver such a ship within one hundred days or assume the one-quarter million dollar cost. The *Monitor* was constructed on Long Island under Ericsson's direction, but the machinery, plates and other iron work were manufactured in Troy. The ship was launched on January 30, 1862 and defeated the *Merrimac* on March 9. Griswold and his associates built six more vessels of the same type.

Iron for the manufacture of the *Monitor* came from several sources including Crown Point, Roth's Forge at North Hudson, and I suspect some from the ore mined by the Port Henry Iron Ore Company.

With the change in management mentioned above, the Port Henry Iron Ore Company immediately set out to investigate and clear all title to the property, purchase all the rights of the lessors to make the company the sole owner of the premises, remove all encumbrances and develop the property to become much more productive. The stockholders agreed with the trustees and readily advanced liberal funds on a pro rata basis without increasing the capital stock. All of these goals were achieved and additional mining lands purchased, including valuable woodlands within a reasonable distance to supply timber and fuel for the company's mining operations.

In the early stages of mining of the Sanford Pit by both companies, wagons were driven directly into the pit and loaded. As mining progressed and the pit deepened, ore was raised by a whim or whimsy. This device was a drum for winding a cable, with two arms to which horses were hitched to turn the drum. The cable was attached to a box which was lowered into the mine on timber slides. Ore was hand shoveled into the box. By 1858 each of the companies mining the Sanford Pit had three whims in operation. At that time the Sanford Pit was two hundred feet north to south, four hundred feet east to west and had reached a depth of fifty feet. North of the Sanford Pit the ore dipped to the southwest and was mined underground. This section became known as Miller Pit.

The Port Henry Iron Ore Company, with financial and legal matters under control, embarked on an expanded development program. James B. Brinsmade, secretary and treasurer, became the driving force of the organization. Operations were pressed forward in the 21 Pit which Storrs had explored years earlier. This was referred to as the South Pit and as operations expanded, the magnitude of the 21 ore became evident. Within a few years nearly all of Port Henry Iron Ore Company production came from this mine. Four whims, each with four horses, raised the ore. These machines were later replaced with steam hoists. By the late 1860's miners were paid two dollars a day. Two and one-half tons per day were mined and raised for each man employed. The company maintained no office, had no salaried officers, no mining engineers and only a superintendent and foreman in each pit in a high pay grade. Ore sales were handled by contract with Witherbees Sherman and Company on a commission basis. This was a lean operation.

Several other shafts were put down including the Tower and Brinsmade. Witherbees Sherman and Company, on their side of the property line developed the Tefft Shaft workings. But of all the mines, 21 was the most spectacular. Standing at the north rim looking south (in the late 1860's) it resembled a giant bowl where the ore had been mined. Below the cap rock massive ore with openings therein was visible on three sides, and work could be done by daylight.

As ore production from the two mining companies increased, the distance from the ore beds to the lake posed a serious transportation problem in meeting demand for the ore. In 1852 a seven-mile plank road was constructed from the various mines to the furnaces and docks on the lake shore. The roadbed was made of three-inch hemlock plank, sixteen feet long, laid on stringers. Wagons carrying ore loads of five to seven tons were hauled by teams over the road. The mining companies contracted with the teamsters who owned the horses. Maintenance of the plank road was costly and area sawmills were kept busy furnishing plank   material. When the wagons were unloaded at Port Henry, the heavy fine ore was washed from the wagons before the return trip up the steep grade to the mines. In its peak period of operation as many as one hundred teams hauled ore daily over the Moriah Plank Road.

Decades later, even through the early part of the twentieth century, when sports competition between the communities was keen, Port Henry teams were called "Wagon Washers" and Mineville teams were referred to as "Iron Ore Eaters."

4

During the early development period of Cheever, Sanford and 21 Mines, other iron ore mining ventures had been moving forward in the Town of Moriah, along the Champlain Valley and westward inland.

Early in the nineteenth century Charles Fisher, who had begun mining on the Cheever property in 1820, commenced mining just south of the Moriah-Elizabethtown town line at what became known as Fisher Hill, and shortly thereafter sold the property to Eliphalet Hall. A long period of sharply contested litigation followed, resulting in a compromise settlement. Finally, the mine was sold in 1863 for $75,000 to a group of eastern capitalists from whom it was acquired in 1872 by the Port Henry Iron Ore Company. The mine had three operating shafts or slopes, with two operating from a depth of 500 and 550 feet. No. 3 slope operated on a breast of ore fifty feet wide and twenty-five feet high. Ore was hoisted by horse power whims.

Port Henry Iron Ore Company production from Fisher Hill Mine began in 1872 and continued through 1893, being idle during years 1876, 1885 and 1886. The final cessation of operations in 1893 was due to the severe economic depression at that time. During the twenty-two year period of operations prior to 1893, the mine operated six hoisting shafts or slopes of 600 to 800 feet depth and produced 217,282 tons of ore, with the largest single year production of 23,672 tons in 1889.

The Burt Lot Mine, just north of the Moriah-Elizabethtown town line on Lot 55 of the Iron Ore Tract, was a continuation of the same geological structure that formed the Fisher Hill Mine. The mine was reportedly discovered in 1840, no doubt following Charles Fisher's activity at adjacent Fisher Hill. There were several openings on the property and four hoisting slopes, with one slope of over 300 feet dipping at an angle of forty-five degrees, with a breast of ore (in 1867) of eighty-five feet by fourteen feet high. The ore was used in the Valley and Kingdom Forges in Elizabethtown.

The Burt Lot property was sold in 1864 for $35,000 to Richard Remington and Jay Cooke, the great industrial financier, who came to Elizabethtown and acquired mineral and iron making interests. In addition to the Burt Lot they purchased the Nigger Hill Mine (Haasz or

Noble Bed) from the Noble heirs for $100,000; the Kingdom Forge on Black River; the Valley Forge at Elizabethtown; the Bouquet Mill in Essex Township; dwelling houses and stores at these locations, and several thousand acres of forest lands. These acquisitions became the Lake Champlain Ore and Iron Company.

The Nigger Hill or Haasz Bed was mined as an open pit and reported to have furnished ten thousand tons of ore for the Valley and Kingdom Forges. Mining on the Burt Lot was not well organized or equipped, and was without steam power for hoisting and pumping. As the mines made considerable water, the slow horse-powered whim and small water box could scarcely allow half-time for production. This type operation was expensive and mine openings were abandoned in ore without reaching any great depth. The estate of Jay Cooke and Company went into bankruptcy, and with other holdings the Lake Champlain Iron Company properties were sold at auction in Philadelphia on June 20, 1890. The Burt Lot Mine passed into the hands of Witherbees Sherman and Company.

The Barton Hill ore bed was opened before 1840 on Lot 34 of the Iron Ore Tract on land of Caleb D. Barton. In 1863 the mine was purchased by the Port Henry Furnaces. The ore was the northern continuation of the New Bed ore discovered in 1844 by D. E. Sanford, and sold to Lee, Hall and Sherman in 1846. The ore was the richest in iron of any ore known. Analysis of the ore showed 71.19% pure metallic iron; 1.12% insoluble silicious material; only a trace of phosphorous; and 27.69% oxygen and moisture. The magnetite crystals of Barton Hill and New Bed ore were well defined and some very large. The greatest known concentration of these very large crystals was in the "Lovers Hole" section of the Barton Hill Mine from which 60,000 tons of crude ore running 70% iron were shipped. One outstanding sample was a large octahedren measuring 1.25 inches on each edge and fitting in its matrix of pure iron ore crystals. This famous perfect sample was called the "Big Diamond" and is now in the Seamen Mineral Museum at Michigan Technological University at Houghton.

The Smith Mine, or Cook Shaft as it was commonly called, was on the eastern part of Lot 47 of the Iron Ore Tract, and was opened in June 1866. The ore in this mine did not outcrop but became known years earlier by an unusual attraction indicated by a compass. Patrick Cook owned the lot and M. T. Smith and an associate arranged with Mr. Cook to open a mine at their expense for which they would receive a two-thirds interest in the property. They sunk a ten-foot square shaft through glacial fill for over one hundred feet and finally through a very thin vein of iron ore. Undeterred by negative comments, and believing the source of the strong magnetic attraction had not been reached, they continued the shaft through hard pan and rock eighty feet further and encountered a fourteen-foot thickness of high grade ore. In 1866 the mine produced 8,000 tons and in 1868 produced 14,500 tons, operating a breast of two hundred feet and a height of fifteen feet. Ore was raised by horse power but pumping was by steam. No separation was required and thirty to forty men were employed. The ore was shipped to Troy and other outside markets.

The O'Neil Shaft was located on the eastern part of Lot 47, a short distance west of Cook Shaft. It was formerly owned by James O'Neil who, prior to his death, leased the lot to J. B. Foltz and Company under the terms that if they sunk a shaft and discovered ore within a certain time they would receive a deed to a one-half interest in the ore. In December 1880 Witherbees Sherman and Company bought the Foltz interest and continued work on the shaft. It was not completed in the time stipulated in the contract between O'Neil and Foltz, and the time was verbally extended. The work then went on to completion and in 1884 ore was developed. The shaft was 630 feet vertical depth with a slope that extended three hundred feet further. At the time of completion it was the deepest shaft in this part of the country. Operations were underway with a productive force of twenty men. The ore was a continuation of the Smith Mine ore and of the same analysis as the Old Bed and 21 ores.

The Smith Mine property was acquired by H. G. Burleigh who organized the Champlain Ore Company in 1884. Officers of the company were H. G. Burleigh, president; B. W. Burleigh, James Morrison, Thomas Caldwell and A. B. Waldo, trustees. The capital stock was $350,000.

The Burleighs filed a claim to the O'Neil Shaft based on rights they obtained from the O'Neil heirs and on the invalidity of the verbal permit of extended time to complete the shaft given to Witherbees Sherman and Company. In the ensuing litigation Witherbees Sherman and Company bought the Smith Mine property. They then discontinued operations through O'Neil Shaft and operated the mine through Cook Shaft.

The Pilfershire group of mines, mentioned earlier in my discussion of Peter Kalm's possible presence on Cheney Mountain in 1749, lay at the foot of the western slope of Cheney Mountain. They consisted of several small openings near Bartlett Brook. Little is known of their original discovery, and to my knowledge no maps exist of the underground workings. D. M. Arnold prepared an area map in 1864 showing the strike of the ore and the various pits. The northern three or four openings were owned by George Pease and called the Pease Mine or Port

Henry Ore Bed. Watson wrote (*History of Essex County 1869*) that the mine was only partially developed and up to 1869 had produced about 1,000 tons. He gave an analysis of 64.15% iron and 6.20% phosphate of lime.

I recall Mr. William J. Murray, a neighbor in his late eighties, told me Pilfershire was a wet mine and one-half of the workday was required to hoist out the water with a water box. Hoisting was with horse and whim.The mine only operated a short period of time. Mr. Murray said the name Pilfershire was given to that area because some of the inhabitants were known to steal cattle.

The Cleveland Mine, formerly known as the Sherman Bed, was opened by Kinsley Sherman, a brother of George R. Sherman. It was acquired by a company in Cleveland, Ohio and operated a few years after 1865 producing eight to ten thousand tons per year which was shipped to Cleveland for puddling purposes. One of the owners was Amasa Stone, a noted railroad builder and public benefactor in Cleveland. One of his daughters married Samuel Mather whose family was engaged in the formation and development of major mining ventures in Michigan.

The Cleveland Mine property consisted of connecting pits south of the Pease or Port Henry Ore Bed. Watson wrote (1869) that a shaft had been sunk about 200 feet and that steam was used for motive power in hoisting ore and pumping the mine, and that thirty to one hundred men worked about the mine and in connection with the business.

I calculated the Cleveland Mine workings to be about three hundred fifty feet along the strike and connected by at least three openings to the surface. It was mined about six feet normal thickness, and the ore dipped about fifty-five degrees. No production figures are available for the Pilfershire mines, but based on information stated above and my personal observations of the mines when the entrances were being sealed, I would estimate that these mines produced from sixty to seventy thousand tons prior to the end of operations. The Pilfershire mine group was later acquired by the Port Henry Iron Ore Company and has been idle since the early 1870's.

The Goff Mine, adjacent to the Cheever, is on the south part of the original Skene Patent. It is the northernmost opening in the area mined by the Cheever Iron Ore Company. The mine was opened in 1845 by Lucius A. Foote and then owned by George W. Goff. About 1865 it was acquired by the Champlain Ore and Furnace Company. Situated near the shore of the lake, the Goff Mine had a separator and dock. The mine was abandoned after a few years operation as the ore was lean and better quality ore was more readily available.

There were numerous other mines, pits or prospects opened during the early 1800's in the Town of Moriah. Some, such as the Foote, Crag Harbor and Dalliba were mentioned by Dr. Ebenezer Emmons in *Natural History of New York* (1842). These mines supplied the early forges and furnaces but were not successful ventures. Others underwent name changes and consolidations and became lasting mines. The Barnum and Hall veins, mentioned in Dr. Emmons' report together with other early named pits such as the Phillips and Colburn, Lemay, Wasson, Alcock and Cooper, Persons, Pearl, Nall and Houston were located on Lot 34 of the Iron Ore Tract. They became the Barton Hill portion of New Bed Mine with surface openings later known as Arch Pit, Lovers Hole, South Pit, North Pit and Orchard. South of Lot 34 the New Bed Mine workings embraced pits on Lots 24 and 32 of the Iron Ore Tract that were called Thomas Mine, Big Pit and Roe Shaft.

The Butler Mines are located south of Moriah Corners and west of Bulwagga Mountain on Lot 32 of Legge's Patent. Watson wrote in his 1869 *History of Essex County* that the Spear and Butler Bed was discovered in 1848. He described it as being opened about ten rods in length and twenty feet deep with a breast of nine feet, widening as it descended. Kemp reported in "New York State Museum Bulletin 119," dated 1908, the mine was opened by Butler and Gillette and continued under the name of Essex Mining Company. I note from an undated old sketch that the Butler was equipped with a whimsey and a tram track. A cross section shows the pit sixteen feet wide at the top and sloping steeply about seventy-five degrees for a vertical depth of twenty feet to water. The ore was magnetite with some hematite.

There were many small early producing mines opened in the 1800's in the townships of Elizabethtown and Westport that may be considered in the same iron district as the mines of Moriah. I will mention these briefly.

The Castaline Bed, discovered about 1800, and the Ross Bed, found about the same time about a mile northeast of the Castaline, were on Lot 72 of the Roaring Brook Tract. The Nigger Hill or Haasz Bed, earlier mentioned, was discovered about 1825-30. Wakefield Pit was discovered about 1845 and opened by Colonel E. F. Williams. Little Pond Ore Bed was discovered about 1840 on Lot 199 of the Iron Ore Tract. The Judd Bed was found about 1845 and operated approximately ten years. Finney Bed was discovered in 1854 on Lot 139 of the Iron Ore Tract. The Gates Bed was found about the same time as the Finney on an adjoining lot. Steele Bed was discovered about 1810 on Lot 189 of the Iron Ore Tract. The Odell Bed with two openings was located in the eastern part of Elizabethtown. Mitchell Bed, on Lot 116 of the Iron Ore Tract,

Burt Lot Mines, 1890. Later part of the Fisher Hill Group.

Port Henry Iron Ore Company "21" Open Pit. Clonan Shaft, Joker Shaft and Bonanza Shaft headframes are shown in the background at surface. Photo circa 1915.

Mill at Arnold Hill, AuSable District, 1870.

North Shaft, Arnold Hill Mine, AuSable District, 1870.

was discovered about 1830. The Buck and Noble Beds were discovered in 1865 on Lots 109 and 110 of the Iron Ore Tract.

Other discoveries north of the Burt Lot Mines on Lot 55 included the Swamp, Foote, Hall, and Sherman Mines on Lot 75 and the Cliff Mines on Lots 74 and 84 of the Iron Ore Tract. East of the Burt Lot Mines on Lot 48 of the Iron Ore Tract, Thompson Shaft and Humbug Mines were located within the Town of Westport. The Campbell or Norway Bed was opened between 1845 and 1850 on Lots 166 and 168 of the Iron Ore Tract. It was worked by Henry J. Campbell and Whalen & Judd who produced several hundred tons in 1852 and 1853. About 1868-69 a road was started from this mine to Westport but it was not finished and the mine became idle thereafter.

The Merriam Bed was opened in 1867 on Lot 165 of the Iron Ore Tract by W. P. and P. D. Merriam. M. P. Smith reported in his 1885 *History of Essex County* that not more than three hundred tons were produced before the mine became permanently idle. F. H. Jackson opened an ore bed about a mile or two east of the Campbell and Merriam Ore Beds but according to M. P. Smith the mine never amounted to anything. As mentioned earlier in discussing the Jackson or Sisco Furnace, Jackson secured ore for his furnace from within Westport, mixing it with hematite from Vermont and Cheever ore from Moriah.

All of the early iron ore prospects, large and small, not only supplied the forge and furnace fires, but by their existence fostered exploration and development for iron ore in the Town of Moriah and its environs that continued through two-thirds of the twentieth century. There were other important iron ore developments beyond the Mineville Iron District in the Champlain Valley during the early 1800's that contributed to the growth of the expanding nation. I will mention them briefly, as in some instances their future became interlocked with plans and operations of mining companies in the Town of Moriah.

Iron ore was discovered in Crown Point by Samuel Renne in 1818 and he began mining in 1822. John Renne operated a forge at Crown Point Center in 1823 using ore from Samuel's mine and from Cheever. Frank Witherbee (*History of the Iron Industry of Essex County, 1906*) credits John Renne with initiating the iron industry in Crown Point. Samuel's mine was later operated by Jacob Saxe and became known as the Saxe Bed.

The Penfield Ore Bed was discovered in 1826 and furnished ore for a forge built by Allen Penfield and his son-in-law, Allen P. Harwood at Ironville in 1828. The Hammond Ore Bed, about a half-mile from the Penfield Bed, was located on Lot 278 of the Paradox Tract. It was discovered in 1821 but was not mined extensively until 1845.

The first Crown Point Iron Company was formed in 1845 by C. F. Hammond and John C. Hammond, Allen Penfield and Jonas Tower who later sold his interest to E. S. Bogue. A charcoal furnace was constructed, but later destroyed by fire and rebuilt about 1860. High quality iron was produced and the first steel rails made by the Bessemer Process in the United States were manufactured at Troy with Crown Point iron. The company also furnished iron for armor plates for the United States ship *Monitor*. The furnace was operated until 1870.

Another early iron venture that held great promise was discovered by Indians about 1822 in the remote Adirondack wilderness area. An Indian brave of the St. Francis tribe approached David Henderson at the Elba Forge near Lake Placid in 1826 and showed him a piece of iron ore that appeared superior to ore being used by Mr. Henderson and his associates at a forge in Keene. The proprietors of the forge accompanied the Indian several miles into the unmapped rugged forest through Indian Pass and beyond the source of the Hudson River until they finally came to an area with masses of rich ore seemingly everywhere, in great boulders, surface veins, mountain masses, the bed of the river and even in a natural iron river dam. The surrounding mountain slopes had a great abundance of timber and hardwoods, the necessary ingredients for iron manufacture.

After careful evaluation of the area Mr. Henderson and his associates hurriedly went to Albany and acquired tracts of land, Townships 46 and 47 of the Totten and Crossfield Purchase, embracing the iron-bearing area they had observed. With title to the property in hand they immediately set out to develop an iron works. They constructed an ore separator, forge, charcoal kilns, housing for the workmen and a road to Newcomb. Satisfied with the iron produced, they erected a puddling furnace in 1837 for producing bar iron and built a road to Schroon River to haul their iron forty miles to Lake Champlain.

In 1844 they built a small blast furnace. Mr. Henderson was the general manager and motivating force of the enterprise. Tests were made with the ore to make steel and a steelworks was planned. However, Mr. Henderson was fatally injured while studying the feasibility of increasing the water power supply from a source several miles above the ironworks. His death was a severe blow to the business and mining community he had built and was expanding. It was also determined that steel could not be successfully produced in a charcoal furnace. In addition, the iron ore with its high titanium content was difficult to manage in the blast furnace. In 1848 a new larger furnace was planned and completed in 1854. Satisfactory iron was made but the company only operated a short time, ending production in 1855. The plant works and village were abandoned and the furnace stands today in a remarkable state of preservation. With the demise of the Adirondac Ironworks and the Adirondac Iron and Steel Company, the unmined mineral wealth of the area lay dormant until the twentieth century.

In the summer of 1939, while on a hiking trip in the Adirondack wilderness area, I came upon a monument set on a base of iron at a desolate place aptly named Calamity Point. The monument is inscribed: "Erected by filial affection to the memory of our father, David Henderson, who accidentally lost his life on this spot by the premature discharge of a pistol, 3d September, 1845."

Seventeen miles southwest of Plattsburgh and four and one-half miles north of the present village of AuSable Forks, iron ore was discovered in 1806 by Samuel Baker on Lots 190 and 200 of Maul's Patent. The property, eventually known as Arnold Hill Mine, was purchased by Baker in association with John W. Southmayd, Dr. Eliphalet Stickney and Elisha Arnold and they began mining as equal partners. In 1812 Baker sold his interest to his partners. They and their heirs continued operation and ownership until March 1864 when the property was purchased by C. G. Hussey and Thomas W. Howe. To that date the mine had produced 154,000 tons.

Two and one-half miles south of Arnold Hill and two miles north of AuSable Forks on Lot 15, Slocum Tract of the Sixth Division of Livingston's Patent, a barren elevation called Palmer Hill rises five hundred feet above the AuSable River. Here ore was discovered prior to 1825 by Zephaniah Palmer, a land surveyor. Palmer produced ore and in 1829 sold part of the hill to the Peru Iron Company and shortly thereafter the rest to other parties.

About 1810 George Griswold built a dam on the AuSable River at Clintonville. He then built a grist mill and a forge with two fires. He used ore from the Winter Ore Bed, about a mile and one-half west of the forge. This was considered to be the first forge erected on the AuSable River. The property passed to a group that formed the Peru Iron Company in 1824. The company began extensive construction including forges, a rolling mill, two charcoal furnaces, improvements at Arnold and Winter Ore Beds which were under lease, and dock facilities at Port Douglass on Lake Champlain. A cable factory and anchor forge were in operation with iron cables and large ship anchors manufactured from Arnold Hill ore.

John and James Rogers had begun producing iron at Black Brook in 1831 and five years later at AuSable Forks using Arnold Hill ore. The Rogers Company used available water power at AuSable Forks to eventually operate a forge of four fires, a rolling mill, nail factory, foundry and machine shop. At Black Brook, the company had twelve forge fires and six more at Jay, making a total of twenty-two.

Palmer Hill eventually was completely controlled by two companies; J. and J. Rogers Company of AuSable Forks mining the south side and the Peru Steel and Iron Company (successor to Peru Iron Company) mining the northeast side of Palmer Hill. A great era of prosperity continued for many years at AuSable Valley, the manufacturing communities growing with the iron industry. Community schools, churches and housing were furnished by the mining and manufacturing companies.

Fourteen miles west of Plattsburgh the hamlet of Dannemora is dominated by the stark gray walls and watchtowers of a maximum security prison that had its origin in the iron industry. Prior to 1842, labor and manufacturing groups in New York State were strongly concerned that prison convict labor was producing products in direct competition with them. Their lobby groups pressured state legislators for a change. The Legislature appointed a commission to study the possible employment of convict labor in mining and smelting iron. A bill passed the Legislature in 1844 to establish a state prison north of Albany for the purpose of mining and manufacturing iron. The location chosen, being in Clinton County, it was named Clinton Prison. In 1846 convicts from Sing Sing and Auburn prisons were transferred to that remote area to work on construction of the prison. Facilities were completed the following year and a mine was opened on the prison property.

Initially the mined ore was sold to forges but in 1853 construction was started at the prison on an ironworks including forge, rolling mill, nail factory and a large blast furnace that was later destroyed by fire. Manufacture of iron was found to be costly, and I suspect badly managed. The ironworks was discontinued in the 1870's and a large part of the four hundred seventy-five convict labor force was diverted to manufacturing hats.

Thirty miles west of Plattsburgh, William Bailey erected a forge in 1803 on the Chateaugay River about five miles below the outlet of Chateaugay Lake. Ore was obtained from the Prall Bed, later known as the 81 Mine. In 1822 a tract of land in Township 5 of the Old Military Tract was divided into three hundred lots, part in the Town of Dannemora and part in the Town of Ellenburg. In November of that same year the part which lay in Dannemora, including the Prall Bed, was acquired by Lloyd N. Rogers. In 1823 an old trapper named Collins discovered ore on the property a few miles east of the Prall Bed in a very remote area.

The discovery did not generate interest due to its wilderness location, far from transportation and with natural obstacles unfavorable for road construction. It would be forty-five years after discovery, in the latter third of the century, before an attempt would be made to develop the property on a productive scale. Yet this ore discovery would eventually prove to be one of the great iron ore mines of New York State that would thrive for a hundred years.

While exploration and development of iron ventures heretofore described were underway in northern New York, the quest for ore was equally vigorous elsewhere. Ore was first discovered on the Upper Michigan Peninsula in 1845 by a chief of the Chippawa Indians and in that same year the Jackson Mining Company was formed. This discovery sparked an intensive mineral prospecting era that defined and brought into production the great Michigan and Minnesota Iron Ranges that would become the nucleus of the American steel industry. Despite the remoteness of these ore discoveries and the long, harsh winter climate, the massive size of the ore deposits and availability of cheap water transportation would in a few years have a profound effect on the competitive position of eastern mines.

Total ore production from mines in the Town of Moriah from their discovery to 1869 was estimated at 1,100,000 tons with one-third of that amount produced during the latter six years. So rapid was mine development in northern Michigan that 650,000 tons were produced from that area in the year 1869 alone—more than half the tons of all the ore that had been produced from the mines of Moriah. And that was fifteen years prior to the opening of the great Mesabi Iron Range.

5

As transportation was a major factor in development of settlements and industry in the Champlain Valley, so it was in the western movement of the expanding American population. The Champlain and Erie Barge Canals facilitated the movement of ore and iron products to the Southeast and Midwest. This generated an increased demand for the high quality abundant undeveloped iron ores of the Lake Champlain Adirondack Region.

Despite the various economic downturns and large volume of European imports in the early part of the nineteenth century, there was a market for domestic iron. However, the American mills lacked the capacity to meet demand. Domestic costs were high. Producers had not applied European technological developments such as the use of mineral fuel in the furnaces instead of charcoal to produce cheaper iron. Nor were transportation facilities such that raw materials could be assembled for efficient production and distribution to a rapidly shifting population. In the 1840's there was an expansion of American blast furnace construction with furnaces east of the Allegheny Mountains being made to use mineral fuel, and furnaces west of the Alleghenies constructed as charcoal furnaces based on available fuel.

By 1840 the railroad boom in England had passed while in America it was just getting underway. Wrought iron rails were dumped into the American market at prices that American rolling mills could not meet. British producers extended credit to the railroad builders. American mills produced superior quality rails but at a higher price. The quality and volume of cheap iron imports in competition with a growing domestic iron industry generated some of the great tariff battles of that period.

Railroad building moved forward rapidly in New York State during the 1840's with some small lines constructed to serve specific areas. In the larger view it was recognized that rail service from Albany northward to Lake Champlain and eventually to Montreal would have tremendous commercial value. During the 1850's railroad expansion was three times the rate of the previous decade. In 1851 rail construction from Albany to the border of Lake Champlain was completed, facilitating transfer to and from water transportation north and south on the lake.

On the northwest side of Lake Champlain a rail connection from Platts-burgh north to Canada was completed in 1854.

As ore production increased from the inland mines of Port Henry Iron Ore Company and Witherbees Sherman and Company, transporta-tion became a bottleneck in meeting market demand. Ore shipments were year-round from the mines over the Moriah Plank road to the lake. When the spring shipping season began, boats waiting to be loaded with ore or pig iron at Port Henry covered several acres of the lake surface. During the lake shipping season daily shipments, including the stocked winter supply at the lake, were three times the daily capacity of the plank road.

A railroad was planned to improve transportation and eliminate the high cost of operating and maintaining the Moriah Plank Road. D. M. Arnold made preliminary surveys and cost estimates in 1857 and in 1863 for construction of a railroad from Cedar Point on Lake Champlain at Port Henry to the Sanford Ore Bed. A charter for construction was granted in 1868 to the Port Henry Iron Ore Company and that company purchased the necessary land for the route. The Lake Champlain and Moriah Railroad Company was formed in 1869. The original stock-holders representing two thousand shares were: Witherbees Sherman and Company, John A. Griswold, the Fallkill Iron Company, H. Burden and Sons, Edward Beck and James B. Brinsmade. The latter five were principals in the Port Henry Iron Ore Company where their shares were eventually passed.

D. M. Arnold estimated construction cost of the railbed, including earthwork, masonry, rails, ties and laying track, at $16,000 per mile. The railroad was built and equipped in 1868-69 for $200,000 which repre-sented its capital stock. The railroad ascended from the lake on an aver-age four percent grade a little over thirteen hundred feet for a distance of nearly seven miles to the mines. There were originally three wyes, or switchbacks, in the railroad to permit back switching to overcome steep grades. Two of these wyes extended north and south on Lot 15 in Small's Patent, and viewed in plan formed the letter "Z." Due to its loca-tion, my grandparents' farm was crossed three times by the railroad main line. All rails, fittings, engines, and cars necessary to build and equip the railroad were delivered by boat to Port Henry as rail service into the Champlain Valley from the south would not reach Port Henry until 1871.

Locomotives of a special design, featuring small diameter driving wheels, were required for the steep grades of this standard gage railroad. Early steam locomotives of the L.C. & M. Railroad were given names as was the railroad custom of the time. The early engines were named

"J. B. Brinsmade," "Champlain," "Witherbee," "G. Sherman," "Alpha" and "Little Giant." These were later followed by "Cedar Point," "Mountaineer," "A. Tower" and "Adirondack." Later engines were referred to by number. Ore was transported in "Jimmy" cars. These were four wheel cars with the body constructed of wood with plate lining. The cars had a carrying capacity of ten tons and were equipped with a long levered hand brake that applied braking to all four wheels.

Ore haulage by the Lake Champlain and Moriah Railroad reduced the cost of transporting ore from the mines to Port Henry from ninety cents to thirty cents per ton. Machinery and supplies were efficiently delivered by rail from the lake to the mines. Grain, timber and passengers were also carried but iron ore was the major source of revenue.

There was strong competition between New York and Vermont railroad interests to establish and control rail service north through the Champlain Valley. Along the west shore of the lake, north from Whitehall, route conditions were far less favorable than on the Vermont side of the lake. However, the expanding iron industry of northern New York offered a high potential freight revenue for year-round rail service.

In 1866 the Whitehall and Plattsburgh Railroad Company was formed to link Whitehall and Plattsburgh by a railroad along the western border of Lake Champlain from Whitehall to Port Henry, thence to the AuSable River near AuSable Forks and on to Plattsburgh. A section was built from inland on the AuSable River to Plattsburgh in 1869. In that same year it was leased to the Montreal and Plattsburgh Railroad Company. The Whitehall and Plattsburgh Railroad Company also built a section from Fort Ticonderoga to Port Henry in 1870, crossing over Bulwagga Bay on a timber trestle, and in that same year leased it to the Rutland Railroad Company. In 1871 control of the Montreal and Plattsburgh Railroad Company was leased to the Rutland Railroad Company, which immediately assigned its leases to the Vermont Central and the Vermont and Canada Railroad Companies. These maneuvers gave the Vermont interests control on the west side of Lake Champlain with the obvious intent of preventing completion of through rail service on that side of the lake.

One of the strongest proponents for construction of a through rail route along the west shore of Lake Champlain was Smith M. Weed of Plattsburgh. Mr. Weed was a highly respected attorney, had been elected to the State Assembly and was influential with state and national officials. In New York City, early in 1872, he met with some of the officers and managers of the Delaware and Hudson Canal Company. He pointed out to them the potential benefits of a through rail system along the west shore of Lake Champlain. The company at that time was expanding its coal mining operations and acquiring various railroad interests to further its overall transportation business. The prospects for coal shipments by rail north to Montreal, with Adirondack ore and iron products rail shipped southward, was indeed an attractive business consideration. As a result of that meeting the New York and Canada Railroad Company was formed. It was incorporated on March 16, 1872 "to build a railroad from Whitehall to the New York-Canada line in Clinton County."

In 1873 the Delaware and Hudson Canal Company purchased the Whitehall and Plattsburgh and the Montreal and Plattsburgh railroad holdings from the Vermont interests. These were merged into the New York and Canada Railroad Company. The consolidation was approved by the New York State Legislature on April 15, 1873. The Vermont Companies realized that the well-financed Delaware and Hudson Canal Company fully intended to complete a through line, even if it meant constructing portions of the line parallel to existing tracks.

The New York and Canada Railroad Company, actually a Delaware and Hudson enterprise, immediately pushed the project forward. They built thirty-nine and three-quarter miles of new railroad construction from Whitehall to Fort Ticonderoga and made some changes in the existing line to Port Henry. On April 18, 1874, ice on Lake Champlain destroyed the timber trestle across Bulwagga Bay at Port Henry. The company decided to relocate about five miles of the railroad. The completed road from Whitehall to Port Henry was opened on November 30, 1874. Tremendous construction difficulties were encountered not only from Whitehall to Port Henry, but northward along the lake shore to Plattsburgh.

On November 16, 1875, President Dickson of the Delaware and Hudson Company hosted a group of prominent railroad, state and national dignitaries on a pre-opening excursion over the completed railroad from Albany to Plattsburgh and on to Montreal the next day. The run from Albany to Plattsburgh was completed in seven and one-half hours. It was entirely fitting that the chairman of the banquet that evening at the Foquet House was Smith M. Weed of Plattsburgh.

Completion of rail service to the Champlain Valley provided the incentive for an expanded iron industry. In October 1872 the second Crown Point Iron Company was formed. This formation encompassed all of the iron interests including mines and forges at Ironville and Hammondville, plus vast woodlands. The initial capital stock was $500,000 represented by 5,000 shares distributed as follows: George T. Olyphant, 1,200; Thomas Dickson, 1,200; Smith M. Weed, 100; and John and Thomas Hammond of Crown Point, each with 1,250 shares (Smith's

History of Essex County). Olyphant and Dickson were executive officers of the Delaware and Hudson Canal Company. In November 1872 the stock was increased to $1,200,000 and in November 1873 to $1,500,000. The company became generally controlled by the Delaware and Hudson Company.

A thirteen-mile narrow gage railroad was built by the iron company from the lake to the ironworks and mines at Ironville and Hammondville. An extensive mining plant was constructed at Hammondville, the forges at Ironville were rebuilt and two blast furnaces were constructed on the docks at the lake. The generally difficult economic conditions of the 1870's, and again in the 1890's, were detrimental to success for the Crown Point Iron Company. In 1893 the Delaware and Hudson loaned the Crown Point Iron Company $150,000 to support its continued operation. Its forges in Ironville had produced excellent bloom iron which was still in demand and the lakeside blast furnaces produced high quality pig iron that was shipped to Troy for the Bessemer process. As with some other Adirondack mining ventures, the Crown Point operation did not survive the 1890's. The last ore shipments from the mines to the separator and furnaces were made in July 1893. The entire operation was later sold to the American Steel and Wire Company and all facilities were dismantled.

Another Northern New York iron ore venture which would benefit by completion of rail service and management decisions by the Delaware and Hudson Canal Company was the Rogers property in the Town of Dannemora on which ore was discovered in 1823 by Trapper Collins. In 1868 Smith M. Weed of Plattsburgh, in association with Henry Foote, Erastus Meade and A. B. Waldo, purchased the property. Sales of the various interests finally resulted in ownership being totally in the hands of Mr. Weed and Andrew Williams.

Mr. Williams operated forges on the Chateaugay River and, having tested the ore in his forge, was well aware of its superior quality. They acquired in addition to the Rogers property, the ironworks and water power at the outlet of Chateaugay Lake and vast timber lands. Ore was mined in a small way in the summer months and stocked. In winter months it was hauled in horse-drawn sleighs over snow-covered frozen ground to the forges on the Saranac River. In 1873 the Chateaugay Iron Company was formed by Weed and Williams and development moved forward. A thirteen-mile plank road was built to connect with the Saranac River plank road for ore to be moved in wagons to the forges. Only the quality of the low phosphorus ore justified the high transportation cost.

Clinton Prison at Dannemora faced transportation difficulties in moving men and supplies twenty miles by teams to and from Platts-burgh. The State of New York constructed, but never incorporated, the Plattsburgh and Dannemora Railroad. It was a narrow gage line built in 1879 and equipped with rolling stock the following year.

The Chateaugay Iron Company, anxious to provide improved trans-portation, incorporated the Chateaugay Railroad Company in 1879 to build an eighteen mile railroad from Dannemora to Lyon Mountain. The railroad company leased the Plattsburgh and Dannemora Railroad from the State of New York and took over its operation. The narrow gage railroad to Lyon Mountain was opened on March 30, 1880.

On May 1, 1881 the Chateaugay Ore and Iron Company was incor-porated. This new company purchased the mining properties and Chateaugay Railroad Company owned by the Chateaugay Iron Com-pany. The Delaware and Hudson Canal Company became financially involved in this venture and eventually assumed full control and owner-ship of the Chateaugay Ore and Iron Company. In 1899 the name of the Delaware and Hudson Canal Company was officially shortened to the Delaware and Hudson Company.

Availability of year-round rail service to the Essex and Clinton County iron districts permitted increased production and shipments. The mines of Moriah continued to ship about twenty-five percent of its ore and pig iron from Port Henry through the lake and barge canal system during the warm weather months. Water shipments, although lacking capacity, were at lower cost. This practice continued well into the twen-tieth century.

While other Northern New York transportation developments were progressing, the Lake Champlain and Moriah Railroad Company im-proved its facilities. A roundhouse was built at Port Henry in 1872 and complete repair shops in 1873. An engine house was built at the mines in 1874 for a switch engine, thus eliminating the use of horses to switch cars.

The expanding iron industry and improved transportation generated a constant flow of immigrants to the Champlain Valley and Town of Moriah. This in turn developed the various communities within the township. The Town of Moriah was partitioned from Crown Point in 1808. (I speculate that Moriah may have derived its name from the up-per part of the Hill of Ophel, the threshing floor of Araunah, upon which Solomon erected the Temple, once called Mt. Moriah [*Encyclopedia Britannica*, 1964].)

In 1836, according to the "Gazetteer of the State of New York" by Thomas F. Gordon, the population of Essex County was 20,690. Moriah was the leader of its then fifteen towns with 2,293. There were post

Crown Point Iron Company train on main line timber trestle, bringing ore from the mines to the furnace at Crown Point, circa 1870s.

Cedar Point Furnace,
Port Henry, N. Y.

*Cedar Point Furnace was built under the direction of Thomas F. Witherbee
and operated from 1875 to 1924.*

offices at Moriah, the center of the township; Port Henry, on Lake
Champlain; and Pondsville, a lumbering section in the North Hudson
area.

For many years after discovery the great inland ore mining area was
referred to as "The Ore Bed." Development of the mines created and
named the communities of Mineville and Witherbee, as Dalliba's iron
venture had named Port Henry. The mines at Mineville were renowned
for the quality of the ore, and the whole region became known worldwide in mining circles as the Mineville Iron District. A United States
post office was established at Mineville on April 20, 1870 with George
T. Treadway as Postmaster. The post office existed previously under the
name of Moriah Centre. The Witherbee post office was established on
April 1, 1891 with William P. Viall as Postmaster. The hamlet of Witherbee obviously was named for the family that created and maintained
the community. From the beginning the mining and furnace companies
built housing for their employees, and that practice continued into the
twentieth century.

While lack of transportation in the early years impeded development of inland mines, the Cheever Mine was ideally situated on the mar-

gin of the lake for shipments by water to the furnaces at Port Henry, the Hudson Valley, Pennsylvania and Ohio. When the main line of the New York and Canada Railroad passed adjacent to Cheever dock facilities the mine had available economic shipping by both rail and water.

Horace Gray, who had leased the Port Henry Furnaces and Cheever Ore Bed from the Port Henry Iron Company in 1845, had been one of the promoters of the New York & New Haven Railroad. Before the failure of his various business ventures in 1847 he had been actively promoting construction of a railroad along the west shore of Lake Champlain. Following Mr. Gray's failure, operations of the Cheever Mine were suspended for a time and finally in 1852 the Cheever Ore Bed and Port Henry Furnaces were sold to Benjamin T. Reed, Samuel Hooper and R. W. Hooper of Boston and Joseph and Lucius Tuckerman of New York City. In 1853 Mr. Reed formed the Cheever Ore Bed Company which took over that mine, and the Port Henry Furnace Company which assumed management of the furnaces.

The Cheever Ore Bed Company contracted to furnish ore to the furnace company at fifty cents per ton above cost. This high quality ore, averaging sixty-three percent iron and 0.3 to 0.4 percent phosphorus, was in great demand as a mixture with other ores at forges and furnaces along the Hudson Valley. The mine produced fifty to sixty thousand tons per year from 1852 to 1884, and thereafter at a diminishing tonnage until 1892. It may be of general interest to quote here in part a description of the Cheever Mine operation as recorded by Watson (*History of Essex County 1869*).

"The ore is found in a regular vein and perfectly developed, from five to fifteen feet in thickness. The vein is reached by five different shafts or pits, one of which descends vertically to a depth of three hundred and fifteen feet. The work of opening has been pursued from the several pits and shafts, until a breast work of nearly one thousand and five hundred feet of ore has been formed and is now worked. From the foot of the perpendicular shaft, four distinct rail tracks have been constructed, which enable cars to transport the ore a distance of about two hundred feet. At the shaft, the ore is tipped into iron buckets, capable of holding about a ton and a half of ore. These are hoisted to the surface where, by the action of appropriate machinery, the buckets are discharged into cars which carry it by a rail road along an inclined plane to the company's wharf, at the lake, or by the same machinery, the ore may be deposited on a platform, ready to be conveyed away by teams. The ore is conveyed on the rail trains in the pits by cars from the breast, and discharged into boxes, which are hoisted up the slide or inclined plane, to the platform above from which it is transported. These slides require ropes seven hundred feet long to connect with the drum in the engine room. Steam is the motive power, created by three stationary engines, for all the movements and elevating of the cars, buckets and boxes with ore about the mine. The rail road which conducts the cars to the lake, is about three fourths of a mile in length. From the wharf it is shipped for exportation. This ore does not require separating. No stones appear in it, except an occasional slight cleavage from the wall rock. . . .

"About two hundred men are constantly employed in this mine. I descended the perpendicular shaft in an iron bucket, accompanied by Mr. John O. Presbrey, the courteous agent at the mine. The stopping of the bucket at the foot was so gentle and noiseless that I was scarcely aware the descent of more than three hundred feet was ended. A strange, weird and thrilling spectacle was revealed. There was no noise but the ceaseless clink of the hammer, and the jarring of the machinery. Along the different chambers a series of twinkling lamps, shining more and more dimly, as the long lines receded in the deep darkness, were sufficient to reveal the low, dark arched roofs supported by massive and glittering doric columns. These columns stand about one hundred feet apart, and average sixteen feet square. They are chiefly formed of solid ore, a most costly material, as each column contains about one thousand tons of ore. At the remotest extremity of one of the galleries I noticed a single light moving and inquired the cause. It was a lantern carried by one in pursuit of powder, kept in that retired spot in small quantities for immediate supply, and to guard against accidents. With every precaution, frequent serious catastrophes occur in blasting, through the carelessness or inadvertence of the workmen. Several years ago, the pillars of ore left to support the enormous burthen of rock and earth above a chamber previously worked yielded to the weight, and the whole mass was crushed together. The concussion is represented to have been not unlike an earthquake, rending the earth and dislocating the massive rocks for acres."

The Goff Mine, located on the former Skene Patent north of and adjacent to the Cheever, and earlier mentioned in connection with the Jackson Furnace, is described by Mr. Watson as follows:

"Goff Bed lies in the vicinity of the Cheever, and possesses a great similarity of ore. It is situated near the margin of the lake, and has connected with it a wharf and separator. This bed was opened in 1845, and was formerly owned by Hon. George W. Goff, but three or four years since was purchased by the present proprietors, known as the Champlain Ore and Furnace Company. Besides its advantageous location on the lake shore, this mine enjoys another great and rare facility in being penetrated by nearly horizontal openings. It has three of these openings, one of which follows the vein almost eight hundred feet. A mule car is employed in the transportation of the ore from the mine. The bed is not at present worked, but when in operation it yields about four thousand tons of ore annually. The ore is magnetic, and about one-half taken from the mine requires separating. It is exported to various markets. When both this bed and the furnace at Westport, owned by the same company, are in operation, they give employment to about one hundred men. This is esteemed a valuable ore."

The long successful period of Cheever Mine operation during the nineteenth century was due in part to economic transportation from the mine to lakeside, and by water to the forges and furnaces. However, high quality of the ore was the major factor.

The Port Henry Furnace Company, under the direction of Mr. Reed, changed the furnaces from charcoal to anthracite fuel with water as the motive power. In 1854 the furnace company built a new iron stack furnace at lakeside under the direction of Wallace T. Foote. This furnace is worthy of special mention as it was reputed to be the first of its kind built anywhere, previous furnaces being built of stone. M. P. Smith (*History of Essex County 1885*) reported that the idea for the furnace as built was conceived by Ralph Crooker and Abial Elliot of Boston. The furnace had an outer casing or shell of boiler iron riveted together and stood upon plates supported by cast iron columns. It was forty-six feet high, sixteen feet in diameter at the top of the boshes, eight feet at the top of the furnace, and was blown through five tuyeres by steam power.

Another similar furnace was built in 1862. Both furnaces were rebuilt in 1866 and 1867 and each made sixty-six feet high by sixteen feet diameter. The tops were enclosed with bell and hopper and the gas conveyed to the ovens and boilers in closed iron tubes instead of brick flues formerly used. A foundry was built in 1866 and operated in connection with the furnaces. The old furnace built (or rebuilt) by Lansing and Powell was dismantled in 1855 and the furnace built by Horace Gray was taken down in 1865.

6

As iron production expanded so did the demand for fuel. During this period the method of smelting iron changed dramatically. Heretofore all Adirondack blast furnaces and forges were fueled with charcoal made in kilns with wood cut from the forests within economic hauling distance. On an average, one acre of forest land yielded cordwood for charcoal sufficient to smelt fourteen tons of ore. This source of fuel became costly as production increased and the forests were cleared. Anthracite was, by this time, the accepted fuel for efficient furnace operations and became available to the furnaces on the lake shore. Inland furnaces and forges, with a sufficient wood supply nearby, continued to operate on charcoal as charcoal iron was in some demand until near the end of the nineteenth century.

Production of charcoal was a major operation. Crews of woodcutters cut trees, limbed them, cut the logs to proper length and hauled them to the burning area or kilns. The logs were stacked upright in a circular area and shaped like a cone, with an opening left in the top; the cone was then covered with dirt. Brambles and chips were dropped down the center of the cone and ignited. Where necessary for proper draft, small openings were made in the sides of the cone. A week or more was required to properly char the cone of wood, and the burning required close attention day and night. Wood that was cut in cold winter weather contained less sap, dried harder and made the best charcoal. When the burning was completed the cooled charcoal was delivered to the coaling area at the furnace. Hauling distance increased as the forests were stripped near the furnaces and the charcoal burning operations were moved near the source of wood supply. In some instances coaling kilns were made at the furnaces and wood was delivered from the forests to the kilns.

Tending the charcoal kilns was a lonely job, and the burner normally had several kilns to tend; he usually had a hut to live in near the kilns during the coaling operation. He had to be skilled in his trade and watch for wind and weather changes that would affect the kilns, requiring changes in the draft to make the wood char properly. It was an around-the-clock operation.

About a mile west of Moriah Center on the south side of the North Hudson Road, the ruins of the Colburn Blast Furnace can be seen today. This charcoal furnace was built in 1848, and little is known today concerning its reasons for being built and its period of operation and final shut-down. I recall being told many years ago that some ore was hauled from Adirondac (Tahawus) during the winter on sleds and given a trial in this furnace. I have not been able to find documentation to support that statement. A Mr. Hodge, writing in the *American Railroad Journal* in 1849, called this the East Moriah Furnace, and reported it produced pig iron for $19.53 per ton delivered at the lake. For a detailed description of this furnace by Mr. Hodge, see Appendix A.

The cost per ton of pig iron at the lake by other furnaces in 1848, according to Mr. Hodge was:

Port Henry Iron Co. Furnace No. 2	$17.19
Jackson (Sisco) Furnace, Westport	18.22
Crown Point Iron Co. Furnace	17.58
Mount Hope Furnace (near Whitehall)	21.00

Cost of raw materials at the furnace and delivered price of iron at the lake for shipment were the economic factors that determined successful iron ventures.

Fletcherville Furnace, the last charcoal furnace built in the region, was constructed in 1864-65 under the ownership of Friend P. Fletcher and S. H. and J. G. Witherbee. It was located in the Town of Westport, north of the Moriah town line, on Lot 48 of the Iron Ore Tract, on the west side and adjacent to the North Pond road leading from Mineville to Westport. Some of the support buildings and facilities were located on Lots 107 and 75.

Fletcherville Furnace was built by Jerome B. Bailey of Plattsburgh who became its first manager. It was first in blast from August to October 1865, then down for repairs, then blown in again in December 1865, continuing in blast until October 1866, producing 1,921 tons of iron from ore yielding 44.8 percent iron, and consuming 223.2 bushels of charcoal per ton of iron.

Fletcherville, about three miles from Mineville, became quite a little hamlet. An 1874 map by D. M. Arnold shows, in addition to the furnace, an engine house, casting house, scales, store and office building, coal house, ten coal kilns, two ore kilns, school, superintendent's house, sixteen employee dwellings and other unnamed buildings. The ruins of the furnace and some building foundations are clearly visible today. For a detailed description of this furnace, see Appendix B.

Thomas F. Witherbee, younger brother of J. G. Witherbee, became assistant to Mr. Bailey, and when Mr. Bailey left to build a furnace in

Alabama, Thomas Witherbee became superintendent of the furnace at Fletcherville and held that position for seven years. His success as a furnace operator and innovator gained him nationwide recognition.

Thomas Witherbee was born October 10, 1843 at Port Henry. After completing a common-school education he entered Rensselaer Polytechnic Institute at Troy but dropped out to enter the Union Army in 1862. Honorably discharged from the army in 1864 he returned to Port Henry. He formed a cornet band that performed for many years, and in the 1880's he sponsored a well-organized baseball team. His achievements as an ironmaster contributed greatly to the developing iron and steel industry.

As assistant to Mr. Bailey, Thomas Witherbee was involved with experiments in ore mix and furnace changes at Fletcherville to produce a high quality iron. Additional pipes were added to raise the temperature of the hot blast, and mixtures of ores from the various mines were used. The ores were all magnetite as follows: Old Bed, New Bed Pure, Old Bed Shaft, Miller Pit, New Bed Lean, Nos. 74, 75, 85, Humbug Hill, and Camel Hill. Iron made from a mixture of New Bed Pure and No. 85 ore contained by analysis:

Iron	92.82%
Silicon	2.64%
Phosphorus	.07%
Sulphur	trace
Carbon	4.05%
Slag and trace of Calcium and Aluminum	.42%
Total	100.00%

This analysis is of particular interest as ore from this blast constituted a part of the first Bessemer furnace charge blown at Troy, New York.

After Mr. Bailey left Fletcherville, Thomas Witherbee continued to modify the furnace to produce high quality iron. The stack of the furnace was raised by a wrought iron shell to sixty feet high, the tunnel head was enlarged to eight feet in diameter and closed with a bell and hopper. Mr. Witherbee established a chemical laboratory at the furnace to analyze and control the product. This is believed to be the first such laboratory attached to a furnace operation.

Part of the first Fletcherville iron produced was shipped to Griswold, Winslow and Holley at Troy and was used in some of the first steel rails made in America. Fletcherville iron was also shipped to the ironworks at Clinton Prison in Dannemora, nail works at Keeseville and AuSable Forks, and various ironworks along the Hudson Valley. The

The Port Henry Furnaces were operated by The Bay State Iron Company of Boston from 1867 until that company failed in 1883. The Port Henry Furnace Company was formed and operated the furnaces for a few years until that company also failed. The plant was dismantled in 1896.

quality of the iron was high but despite the innovations at Fletcherville, including introducing anthracite fuel, freight costs and other economic factors were not favorable for a secure future operation. A severe drop in the price of Fletcherville iron from sixty to thirty dollars a ton in the depressed period in the early 1870's contributed to the early demise of the furnace. Upon the death of Mr. Fletcher in 1874, the furnace was closed down permanently and the property later passed into the hands of Witherbees Sherman and Company.

In 1867 the anthracite furnaces at Port Henry and the Cheever Ore Bed lease, held by the Port Henry Furnace Company, were acquired by the Bay State Iron Company, a company with a rolling mill and other holdings in Boston. This transaction also included the Barton Ore Bed which the Furnace Company had purchased in 1863. The Bay State Company operated the furnaces until it encountered financial difficulties and failed in 1883. Shortly thereafter a new Port Henry Furnace Company was formed by Wallace T. Foote, the Burleighs of Ticonderoga and Witherbees Sherman and Company. This group operated the furnaces for a few years until financial difficulties resulted in a sheriff's sale and the property was acquired by Witherbees Sherman and Company. That company operated the No. 3 Furnace until 1890 and the

No. 2 Furnace until 1892. In 1896 the plant was dismantled.

In the 1860's Witherbees Sherman and Company furnace ownership was at Fletcherville, the furnaces at Port Henry being under control of Mr. Reed and the Port Henry Furnace Company, and later the Bay State Iron Company as successor. Anticipating the eventual shutdown of the Fletcherville operation for economic reasons, the company made plans for a new and larger furnace to be built at the lake shore. Valuable experience in furnace design and management had been gained at Fletcherville which enhanced and favored the plan.

The Cedar Point Iron Company was formed in 1872. Among its first directors were S. H. and J. G. Witherbee, A. B. Waldo, G. R. Sherman, Dr. R. E. Warner, H. B. Willard and Walter Merrill. A site was selected for a new modern blast furnace on the lake shore at the south end of the village of Port Henry. Thomas F. Witherbee was placed in charge of the project.

In 1872 he began construction of the Cedar Point Furnace and incorporated in its design not only the experience gained at Fletcherville, but the latest concepts in furnace design nationally and abroad. He installed the first Whitwell fire-brick stoves ever erected in this country, importing the brick and castings from England. It was here that he introduced the Witherbee bronze tuyeres, his own invention. He was the first in America to use the Lurmann water-cooled cinder notch; he invented and used the kerosene blowpipe for opening closed tuyeres and tapholes. He was the first to remove scaffolds and other obstructions in the blast furnace with dynamite and for this he was sometimes called "Dynamite Tom."

The Cedar Point Furnace was built in 1872-74 at a cost of $600,000, but due to the financial depression of 1873-74, the furnace was not put in blast until August 12, 1875. The best description of the construction of this blast furnace plant is recorded in a paper "The Cedar Point Iron Company's Furnace No. 1 at Port Henry, Essex County, N.Y." by T. F. Witherbee which appeared in *Transactions of the American Institute of Mining Engineers*, Vol. 4, 1876, and is quoted in part in Appendix C.

The Cedar Point Furnace produced forty-one tons of iron per day from the beginning of operations, running on Mineville ores although other Adirondack ores were occasionally used. Thomas Witherbee was the guiding force and his achievements as a furnace operator were nationally recognized. He remained in charge at Cedar Point until 1887. He then went to Durango, Mexico as superintendent of a large ironworks. From 1898 to 1900 he managed furnaces in Chicago and Mayville, Wisconsin. He was recalled to Durango where he remained until his death in 1909. Thomas Witherbee's contributions in refining the skills of the Ironmaster were many, including fifteen technical papers published in *Transactions of the American Institute of Mining Engineers* during his thirty-eight years membership, beginning in 1871, the year the AIME was formed.

The Cedar Point Furnace was taken over by Witherbees Sherman and Company in 1885. It was later leased to Slayback, Robinson and Dickey of New York, who added a Clapp-Griffith steel plant to the furnace. This was not a success and the steel plant was removed to Pittsburgh. The furnace was later leased to Pilling and Crane of Philadelphia, who operated it in the early 1900's.

One of the engines from the old Bay State furnaces and some of the hot blast stoves from the Crown Point furnaces were added at Cedar Point. With this additional equipment and some other improvements, furnace production was increased to 175 to 200 tons per day of high quality iron.

It is difficult today, over a century later, to visualize the water of Lake Champlain touching the eastern bounds of the Delaware and Hudson Railroad main line at Cedar Point at the south end of the village of Port Henry; also to visualize the 1,200 feet of railroad trestle over the water to the furnace plant built out into the lake. The shore of Lake Champlain was extended several hundred feet east of Cedar Point in subsequent years into the 1930's as cinder or slag from furnace operations was dumped on Lake Champlain land under water granted to the iron interests.

The Cedar Point Foundry, operated by Andrew Tromblee, was built in 1879 near the Cedar Point Furnace, and located on the west side of the highway just south of Meacham Street. It produced castings for paper mill and mining machinery. The high quality of the castings created a demand that kept the foundry operating at capacity, even through the depressed years of 1893-98 when many industries were shut down. The foundry was destroyed by fire in 1903 and the business was moved to Plattsburgh. The successor to that business was the Plattsburgh Machine and Foundry Company.

7

Economic forces at work in nineteenth century America were both a help and a hindrance to the local iron industry. Financial panics of 1837, 1857, 1873 1893 and the aftermath of those years, brought financial ruin to some while the survivors grew stronger. In the growing American nation, when the panics hit the industrial northern states, American workers and farmers picked up and moved to the western frontiers to build a new life.

As business improved, industries found an adequate number of immigrant workers ready to fill any jobs that were available. They had left their homelands by the thousands because there was no undeveloped frontier where they could rebuild their lives. It was fortunate for America that they came, for they dug the canals and built the railroads that made the nation grow. They manned the factories and mines; they were often exploited. The ten and twelve-hour workday was considered by the industrialists to be best for the workers as too much idle time on their hands would be morally bad. Pressure was maintained on political leaders to support this philosophy.

The immigrants came to the Champlain Valley, to Mineville, Witherbee and Port Henry. They were from many nations. Their customs, speech and dress were different; there was a language barrier and they were considered inferior to their American-born counterparts and were for the most part uneducated. But they mined the ore and manned the furnaces, becoming skilled in their trade; and they and their families shaped the communities.

The growth of the West and development of the great Michigan mines, with cheap water transportation to Great Lakes ports and rail shipments from there to the steel plants of the Midwest, Ohio and Pennsylvania, controlled that market area. The market for Lake Champlain ores was thus generally confined to plants in southern New England, the Hudson Valley, New Jersey, eastern Pennsylvania, and Ohio. This market area, however, was a constant target for cheap foreign ore imports at east coast ports.

Following completion of improved year-round rail transportation, the two major mining companies in the Town of Moriah, Witherbees

Sherman and Company and the Port Henry Iron Ore Company, increased the development of their mines and became major eastern iron ore producers. However, executive management of the two companies differed. Witherbees Sherman had more on-site control with the highest executives maintaining residences locally; Port Henry Iron Ore Company top executives and officers lived elsewhere and were involved with other iron and steel ventures. Witherbees Sherman was a minority stockholder in the Port Henry Iron Ore Company and, under contract with that company, handled the sales of its products.

The Port Henry Iron Ore Company "21" Mine was at one time one of the largest and most impressive iron mines in the world, being mostly mined as an open pit with underground openings from the pit to the south and east. The ore vein was from three hundred to four hundred feet thick, whereas the typical good ore vein was perhaps fifteen feet thick. The ore as mined averaged about 60 percent iron and 1.25 percent phosphorus. Adjoining the "21" Mine and contiguous to the main ore structure, the company opened and mined the Brinsmade, Nolan and Welch Mines, and had mined the "23" Mine and ore on Lot 24 of their ownership next to Miller Pit Mine of Witherbees Sherman and Company. As mentioned earlier, the Port Henry Iron Ore Company mined the Fisher Hill Mines from 1872 to 1893.

Witherbees Sherman and Company mining operations also expanded during this same period. In addition to the Sanford and Miller Pits, the Tefft Shaft workings and Joker and Bonanza Mines were developed. They were on Witherbees Sherman property, but were a continuation of the "21" ore mined by Port Henry Iron Ore Company. Witherbees Sherman and Company had also acquired Burt Mines at Fisher Hill, Cook Shaft or Smith Mine property, Barton Hill and New Bed Mines. In addition, they acquired several thousand mineral acres embracing lands formerly held by the Jay Cook Estates, including some small mines near the Fletcherville Furnace.

The Tefft Shaft Mine must have been a more hazardous operation than other mine workings as indicated by the following document.

Mineville, N.Y., January 1884

"We have and do hereby apply to Witherbee's, Sherman, & Co., for and accept employment in their mine known as "Tefft Shaft," and recognizing that labor in and about said shaft may be dangerous, in consideration of the wages paid, we hereby agree to accept and run all risk of death or injury in said mine or work connected therewith or arising from any defect in mine, or machinery or appliances used therein, especially from any defect of roof, wall, track, cars, or any instrumentality used in said work, and we further agree in considera-

tion of our employment to make no claim against said company for
any injury received in said mine or in work connected therewith. And
it is understood that said company gives us no assurance of the safety
of said mine, machinery or appliances."

From January 1, 1884 through June 30, 1885, forty-nine men signed
the above statement as a condition of employment by Witherbees Sherman and Company for work in the mining area known as "Tefft Shaft."
Nineteen of the signatures had an "X" denoted as "his mark," between
the given and surname of the signature. All signatures were witnessed
by L. S. Collins. I sent a copy of this document to Mr. John L. Shea who
had worked for Witherbees Sherman and Republic Steel continuously in
accounting and employment from about 1915 until his retirement in
1960. From his early years Mr. Shea remembered three of the men who
had signed the document. He also noted that L. S. Collins was a cousin
of Mrs. F. S. Witherbee, and had been timekeeper and paymaster at
Mineville. He commented on the document the men signed.

"I was dumbfounded to read what the men had to sign to be
accepted for employment at W. S. & Co."
"I am still astounded at the requirement W. S. & Co. demanded
for a man to be accepted for employment. I thought the Civil War
abolished slavery. I cannot understand how a company could be so
callous. I did think W. S. & Co. repented a little in later years. I know
they did bestow pensions of the large sum of $30 a month to a few
old employees not able to work any longer. I think bestow rather than
give is the correct word and they perhaps thought they were doing a
big favor. In one instance an old couple was given $30 a month
whose son was killed in the mines. I delivered the check to them and
took a receipt. I remember several cases where they paid $1,500 to
the widow of a man killed in the mines. . . ."

The financial depression of 1873-74 affected mining operations and
the hundreds of employees of both mining companies. On November 30,
1874 the companies posted a notice to their employees stating that the
iron business was growing worse and worse, and times looked so bad
that they were obliged to either close the mines or reduce wages and,
after much consideration they decided not to close, but to reduce wages
on December 15. The notice included a reduced wage schedule for a
ten-hour workday by which pit foremen would be paid $2.25, the high-
est daily wage, and drill boys would be paid $1.00, the lowest daily
wage on the schedule.

Despite the cyclical nature of the iron and steel industry and recur-
ring recessions, the mining companies kept abreast of technical and
equipment developments to update operations and remain competitive.

The use of compressed air for drilling to replace hand drilling was introduced into the mines at Mineville. Previously hand drilling was accomplished by a three-man crew, with one man holding and turning the drill and two men alternately striking the drill with twenty-pound hammers.

In 1874 advertising circulars for the Rand, Waring and Ingersoll Rock Drill Companies reported competitive tests on their drills at the mines at Mineville. Each claimed superior performance. One circular, featuring Waring's "Improved Self-Feeding Rock Drill," showed a hand-crank rock drill mounted on a tripod with weighted legs. This feature was a forerunner of tripod-mounted hand-crank rock drills that were used in Mineville mines up to 1940.

A pillar blast was scheduled for April 19, 1877 at the Port Henry Iron Ore Company's "21" Mine. For four years the company had been removing a portion of the mine roof to surface which was supported by three pillars of iron ore. The pillars were from 140 to 170 feet high, 30 to 50 feet in diameter and estimated to contain 79,800 gross tons of ore. Drilling had been completed in preparation for loading explosives. Mr. William Murray told me many years ago that he was a drill boy at the mine and was supposed to carry blasting powder up on the pillars that day. There was a two-inch snowfall the night before and he stayed home sick as he thought it would be slippery and dangerous.

The blast was considered a major event in mining circles and was widely publicized. Distinguished guests came by special train to view the blast. The 140-member group included Eastern Ironmasters, members of the press, W. A. Roebling, the bridge builder, David H. Cochran, president of Brooklyn Polytechnic Institute, railroad officials and others. At Port Henry, the train was divided into two sections and coupled to the engines Brinsmade and Sherman to ascend the steep grades of the Lake Champlain and Moriah Railroad. Following a luncheon at the railroad shop facilities, and arrival at Mineville, the guests assembled on a platform constructed for them on the north bank of "21" Mine. Here J. B. Brinsmade, secretary and treasurer of the company, with his wife and daughter present, explained the work to be attempted on the section of the mine that lay in full view of the group.

Final loading of explosives had been underway since three o'clock that morning. This was to be a spectacular blast initiated electrically to blast the three pillars and roof section simultaneously. Wires were insulated and connected to Smith and Farmer batteries. The signal to fire was given to the men at the batteries and in the ensuing explosion fragments from the blast fell among the people in the stands. The amount of fly-rock and ore varied according to various sources, but I know of no injuries reported. As the onlookers crowded to the edge of the bank they could see that forty feet off the top of the west pillar with parts of the roof and arches had been blasted down.

The middle pillar was cracked but remained standing and the third pillar with the roof it supported was undisturbed. Wires were again connected to the batteries and a second blast initiated, this time demolishing the standing west pillar. Before the second blast however, the observation platform was vacated. It is fortunate that the initial blast failed for if all the pillars and roof had been blown simultaneously, there could have been serious injury to the observers. The visiting guests were returned to Albany by special train to make other evening train connections.

The next day, April 20, a second blast was made in the east bank of the mine to remove a large mass of loose ore. The concussion from this blast was so severe that it shattered windows in the nearby Witherbees Sherman office. This was the only real damage that occurred from both blasts. Plans were made to blast the third pillar and the roof it supported in July.

Not long after Edison invented the incandescent lamp, a dynamo and twelve electric lights were installed in the underground workings of the Port Henry Iron Ore Company. This was one of the first, and possible the first, use of electric lights in an underground mine. By the late 1880's the company had efficient mechanical installations to produce large tonnages. One central power station, on the north bank of the "21" Mine furnished all the motive power for hoisting, pumping and compressed air. There were three large hoisting engines, one shop engine, one pumping engine, four duplex air compressors, three lift pumps, sixteen steam pumps, air drills, etc. The office, boiler house, coal shed, storehouse, shops and water reservoir facilities were located east of the Welch, Brinsmade and Nolan shafts. These shafts mined portions of the same ore structure that produced the massive "21" Mine. During this same period Port Henry Iron Ore Company also operated Fisher Hill Mine, two miles north of "21" Mine.

Old Bed ore, mined underground by Witherbees Sherman and Company, was hoisted to the surface through Bonanza and Joker shafts. For a description of these two shafts, see Appendix D.

The Joker and Bonanza shafts, hoisting Old Bed ore, became the major producers for Witherbees Sherman and Company. Production from all their mines and from Port Henry Iron Ore Company mines rose steadily, except during the depressed years, as illustrated in the twenty-year period of 1870-1890 showing yearly tons produced at five year intervals:

	Witherbees Sherman and Company			
1870	**1875**	**1880**	**1885**	**1890**
81,681	118,582	191,781	105,750	269,587
	Port Henry Iron Ore Company			
82,227	100,926	170,951	74,474	139,201
		Totals		
163,908	219,508	362,732	180,224	408,788

The financial strength of these two companies permitted them to survive the depressed years of the 1890's which witnessed the end of many mining operations. So severe was the local impact of the 1893 depression that only a total of 45,178 tons were produced during 1894 by these two companies. Witherbees Sherman and Company idled certain of their operations, concentrating their efforts on the richer and more productive mining sections. The Port Henry Iron Ore Company terminated operations at Fisher Hill and only continued to produce ore from the "21" Mine.

Continued family-owner on-site management of Witherbees Sherman and Company operations had fostered sustained growth of the company. Sons of the founders followed the footsteps of their fathers. Walter C. Witherbee, son of S. H. Witherbee became involved in the company and, following the death of his father, continued to be active during his lifetime. Jonathan G. Witherbee, nephew of S. H. Witherbee and one of the original founders of the company, was also a director of the Port Henry Iron Ore Company and president of the Cedar Point Iron Company. He became president of the First National Bank of Port Henry and first president of Port Henry Village following its incorporation.

Jonathan G. Witherbee died in Port Henry on August 25, 1875 at age 54. On his death the *New York Tribune* noted,

> "Mr. Witherbee began life without means, and succeeded in amassing a large fortune, owning one-third of the firm of Witherbees Sherman and Company. . . .

> "Mr. Witherbee would be best remembered for his large-hearted generosity, multitudes of poor families having been supported by his bounty, bestowed without the knowledge of others. Young men starting in business, as well as many persons afflicted with distress or perplexity, have found in him a sympathetic friend, a wise counselor, and a practical helper."

Perhaps the best tribute of all paid to Mr. Witherbee was the presence of the long lines of miners who lined both sides of the road as his funeral cortege reached Union Cemetery.

Frank S. Witherbee, son of Jonathan G. Witherbee, was graduated from Yale University in 1874. Upon hearing the news of his father's death, he came home and at age 23 assumed the management of his father's estate. He became an active member of the firm of Witherbees Sherman and Company. As an ambitious, educated young man who had travelled worldwide, Frank Witherbee brought to the company an understanding of the changing nature of the iron and steel industry and the economic forces at work in the latter quarter of the nineteenth century.

Development of the great Mesabi Iron Range in Minnesota, with cheap water shipping to steel plants at Great Lakes ports, increased the competitive pressure against Lake Champlain ores. The Mesabi and Michigan Iron Ranges, with tremendous readily available ore reserves strategically located, became the major source of iron ore for a rapidly expanding steel industry in step with the industrial development of the nation.

The economic importance and decline of Mineville ores as a major source of supply can be illustrated as follows: In 1875 two and one-half million tons were mined in the United States and 8.8 percent of that amount was produced at Mineville. By 1905 production from Mineville mines had increased three times the 1875 rate, but this amounted to only 1.3 percent of the 50 million tons of United States ore mined.

Lake Champlain ores were generally magnetite (Fe_3O_4) and as mined ranged from 25 to 65 percent iron, with the lower grades requiring separation to improve the quality. These ores enjoyed certain metallurgical qualities which helped maintain their competitive position. The high grade hand-sorted lump ore from "21", Joker and Bonanza mines of both mining companies worked well in the furnaces. When added to a furnace charge of lower grade hematite ore, these ores improved the operation of the furnace through reduced heat time. The lean ores, upgraded to 60 percent iron, also worked well mixed with other ores in the furnace charge.

Iron ore was mined, shipped and sold by the long ton (2,240 pounds). Due to the varying iron content of ore from the many mines, the competitive price was based on an iron unit; one unit of iron representing one percent of iron in the ore. If a 50 percent iron ore had a value of $5.00 per ton (ten cents an iron unit), a 60 percent iron ore would have a value of $6.00 per ton. Higher iron units per ton and a metallurgical advantage in furnace operations helped soften the impact of high rail freight costs for shipping Mineville ores.

Witherbees Sherman and Company plowed vast sums from profits back into the business, equipping their mines and plant with the latest machines available. On June 1, 1875 they occupied their new main office building at Port Henry, built and completely furnished for $20,000. This overlooked the lake shore docks, the new Cedar Point Furnace and the main line of the recently completed New York and Canada Railroad. The company maintained a continuous diamond drill exploration program to block out the ore reserves and in depressed years of the 1890's was thus able to concentrate capital expenditures and mine production schedules in the richer Joker-Bonanza low cost mining area. In 1897 Witherbees Sherman mined only 85,099 tons, and in 1898 only 38,188 tons, whereas in the year 1890 the company mined 269,587 tons.

In 1898 Charles Cady, general manager for Witherbees Sherman and Company, described the mine operations and support facilities in detail. See Appendix E.

Support facilities for mine operations listed by Mr. Cady included a carpenter shop, a machine shop and blacksmith shop constructed of brick with metal roofs, and both equipped with modern tools, an ore concentrating plant with a capacity of 150 tons per day, a warehouse, barn, office and 84 tenement houses at various locations.

Mr. Cady listed the various ore deposits of the company in 1898 and included in the non-Bessemer group Bonanza-Joker, Old Bed, Miller Pit, Miller Pit Red Ore Vein, Tefft Shaft, Cook Shaft and O'Neil Shaft workings. He listed the Bessemer group including Burt Lot, New Bed, Barton Hill and Mt. Tom East Slope Exploration. Although none of these non-Bessemer and Bessemer deposits were in operation, with the exception of Joker-Bonanza, the Mt. Tom East Slope Exploration was being carefully prospected and evaluated as a potential mining operation. This particular structure did not outcrop at the surface as had other ore deposits, but was indicated by magnetic attraction to the compass and then confirmed by diamond drilling. (According to John L. Shea, the American Steel and Wire Company previously held an option to diamond drill that particular area but did not strike ore. The option was not renewed and Witherbees Sherman and Company drilled and found the ore.)

The field enclosed by diamond drill, as reported by Mr. Cady in 1898, showed an average ore vein thickness of 29 feet over an area of about 600 by 900 feet, capable of producing 1,572,981 gross tons. However, magnetic survey work indicated an area 1,800 feet long and 1,000 feet wide, including the drilled area, showing an overall average ore vein thickness of 20 feet that would produce 4,821,333 gross tons. Within the drilled area ore was encountered 238 feet below the surface, indicating a low cost shaft at that location to reach the ore. Drill core samples showed some of the ore could be shipped direct and some

Central Power House, a coal-fired power generating station near New Bed Mine, was placed in operation in 1903 and in that year furnished power to A and B Power House near Harmony Mine.

Witherbee Memorial Building built in 1893 by the Silas H. and Jonathan G. Witherbee families in memory of their father.

Mineville Hospital constructed from a converted shop building and supported by the Witherbee Sherman and the Port Henry Iron Ore Companies. Photo circa 1908.

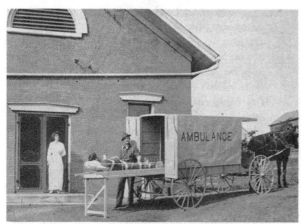

Horse-drawn ambulance at hospital in 1910. Note bell on dashboard and nurse standing in the hospital doorway.

W.S. & Co. concrete block tenant house, early 1900's.

would require milling to bring it up to satisfactory grade.

Although the Mt. Tom East Slope Exploration offered an excellent mine development potential, the project had been delayed for some time by serious disagreement among the officers and directors of the company. Some favored increased mine development to improve ore sales while others felt more capital funds should be spent to increase blast furnace production of pig iron.

In 1900 events occurred that determined the direction of the company for two decades.

The company was incorporated under the name of Witherbee Sherman and Company, dropping the "s" from the former name. Frank S. Witherbee became its first president, a position he would hold until his death in 1917.

The Lackawanna Steel Company of Buffalo purchased George Sherman's one-third interest in the company. Directors of the company were W. C. Witherbee, W. T. Foote, Jr., L. W. Francis, F. S. Witherbee, Moses Taylor and E. A. S. Clarke. Messrs. Taylor and Clarke represented the Lackawanna interest. (John L. Shea told me this transaction appeared favorable as it was understood Lackawanna would purchase 200,000 tons of ore per year from Witherbee Sherman and Company, but the arrangement ended later when Lackawanna Steel Company was purchased by Bethlehem Steel Company.)

Development of the Mt. Tom East Slope Exploration was pushed forward and "A" Shaft was sunk to the ore. In 1901, 9,900 tons were produced, and 25,330 tons in 1902. "B" Shaft was sunk in 1902 and completed in May 1903. In that year 44,229 tons were produced from both "A" and "B" Shafts, including 4,466 tons of ore produced while developing "B" Shaft. Two-thirds of the ore was pure ore that could be shipped direct, the remaining one-third being lean ore that was shipped to the separators.

The high quality of this ore found a ready market for all that could be produced. The officers and directors of the company were so euphoric with the success of the venture that, as Mr. Shea told me, their disagreements vanished and they decided to "kiss and make up." They thus named the Mt. Tom East Slope Exploration "Harmony Mine."

Electric power and compressed air for developing Harmony "A" and "B" Shafts were furnished from No. 1 Power House, constructed in 1896-97 to serve Joker and Bonanza Mines. This source became inadequate as mining operations expanded. An aggressive Witherbee Sherman mine development program to reopen New Bed-Barton Hill and Smith Mines required more power facilities. In addition, the variety of ores, varying in chemical analysis, led their engineers to test various methods of ore separation for Bessemer and non-Bessemer furnace feed.

Central Power Plant, a coal-fired steam boiler system near New Bed-Barton Hill Mines, was completed and fire laid under the boilers on October 31, 1903. The plant began furnishing power to Separator No. 2 on November 30. "A" and "B" Power House, constructed to serve Harmony Mine, was completed with power first turned on from Central Power Plant on December 4, 1903.

For the year 1903 Witherbee Sherman spent $217,542.26 for new construction. In addition to the power facilities, the cost included construction work at Mills 1 and 2, "B" Shaft, plant railroad work, miscellaneous mine and yard tracks at Mineville, laying the railroad to Smith Mine, and the expense at Smith Mine for un-watering and re-timbering Cook Shaft, overhauling mine tracks, and repairs to mine buildings and machinery.

During 1903 Witherbee Sherman mined 212,887 tons from Old Bed and Harmony Mines and purchased 20,044 tons from Port Henry Iron Ore Company. They shipped 206,796 tons including 65,611 tons of crude ore and 141,185 tons of concentrates. The Witherbee Sherman work force that year averaged 261 with an average daily wage of $1.92. Although the labor cost was 67.8 cents per ton for 1903, the cost of new construction was $1.02 per ton.

These statistics reflect favorably on the directors of Witherbee Sherman and Company and its president Frank S. Witherbee. The 1890's and the turn of the century were years of recession and widely fluctuating ore prices during which many mines failed. Despite these conditions, Witherbee Sherman plowed back funds to ready the company for the economic recovery that was certain to come. The soundness of the planning would be proved during the ensuing fifteen years.

The Smith Mine property, located about two miles north of Mineville and including Cook and O'Neil Shafts, had been purchased by Witherbees Sherman and Company in the 1880's but had been idle for many years. About 200,000 tons had been previously mined but the mine workings were flooded. The ore mined was of the same general character as that of the Joker-Bonanza. Analysis of lump ore was 62.80% iron and 0.87% phosphorous. Fine ore was 62.86% iron and 0.94% phosphorous. Ore left in the side walls of the mine by the former owners and magnetic surface attractions indicated the mine covered a large undeveloped area. The railroad was extended to the mine during 1903-04. The electrical, compressor, and hoisting plant was completed; a large new shaft house was built and a gyratory crusher installed. Electric power was furnished from a hydro power plant at Wadhams Mills, about thirteen miles distant.

Under a long-standing agreement, Witherbee Sherman acted as sales agent for Port Henry Iron Ore Company. The latter only produced crude ore, lump and fines which were shipped direct to customers; they operated no concentrating mills. Under the terms of the ore sales agreement, orders for crude ore were to be apportioned equally between the two companies. Witherbee Sherman was paid a fee for handling the sales for Port Henry Iron Ore Company. Sales of concentrated ore by Witherbee Sherman were outside the sales agreement, and Witherbee Sherman did not always have available enough crude shipping ore to satisfy its half of the orders. This permitted Port Henry Iron Ore Company to supply the portion not furnished by Witherbee Sherman. One of the considerations for reopening Smith Mine was to supply additional crude shipping ore to fill the Witherbee Sherman portion of sales of crude ore.

About a half mile north of Smith Mine the Humbug Mine had been opened in a small way in the 1850's. Studies indicated it was within the Bessemer limits for phosphorus and probably half the ore could be hand-cobbed to about 60% iron for shipment as crude ore. The balance could be shipped to No. 1 Mill for concentration. During 1904 the Humbug Mine was un-watered and an air line installed from Smith Mine compressor plant. An electric hoisting plant was ordered to develop the ore deposit, hoping to open a substantial body of ore.

Humbug Mine produced 746 tons in 1904 of which 575 tons were treated at No. 1 Mill and 171 tons were treated at No. 2 Mill. During 1905 Humbug produced 2,186 tons from which 251 tons were crude shipped and 1,935 tons were shipped to the separators. By comparison, Smith Mine produced 27,903 tons during 1905 from which 27,326 tons were crude shipped and 577 tons were shipped to the separators. In addition to a low percentage of crude shipping ore, Humbug production cost per ton was 43% higher than Smith Mine. High costs and unsatisfactory development of crude shipping ore brought an end to renewed operations at Humbug Mine.

The first nine months of 1904 was a period of declining ore prices and reduced business activity nationwide. Many mines in the Lake Superior region were shut down and few, if any, operated at full capacity. However, Witherbee Sherman was able to operate its mines and mills full time, producing 339,503 tons. By year-end ore prices advanced 50 to 75 percent above the mid-year rate. The Port Henry Iron Ore Company mined 96,239 tons during 1904. Of the total 435,742 tons mined by the two companies, Witherbee Sherman produced 77.9%. This was possible because Witherbee Sherman produced, in addition to crude ore, Old Bed concentrates and Harmony low phosphorous cobbed and crude ore. The increased sales justified the expenditures made to produce the various grades of ore.

While management decisions by Witherbee Sherman and Company at the turn of the century placed the company in a position to take advantage of growing demand for its varied high grade magnetite iron ore products, similar decisions were lacking within management of the Port Henry Iron Ore Company. This may have been due to historical complacency and satisfaction with the abundant profits achieved by the very nature of the "21" Mine. Its massive ore body, not deep underground, furnished a non-Bessemer lump ore product desirable for furnace operators.

From the early organization of the Port Henry Iron Ore Company the ranking officer in charge of affairs was the secretary-treasurer, certainly competent but lacking a proper title to enhance the position in the minds of leaders in the iron ore industry. No company directors or officers ranking higher than mine superintendent maintained a local residence, with the exception of a Witherbee Sherman and Company member on the board of directors.

In contrast, all but two Witherbee Sherman directors and officers maintained local residences and were active in the company locally. Frank S. Witherbee, president, was a state and national figure, having served as a member of the Electoral College from New York State. Wallace T. Foote, a Witherbee Sherman director, had served in the U.S. Congress. This is not to infer that Port Henry Iron Ore Company's top executives lacked stature. To the contrary, they were for the most part nationally recognized industrialists with diverse business activities in which the Port Henry Iron Ore Company was a part. They may have lacked the "hands-on" knowledge to assess the opportunities available in the changing iron ore market.

Had Port Henry Iron Ore Company acted at the turn of the century and reopened their Fisher Hill Mine property that was shut down in 1893, and at the same time built a concentrating mill to treat Fisher Hill ore and "21" Mine fine ore, the company could have furnished, in addition to lump ore, high grade Bessemer and non-Bessemer concentrates to the fast-developing market for those ores.

8

Concentration of magnetite iron ore was a necessary process for some of the Mineville ores. I mentioned earlier the magnetic separator used in 1852 to separate iron ore from apatite or "red sand" in the Old Bed "21" ore. Other early methods of separating crystals of ore from rock included roasting the ore, then crushing it and placing the crushed material in various type tanks or troughs with flowing water to liberate the lighter non-iron material.

Witherbee Sherman and Company continually studied and developed separation methods, and at one time was reputed to be the largest producer of magnetically separated iron ore in the world. The concentrating mills at Mineville were designed to upgrade the ore mined to an acceptable product for the furnaces. Old Bed ore in place was usually sharply defined with a clear boundary between ore and rock. New Bed, Barton Hill, Fisher Hill and Harmony ores were not so clearly defined in place. In some areas the ore was massive, very rich and often called "pure ore," being 70% iron. Generally though, the bounds of these ores tapered off into the adjacent rocks in decreasing content of iron. Volume of tons and other factors determined the economic overall grade that could be successfully mined and concentrated.

Crude ore hoisted from Old Bed Mines was hand sorted, with chunks of pure ore going to a bin for direct shipment to the furnaces. The remainder was fed to the crushers and separators. The two mills at Mineville were taxed beyond capacity by opening Harmony and Smith Mines. No. 1 Mill, treating only Harmony ore, was practically rebuilt during 1904, while being operated at the same time. The mill was simplified and strengthened. Additional crushers and rolls were added to increase its capacity. No. 2 Mill, treating Old Bed ore, was running efficiently in 1904 but anticipation of increased Old Bed Mine production indicated that No. 1 Mill would soon be required for treating Old Bed ore. Plans were initiated for construction of a new mill to be located at Harmony Mine to serve both "A" and "B" Shafts. This would eliminate surface rail transfer of ore from Harmony to No. 1 Mill.

At that time Witherbee Sherman and Company was fortunate to have Sheldon Norton as general manager, succeeding Charles Cady. Mr.

Norton had broad experience in eastern mines and held, and was co-holder of, certain patents on magnetic separators. It was during his tenure at Mineville that the concentrating process was refined and the mills brought to a high state of efficiency. Ball and Norton magnetic separators were installed in the concentrating circuits, in conjunction with other separators, resulting in an improved grade of iron ore concentrate.

The large capital funds expended by Witherbee Sherman and Company for power and milling capacity, following the opening of Harmony Mines, not only increased the volume of business but brought to the iron ore market several grades of product that found a ready demand by furnace operators.

Harmony and Old Bed Mines and Mills 1905, are discussed in detail in Appendix F.

Research in iron ore concentration had been underway for several years by Witherbee Sherman and Company. With the outlays of large capital funds after 1900 the mills at Mineville were completely rebuilt. Results for the year 1905 established the company as a leader in development and production of magnetic iron ore concentrates. Production of crude ore from the mines and products produced are shown in long tons for the year 1905.

Mine Production and Crude Ore Handled, 1905

Mine	Hoisted	Direct Shipped	Sent to Mill 1	Sent to Mill 2
Old Bed	275,113	40,350	4,940	229,823
Harmony	150,734	39,647	113,703	625
Smith	27,903	27,326	222	355
Humbug	2,186	251	1,871	64
Barton Hill			1,560	
Surface Ore			28	
Port Henry I.O. Co.				17,748
Totals	455,936	107,574	122,324	248,615

Witherbee Sherman and Company occasionally purchased "21" Mine fine crude ore from Port Henry Iron Ore Company (17,748 tons above), and concentrated it, recovering iron and apatite. Ore produced during shaft sinking, mine development, and exploration work was placed in stockpiles and fed into the milling process when convenient (Barton Hill and surface ore above). These ores plus the crude ore hoisted made a total of 475,272 tons of crude ore handled by Witherbee Sherman and Company in 1905.

Witherbee Sherman and Company Mills 1 and 2 built and improved in the late 1800's. Bonanza Shaft at left, Joker Shaft at right.

Mills 1 and 2, and Cobbing Plant were destroyed by fire June 17, 1914. Joker shaft at left, Memorial Hall at right.

Witherbee Sherman Power Generating Station at Port Henry placed in operation in 1910.

Power Plant and Steam Ferry G. R. Sherman *in foreground. Ferry provided transportation from Port Henry to Vermont prior to construction of Champlain Bridge at Crown Point.*

Shipping products produced by the company consisted of direct shipping crude lump ore, iron ore concentrates of non-Bessemer and Bessemer grade, apatite of first and second grade, and ore tailings consisting of crushed stone and sand.

The year 1905 was a year of great activity in the iron trade with improved prices. Although Witherbee Sherman and Company operated the mines and mills at full capacity they were unable to meet the demand for their products. Their total shipments of 408,806 gross tons stood as a record. Frank Witherbee commented that 289,856 tons of the total shipments represented the output of the two separating plants and justified the money they had spent in their Separating Department. He also commented that they were only able to ship 27,423 tons out of the 107,800 of crude Old Bed "21 Furnace Ore" to which they were entitled under the sales agreement with the Port Henry Iron Ore Company. This justified the expenditure for un-watering and reopening Smith Mine to increase their output of this grade ore.

The Port Henry Iron Ore Company produced 199,296 tons from "21" Mine during 1905. Under their sales agreement with Witherbee Sherman to share on an equal basis orders for "21 Furnace Ore" they were entitled to ship 107,800 tons. However, due to increased concentrate production, Witherbee Sherman could not provide 80,377 tons of their share of "21 Furnace Ore." Port Henry Iron Ore Company was able to furnish those tons bringing their total shipments of this grade ore to 188,177 tons. Tonnage Witherbee Sherman was unable to furnish represented 40 percent of the total Port Henry Iron Ore Company production for the year 1905.

It appears to me the handwriting was on the wall for Port Henry Iron Ore Company executives to see in 1905. Witherbee Sherman was taking steps to provide their share of "21 Furnace Ore." Success of the concentrating process demonstrated the lower grade Bessemer ores could be concentrated. Fisher Hill Mines, owned by Port Henry Iron Ore Company, could be reopened to produce these ores in quantity. In this time of great demand for those ores an efficient concentrating mill to treat all their ores could be patterned after the Witherbee Sherman Mills and quickly put in operation. This would furnish a good product mix and spread recovery of ore reserves over a great number of years.

I can only presume these matters were weighed by Port Henry Iron Ore Company executives. Their failure to act was, in my opinion, a severe case of mismanagement that was detrimental to their mining properties, their employees and the community.

I chose the year 1905 to describe in detail (see Appendix F) the facilities and operations at Mineville as it was a pivotal time that set the pattern for years to come. Witherbee Sherman and Company, although having spent very large sums for improvements, was in good financial condition. Regular dividends were paid to the stockholders, and the company had accumulated a surplus of nearly $400,000. Port Henry Iron Ore Company "21" Mine was in good operating condition with several years' reserves at the present rate of production. Prospects did indeed look bright for the years beyond 1905. Tons mined for the years 1906-10 by the two mining companies shown below illustrate the trend.

	Witherbee Sherman	Port Henry Iron Ore	Total
1906	537,039	110,411	647,450
1907	566,037	183,086	749,123
1908	390,935	111,728	502,663
1909	609,461	176,012	785,473
1910	721,859	231,634	953,493

For Witherbee Sherman and Company it was a prosperous time in the iron industry. I was told many years ago that Mr. Witherbee hosted a dinner early each year in New York City for their principal customers and their ladies. After the dinner Mr. Witherbee would ask the ladies to excuse the men for a few minutes to discuss a little business. The gentlemen would retire to another room and enjoy cigars and a chat. Finally Mr. Witherbee would take a slip of paper from his pocket and inform them how many tons Witherbee Sherman expected to mine during the year. He would then tell how many tons each customer would be able to purchase. The men would then rejoin the ladies. It was truly a seller's market.

The expansion of mining facilities and increased production from the mines at Mineville placed a heavy demand on the Lake Champlain and Moriah Railroad. Roadbed and equipment, adequate for the 1880's and 1890's, had to be improved and strengthened to keep pace with mining and milling operations. Rail sidings had to be built to serve the Harmony Mines and a new two-mile main line laid to Smith Mine. During 1903-04 the main line from Port Henry to the mines was re-laid with heavy 90-pound rails and the bridges replaced with new and stronger structures.

Large sums were expended to renew the railroad rolling stock. In 1906 it consisted of eight steam engines, 312 ore cars and a limited amount of equipment for hauling passengers. Three types of ore cars were used. The larger number were 10-ton capacity, four-wheel, wood and plate lined "Jimmy" cars, earlier described. A larger 20-ton capacity redesigned steel "Jimmy" car featuring the same four-wheel hand operated brakes as the 10-ton car was put in service. New special design 55-ton capacity steel gondola cars, manufactured by the Pressed Steel Car Company and equipped with air and hand brakes, were purchased for their large carrying capacity. The "Jimmy" cars had a greater braking capability per ton than the large 55-ton capacity steel cars, and were normally added to the trains with the larger cars to assist in controlling the speed of the ore trains down the steep grades to Port Henry.

The L. C. & M. Railroad also had a director's car. I am not certain just when it was acquired but I recall in the late 1920's there were a couple of occasions when it was switched to a siding at the lower "Y" just north of my grandfather's farm and the officials held a meeting in the car. This was probably during an inspection of the road. Those meetings were believed to have been the source of several empty whiskey bottles noted near the tracks at the lower "Y."

Railroading was an exciting occupation during the nineteenth and early decades of the twentieth centuries. The L. C. & M. Railroad with its special steam engines, ore cars and steep grades offered a challenge to young men who hired on as track laborers hoping to become brakemen, firemen, conductors and finally engineers. In these occupations there were occasional accidents resulting in fatal or serious injury. In all industrial accidents of that period, settlements for death or injury were meager.

In 1904 a young man, age 18, suffered a crushing injury to his right knee that left his leg stiff the rest of his life. The railroad company gave him a full cash settlement of thirty-seven dollars and fifty cents, but he could no longer qualify for employment with the L. C. & M. Railroad. In that same year, a tragic fatal accident occurred involving a locomotive. The locomotive, moving ore cars at Bonanza Mine, was parked under the bin in the shaft house. The engineer and fireman were in the engine cab when, for some unknown mechanical failure, the boiler on the locomotive exploded, killing both men in the cab. The explosion also blew out most of the windows and some of the corrugated sheeting covering the shaft house.

Perhaps the most spectacular railroad accident of that period involved a runaway train on February 16, 1905. Delaware and Hudson Railroad engine No. 104, leased or loaned to the L. C. & M. Railroad, was scheduled on the evening shift that day to haul a train of seven 55-ton capacity loaded steel ore cars and ten loaded "Jimmy" cars from the mines to Port Henry. The L. C. & M. crew consisted of John Howe, yardmaster; William Howard and Seward Foote, engineers; William Fountain and Michael Sweeney, firemen; and brakemen George Pelsher, Michael McGarry and George Riddle. Engineer Howard was in charge

Wreck of runaway Locomotive 104 with seven loaded 50-ton steel gondola cars. End of the track at Upper "Y" is shown at left. Photo taken February 16, 1905.

Engineer M. Sweeney and No. 17.

Lake Champlain & Moriah Railroad Main Line Engines 16 and 17.

Lake Champlain & Moriah Railroad Switch Engines 15 and 18.

Lake Champlain & Moriah Ore Cars, 20-ton and 10-ton load four-wheel cars with handbrakes.

Storehouse and shops, No. 3 Mill, Harmony "A" Shaft in 1918.

Apatite Mill, No. 5 Mill, Clonan Shaft, Joker Shaft in 1918.

of 104, but Foote, his assistant, was running the engine. Fountain was the working fireman and Sweeney was on the engine to ride to Port Henry for a work assignment that night.

Between six and seven o'clock in the evening, getting dark except for a full moon, the crew commenced to make up the train. The engine coupled to the seven loaded steel cars and attempted to pull them up-grade on the Joker track from the separators to the main line to couple to the "Jimmys" on the main line west of the switch. Riddle was on the end "Jimmy" car waiting to couple them to the train. The first attempt to pull the train failed and the train backed on the Bonanza siding to make another attempt. Engineer Foote opened the throttle full to pull the train up the grade and, as it reached the top of the grade, he attempted to close the throttle to reduce speed but was unable to do so. He pounded on the handle with a hammer but could not close it, nor could he apply the air brakes on the cars as the air cylinder on the engine was not in working order. He blew the locomotive whistle, signalling the brakemen to apply hand brakes, and then threw the lever to reverse the engine.

As the train reached the top of the grade McGarry set the brake on the seventh car and was setting the sixth, at the same time Howe was setting brakes on the first and second cars. Pelsher set the brakes on the third and fourth cars. By this time the engine, under full power, was gathering speed. Howard, seeing that Foote could not close the throttle, told them to jump off the train. Fountain, Sweeney and Howard jumped from the engine while Foote was still trying to close the throttle. The brakemen jumped from the cars and only Foote remained on the train as it reached the main road crossing north of the Mineville post office.

Foote jumped off the engine on the east side of the crossing and the unmanned train, under full steam and completely out of control, roared down the two-mile steep grade to the upper "Y." Here the train tore away the bumping block and literally flew through the air from the end of the track. The train remained as a unit, the locomotive striking the ground 340 feet distant and fifty feet below the end of the track, the engine finally coming to rest 180 feet further. The last car of the train struck the ground 172 feet from the end of the track.

An examination of the wreck revealed the engine control lever was in reverse, and the throttle valve was impossible to move with a heavy wrench. The engine was destroyed but the seven cars were repaired and put back in service. Fortunately, in this accident no one was injured.

9

Capital expenditures by Witherbee Sherman and Company from 1900 through 1904 amounted to $600,000, all paid out of profits from ore and pig iron sales. The healthy market demand for Mineville ores fostered a continuing capital program for support facilities and long range planning. Expanded operations increased employment by the company as shown below:

Average Number of Men Employed and Average Daily Wage

	1903	1904	1905	1906
Men	261	378	626 ·	747
Daily Wage	$1.92	$1.88	$1.93	$2.01

With the work force nearly tripled in four years, employee living accommodations had to be provided by the company. An Italian boarding house to accommodate sixty men was constructed in 1905. A concrete block four-tenement house, built in Witherbee during 1906, served as a Hungarian boarding house. In that same year six new concrete block single family dwellings were built for a total of $12,123 on a new street named Norton Avenue, more popularly known as Bridal Row. I was told the first inhabitants of the new houses were young newlyweds— hence the name. A monolithic concrete house and adjacent jail, complete with steel cells and the upper floor furnished for a justice court, were provided for the company-paid police officer.

The concrete block houses, designed by company engineers, were selected as being less costly to maintain. The blocks were made from iron ore tailings and featured rough rock face as well as smooth face. The roofs were covered with slate. The various designs were two-story, for single and two and four family occupancy. A few of these houses, more elaborate than others, were assigned to department heads.

In requesting new construction funds for 1907, general manager Sheldon Norton commented on housing as follows:

> "The first and most important improvement, in addition to your present Mining Camp, is more houses for employees. There is little use to add to your machinery or plant until you provide sufficient

places for men to live.

"To provide houses, sufficient to take care of the present force, with what additional men we will need for the coming year, will cost somewhere in the neighborhood of $50,000. There is no question, but that if we wish to keep men we will have to provide this additional room. The houses are so crowded that it is uncomfortable, and good men will not stay. We are also occupying ten tenements of Port Henry Iron Ore Company, which they will need, if they enlarge their output."

In positive response to the situation as outlined by Mr. Norton, Witherbee Sherman and Company expanded housing construction in 1907. Seven single-family, six-room concrete block houses were built on Joyce Road; a six-room concrete block house was built on Plank Road; three frame houses with stucco finish were built on Wall Street; a four-tenement concrete block building was built, and construction of a second similar building begun in Witherbee for foreign labor. These were followed during 1908 by five single-family concrete block houses along a north-south road connecting Wall Street and Joyce Road. Three six-room houses were built along the north side of Wall Street. One seven-room concrete block house was built on the northeast corner and west side of the street connecting Joyce Road and Wall Street. One double concrete block house, each tenement with seven rooms, was built on the south side of Joyce Road. Housing construction by the company continued unabated for the next several years.

The mining companies, as was the custom in Industrial America during the period, accepted responsibility for providing education and recreation facilities for employees and their families in company towns. The Witherbee Memorial Building was constructed by heirs of S. H. and J. G. Witherbee at Mineville to serve as a community activity center. It was built of stone and contained an auditorium, two schoolrooms, bathrooms, a hospital, reading rooms, a billiard room and bowling alleys. A cooking school, sewing school and kindergarten were conducted in the Memorial Building. The mining companies built an eight-room concrete school building adjacent to the Witherbee Memorial Building. Owning nearly all the property within the school district, they paid over 90 percent of construction and operating costs through their taxes. I first attended school in that building in 1924.

Increased ore production during the first decade of the twentieth century created electric power demands that exceeded capacity of existing facilities. Witherbee Sherman and Company was utilizing the entire steam and electric power generated at Mineville, and in addition about 500 electric horsepower generated by the D. F. Payne hydro plant at

The Witherbee Memorial Building, circa 1910. The Mineville-Witherbee Grade School is seen at the right.

Witherbee Sherman and Company Mineville Office Building viewed from Memorial Hall, circa 1910. Note bandstand just above highway at left and tenant housing behind office building.

Wadhams Mills. With no surplus available for future development or for use in case of breakdowns, the company decided to build another electric power plant of 1,000 horsepower capacity at Port Henry and transmit the power by wire to Mineville. Power could be generated more cheaply at Port Henry as coal could be delivered there at far less cost. In addition, it was hoped to supply the village of Port Henry with electric power for lighting and power purposes at a figure that would pay for the operation of the power plant.

Before deciding to generate power by steam at Port Henry, Witherbee Sherman engineers investigated use of available water powers of North Hudson, Paul Smith's, Raquette River and AuSable Chasm. As the company had variable load factors to contend with which would require a considerable excess of water at times, they concluded to adopt steam generation for their electric power as being more reliable. Hydro power transmission lines would have to be maintained in the winter through the forests and wild country of the Adirondacks. The Port Henry power plant was put in operation in July 1907, with final completion during 1908 at a total cost of $115,000.

Witherbee Sherman and Company maintained a sales office in New York City. The local corporate office was the imposing structure built at Port Henry in 1875. The company also maintained an office at Mineville to serve mining and milling demands. It was located near the property line and adjacent to the Port Henry Iron Ore Company "21" open pit mine. A cave-in of part of the "21" Mine in 1905 rendered the office unsafe. Many years ago Mr. Edward Dudley told me that one morning when they came to work, the office force found that one corner of the building was cracked and settled.

Due to the unsafe condition and inadequacy of the Mineville office to serve the expanding clerical force, the company constructed in 1906-07 a new two-story concrete office building with a full basement at a total cost of $22,877. Three concrete walk-in vaults were built one over the other in the center of the building to house valuable maps and records which had been a concern for possible loss in case of fire. A testing laboratory for making mill tests was installed in the basement of the office building. It included a crusher, rolls, screen and magnetic separator.

A steam-powered sawmill, located near Central Power House and equipped to supply timber from logs harvested on company-owned forest lands, was converted to electric power in 1906. Here, common rough lumber was produced at a saving of $1.00 per thousand board feet. An adjacent carpenter shop, equipped with a planer and matcher, wood turning lathe, band saw and cut-off saw, produced all types of finished lumber and flooring at a cost saving of $7.00 per thousand board feet. These woodworking facilities and company operated electric, plumbing, and machine shops produced the materials, and skilled company craftsmen provided the labor to maintain the plant and to construct housing.

Concurrent with surface plant and housing construction, mine development and improvement expanded. For details of new mine development and support facilities see Appendix G.

The year 1908 was an example of the cyclical nature of the iron ore business; 502,663 tons produced by the two mining companies was 240,460 tons less than the 743,123 tons mined in 1907. However, production rebounded in 1909 and the two companies produced 785,473 tons. On December 1, 1907 there had been a reduction in operations with about four hundred men laid off. On January 1, 1908 Witherbee Sherman cut the daily wage rate ten cents, and on June 1st, five cents more. The average daily wage rate for all men employed during 1908 was $2.02 versus $2.13 for the previous year. The program of mine development and plant and housing improvement was not curtailed. The company wisely took advantage of a lull in ore sales to prepare for the certain renewed demand for ore. On December 31, 1908 Witherbee Sherman had on hand on the dock at Port Henry 38,367 tons including Old Bed crude ore, Old Bed concentrates and Harmony concentrates, all with a total book value of $85,648.30.

From the beginning of his service as general manager of Witherbee Sherman and Company, Sheldon Norton had urged a systematic exploration and evaluation of company mining lands to insure adequate ore reserves. At the same time he advocated a mine development program to provide mining areas readily available to meet any surge in market demand. Production was increased to fill orders regardless of future developments. At the start of 1908 the Witherbee Sherman directors had authorized an increase in mine development. During that year $109,640 was spent underground for ore handling and access to additional mining areas. Witherbee Sherman ore reserves stated on December 31, 1908 are shown below.

Mine	Ore Developed	Probable Ore
Joker-Bonanza	1,410,000	9,000,000
Harmony	540,000	8,000,000
Barton Hill-New Bed	200,000	2,000,000
Smith Mine	50,000	200,000
Lot "75"		1,000,000
Total Tons	2,200,000	20,200,000

Ore developed was based on actual measurements and computations; probable ore tons shown was based on an examination of various factors which entered into the possibilities of other ore bodies being found on company-owned property, but which up to the time of the estimate had not been actually tested. The tons shown developed was nearly the same as the total amount mined during the previous five years. In his annual report for 1908 Mr. Norton commented as follows:

> "The present outlook of your property as an ore producer is certainly very bright. I am thoroughly acquainted with all of the magnetic ore mines in New Jersey and New York, and would unhesitatingly state that the body of ore known as the Old Bed, or which is worked by your Bonanza and Joker Shafts, is of far greater value than any other at present known body of magnetic ore. In fact, if you take your Harmony Mines, or the ore body developed in the west wall of the Bonanza, or your Barton Hill, either one of these taken by itself is of more value than any other magnetic ore mine in New York or New Jersey at present developed; and taking the aggregate value of your whole workings and property, it is greater than the far-famed "Cornwall Banks" ore property of Lebanon, Penna."

Geological exploration, mapping and diamond drilling on company-owned lands was carried on extensively by Witherbee Sherman during the early 1900's. This was in addition to the on-going program at operating mines. Frank Nason, consulting geologist, was engaged to work with company engineers to coordinate and evaluate the work and served in that capacity for many years. The area north of Fisher Hill and Smith Mine stretching north beyond Lincoln Pond, and to the south and west beyond Crown Point and Paradox Lake, embraced many small ore prospects mined in the previous century. These were carefully examined in hopes of finding a large ore body. Samples from outcrops, old pits and waste dumps were carefully collected and analyzed at the company laboratory in Mineville.

The Cheever Mine, located two miles north of Port Henry near the lakeshore, had been a major producer during the nineteenth century but had been idle since 1893. The property was owned by the Cheever Iron Ore Company and consisted of 200 acres of surface land and 400 acres of mineral ownership. The company, represented by 2,500 shares of stock, was owned by Oliver S. Presprey and his sons. About 1906, Mr. Presprey attempted to reopen the mine, but only managed to receive orders for about two carloads of ore per day—certainly not enough for an economic operation. In 1907 Witherbee Sherman and Company purchased 1,210 shares (48.4%) of the stock for $121,000. The remaining 1,290 shares (51.4%) were purchased for $150,000 in 1909 by Bethlehem Iron Mines Company, an instrument of Bethlehem Steel Company.

With this change in ownership of the Cheever Iron Ore Company completed, H. S. Snyder of the Bethlehem Company was named president and F. S. Witherbee of Witherbee Sherman and Company was named vice president. A. E. Hodgkins became general manager of the Cheever Iron Ore Company and Sheldon Norton, general manager of Witherbee Sherman and Company, served as a consultant on engineering and operations matters. By a negotiated agreement, all tons mined were to be delivered to the Bethlehem Company at cost. Witherbee Sherman, owning 48.4% of the Cheever Company, would receive a royalty payment from the Bethlehem Company on 48.4% of all tons shipped. The royalty was on a sliding scale based on the percentage of metallic iron in the crude ore with a minimum of fourteen cents per ton on 30% iron to a maximum of sixty cents per ton on 60% iron. The agreement was for twenty years with an option to Bethlehem for renewal.

There were no accurate maps of the mine workings nor sound geological data available in support of the venture. Engineers of both companies made cursory examinations of the underground workings, but the decision to acquire the Cheever Iron Ore Company seemed to be based on the economic status of the Eastern Iron Ore Trade and other factors, than on a technical evaluation of the property potential. The mines were developed and equipped to produce 165 tons in a ten-hour shift. The mill on the property could handle 400 tons in a single ten-hour shift. Ore hoisted to surface was all milled. Recovered concentrate tons were lowered via track on a decline plane to the railroad at dockside or to the Cheever Dock for either rail or water shipment. Capital funds were required to properly equip the mine and plant for increased production, and for defining the ore reserves.

In Chapter 5 I quoted a description of the Cheever Mine as written by Watson (*History of Essex County 1869*). He reported at that time about 200 men were constantly employed in the mine, and the vein was reached by five different shafts or pits.

Solomon LeFevre, chief engineer for Witherbee Sherman and Company, visited the limited renewed Cheever Mine operation in December 1908. His comments on the mine and plant are described in Appendix H.

The stockholders advanced the necessary funds to equip the mine to operate at mill capacity. They also funded an exploration and development program to define the ore reserves. During the years of extensive mining in the previous century, mining had been confined to high grade seams of ore. This left lower grade unmined ore seams in the roof and on the footwall of large stoping areas. Under conditions of reopening the mine these seams of ore were not only considered economic for production purposes, but the lean ore left in the mine roof created an unsafe roof condition that had to be corrected. In addition to this, pillars that were left to support the roof were small and widely spaced, and the miners were afraid to work in some areas of the mine.

With the mine equipped to furnish sufficient tons to the mill, the Cheever Iron Ore Company produced and shipped iron ore concentrates through 1918. During the years 1911 through 1918 the mine produced 763,290 tons of crude ore from which 291,816 tons of concentrates were recovered. The plant was shut down during this period from mid-1914 through mid-1916, but during seventy-three months of operation an average of 10,456 tons of crude ore were mined yielding 3,997 tons of shipping product per month. Although operating statistics varied somewhat from year to year, figures for the years 1912 and 1917, shown below, portray the operations and could be considered typical.

	1912	1917
Tons crude ore mined	117,971	130,194
Tons concentrate produced	48,113	43,214
Percent iron - Crude ore	32.01	26.54
Percent iron - Concentrate	62.89	60.09
Percent iron - Tailings	10.72	9.86
Ratio - Tons crude to concentrate	2.45	3.01
Tons per man per day - Mine	6.02	4.95
Average number men - Total force	129	152
Tons per man per day - Total force	4.92	3.86
Average Daily Wage - 10 hours	$2.25	$3.33

The Weldon and Tunnel Pits, mentioned by Mr. LeFevre in his report, were mined out by 1912 and work thereafter confined to the old workings and unmined areas to the north, referred to as the Witherbee Mine. Diamond drilling indicated good ore in unmined areas beyond the old workings. Recovery of lean ore from the roof of the old workings, to make the mine safe for hand tramming ore through these areas, was continuous. With this dangerous condition, accidents did happen.

There were three fatalities in 1917 from falls of ground. One man working on the roof walked under a large slab he had been trying to take down. The slab fell on him, killing him instantly. In another accident, two men pushing a tram car of ore were instantly killed when struck by a large thick slab that fell from the side of a pillar.

The Cheever Mine was permanently shut down at the end of 1918. Geological studies through 1917 revealed over 2,000,000 tons of ore in sight (proved) and an additional 3,000,000 tons considered probable and possible ore. Studies also revealed the unmined ground faulted, suggesting a costly operation with unsafe roof conditions. In addition to these factors the general ore handling layout of the mine workings would require a new vertical shaft from surface to a central ore gathering location, thus eliminating ore haulage through old workings with poor roof conditions.

Lovell Lawrence, engineer at Cheever Iron Ore Company, in comments on conditions at the time of closing the Cheever Mine noted that an effort was made in 1917 to obtain an appropriation for sinking a vertical shaft from surface to the "bottom of the bowl," where the low point of the ore body had been determined by extensive diamond drilling. He also advised sinking the shaft if a future operation would be considered. He stated that based on diamond drilling records, reports and sidewall conditions in the mine, there was every assurance the developed tonnage could be mined and held to 29 percent soluble iron content.

Although the twentieth century operation of the Cheever Mine was of short duration, it demonstrated successful concentration of low grade magnetite ore. From its infancy until about 1910, study and practice in the concentration of magnetite iron ores had been devoted to treatment of ores running from 45% to 55% iron to produce 65% iron concentrates. Cheever claimed to stand alone in the lean ore magnetite field as the only operation in the country handling a 27% crude magnetite ore with efficient recovery at a low milling cost of $0.278 per ton of crude ore.

Cheever Iron Ore Company had access to successful mining and milling practice at Mineville and consultation of Witherbee Sherman and Company engineers. There was an advantage in the distance from the mine to dock and mainline rail facilities, and in the shallow depth of the underground mine workings. Major disadvantages were the low grade of developed ore, a difficult costly underground ore handling system, low production capacity, and a serious unsafe underground roof condition. To my knowledge, reopening the Cheever Mine was never again considered.

Cheever Iron Ore Company was a separate entity and not a part of Witherbee Sherman and Company or Bethlehem Steel Company operations. Production, cost and employment data were not co-mingled with similar data of the two companies. Witherbee Sherman in 1918 purchased the Bethlehem Iron Mines Company shares of Cheever Iron Ore Company stock and became sole owner of the idle Cheever property.

10

During the first decade of the twentieth century Witherbee Sherman and Company was in good financial condition as indicated heretofore. The company held a strong position in the eastern magnetite iron ore market. In line with a vigorous evaluation of their own mineral lands, they studied other iron ore prospects throughout New York State.

Witherbee Sherman acquired large tracts of surface and mineral lands in the AuSable area of Clinton County, New York. These included former mines known as Battie, Arnold Hill, Jackson Hill, Palmer Hill, Indian, Finch, Cook, Dills Lavake, Winter and Mace. Large sums were spent on geological field work. A magnetic survey was made in 1910 followed by test pitting and diamond drilling under the direction of Witherbee Sherman engineers Norton, Lefevre and Stolz, and consultant Professor H. L. Smythe of Cambridge, Massachusetts assisted by the eight-man graduating class in mining at Harvard University. These young men checked by survey the location of test pits and openings and sampled the exposures. The studies proved up a large tonnage of lean ore, but no capital funds were committed for mine development. Market demand and costs would determine any future operation at the AuSable mines.

Witherbee Sherman studied eastern ore prospects outside its region to determine their effect on its own market area. See Appendix I for further details.

Witherbee Sherman and Company owned or held mineral rights on about fifty square miles in the Mineville District of which less than ten percent had been carefully explored. The entire 6,000 square-mile Adirondack region contains, for the most part, iron bearing rocks, although none known or developed to the extent of the massive Mineville deposits. The Chateaugay Ore and Iron Company operation at Lyon Mountain was a producer of magnetic iron ore but at far less tonnage than Mineville. Possibility of renewed operations at the Crown Point mines would offer competition. The AuSable mines, owned by the company, enhanced Witherbee Sherman reserves. The MacIntyre Iron Company's Lake Sanford ore in the remote Adirondack wilderness was high in titanium and considered unsuitable by furnace operators.

Of the magnetic iron ore mines east of the Mississippi River, Mineville mines led in production. If, as expected, demand for magnetic ores increased, Witherbee Sherman intended to remain the leading domestic supplier.

Acquisition of additional mineral lands by Witherbee Sherman and Company outside the Mineville area appeared not only an effort to reinforce the company's ore reserves, but to minimize the threat of additional competition in the market area. As mentioned earlier, Witherbee Sherman handled their own ore sales and sales of ore produced by the Port Henry Iron Ore Company. Direct shipping ore consisted of hand-picked lump ore and some fines produced as mined. Concentrate ore was lean ore milled to raise the grade and produce a uniform size product. For Witherbee Sherman all crude ore mined and not shipped as lump ore was milled. Concentrates produced grew from 101,253 tons in 1901 to 590,797 tons in 1910. Uniform high-grade iron concentrates in very low and high phosphorus content were produced to suit customer requirements. At that time, imports from Sweden could not match Witherbee Sherman ore concentrates in quality.

A small percentage of Witherbee Sherman ore was converted to pig iron in the company-owned Cedar Point blast furnace at Port Henry. The remainder, including Port Henry Iron Ore Company ore, was shipped from Port Henry over the Delaware and Hudson Railroad, or by barge through Lake Champlain and the New York State Barge Canal to furnaces in the eastern iron ore market area. It was this area Witherbee Sherman and Company hoped to dominate.

In 1910, Frank Nason, consulting geologist, estimated Witherbee Sherman and Company ore reserves as follows:

Region	Tons
Mineville Division	198,141,204
AuSable Division	44,000,000
Camaguey, Cuba	203,000,000
Total	445,141,204

Eighty-nine percent of these reserves were controlled by Witherbee Sherman and Company and the remaining eleven percent by outside ownership. Only about five percent of these total reserves were proved rich ore, the remainder being lean ore and probable rich and lean ore, with the grade to be determined by future exploration and drilling.

The second decade of the twentieth century was a prosperous time for mining companies and communities in the Town of Moriah. Witherbee Sherman and Company and Port Henry Iron Ore Company mined nearly ten million tons from Mineville mines and exceeded one million annual tons in years 1916 through 1920 as shown below.

Year	Witherbee Sherman & Company	Port Henry Iron Ore Company	Total
1911	567,353	167,104	734,457
1912	509,113	166,399	675,512
1913	684,690	221,709	906,399
1914	441,459	87,748	529,207
1915	661,711	125,319	787,030
1916	1,238,542	194,157	1,432,699
1917	1,320,217	159,648	1,479,865
1918	990,922	107,597	1,098,519
1919	932,193	115,801	1,047,994
1920	925,744	112,085	1,037,829
Total	8,271,944	1,457,567	9,729,511

Of the total tons mined at Mineville during the ten-year period, Port Henry Iron Ore Company mined fifteen percent, but on a declining share from the 24.3 percent mined in 1910. The company continued to operate only the "21" Mine. It did no development of its Fisher Hill property. It did not build a concentrating mill, but continued to ship crude ore as mined.

Witherbee Sherman and Company met the demand for its products by increasing productive capacity. It operated Old Bed, Harmony, New Bed and Smith Mines.

No. 3 Concentrating Mill was built in 1910 between Harmony A and B Shafts for greater productive capacity. No. 4 Mill was built north of the Central Power House for New Bed Mine. Following a fire which destroyed Nos. 1 and 2 Mills in 1914, No. 5 Mill was built near Joker Shaft. For a detailed description of these mills and their operating conditions, see Appendix J.

As part of the overall expansion program in 1916, Witherbee Sherman began development of Sherman Mine, about a mile north of Smith Mine. A hoist building with a double drum hoist, headframe with crusher and bin, compressor building, shops and change house were built and a double track incline shaft sunk in ore from the surface outcrop. The Sherman Branch of the L. C. & M. Railroad was extended from Cook Shaft, which involved building a long timber trestle over a gully. I recall Mike Sweeney, railroad engineer, told me he drove the first engine over the trestle to the mine in 1916. Ore production from Sherman Mine began in 1916 with 16,714 tons produced that year; 27,674 tons produced in 1917 and 1,584 tons produced in 1918. Ore was primary crushed at the mine, then rail shipped to No. 5 Mill at Mineville

B Shaft, 3 Mill, A Shaft, Shops and Warehouse, circa 1915.

for concentration. Sherman Mine was shut down in 1918 and never re-opened.

The short life of Sherman Mine was probably due to several factors: Shortage of manpower during World War I; adequate mine capacity at Mineville to meet demand; consolidation of mining at a more economic central location; and a higher production cost through shipping product from Sherman Mine.

Along with industrial expansion Witherbee Sherman and Company continued to construct housing for employees, and facilities for the general welfare of the communities. During those years social life centered within the community. Local churches and the Witherbee Memorial building were central to many activities. The mining companies jointly hired a social director who worked with the clergy and group leaders to coordinate activities. A volunteer Mineville and Witherbee Fire Department and uniformed community band were sponsored with equipment furnished by the companies. A hospital, primarily for treating employee injuries, was maintained by the companies. At that time, all patients were treated free of charge. A district nurse was hired to visit employees' homes on a regular basis to monitor general health of not only the employees but also their families.

There were Catholic, Presbyterian and Baptist churches in Mineville serving Mineville and Witherbee. In Witherbee there was a large Polish-Lithuanian immigrant population that formed a Polish Society, one purpose being to build their own church with a Polish-speaking priest in residence. Witherbee Sherman and Company deeded a parcel of land on the main street of Witherbee to the Society where the present

St. Michael's Catholic church now stands. Frank S. Witherbee, Silas H. Witherbee and George C. Foote personally guaranteed their loan of $20,000 from the Glens Falls Insurance Company so they could build the church, but the people of the parish paid for the building.

In this time of bustling expansion all was not smooth and without problems. The large influx of labor and lack of firm, fair labor relations policies became a breeding ground for discontent. The mining companies provided good housing at very low rent which did not cover maintenance costs. They paid the highest mine wages in eastern mines. They provided change houses for the miners to shower and change at the end of the work shift, and put in safety programs to reduce injuries. However, in those days what was considered a safety program would be considered shocking by today's standards.

The miners were segregated by nationality partially due to the various languages spoken. Safety and direction signs underground were printed in several languages. One company report of the period stated that these groups, by nationality, had a sense of competition that was beneficial for production, but this was certainly not helpful in social contacts among the groups. The foreman on the job held a lot of authority over men not allowed even to mine captains in later years. Rumors of graft by bosses in charge of muckers or drillers were rampant. One story I heard years ago concerned a miner who was promoted from hand mucking to drill runner. The drill boss told him he had to pay for the drill machine by giving him a certain amount each payday. This went on for some time until the man quit to leave the area. He insisted on taking his drill with him as he said he had paid for it. There were also reports that muck bosses received payment from men they assigned to the best muck locations. These and other incidents uncovered the graft situation. Top company officials thoroughly investigated and took corrective action.

In a period of discord in 1912-13 the Mineville Miners Union officers made serious charges against the company that were quoted in New York newspapers. Witherbee Sherman denied the charges and discharged two employees. A short strike, called by the union officers followed. The actions of the union officers and company officials in this matter are detailed in Appendix K.

Port Henry, Mineville and Witherbee were company towns, established by the iron industry, most of the taxes paid by the iron industry and the population growth and economic well-being sustained by the iron industry. As was the case in most industrial communities in the latter part of the nineteenth and early part of the twentieth centuries, company officials held enormous control. For the most part, they accepted a social responsibility but maintained their own select social status in a tight-knit group. Local elected officials deferred to them in most matters as their financial support was vital for community improvement. They could supply the talent to solve problems and in many instances furnished labor and material for civic purposes. Employees and their families generally supported company approved local office seekers, partially because they respected their judgment, also perhaps because opposition would reflect unfavorably at work.

On the plus side, company benevolence filled voids that would be non-existent in later years. There were no public social welfare programs to aid the sick, the widow or orphan. Hardship cases were frequently the beneficiaries of company assistance unknown to the general public. There were no public scholarship or student loan programs available for young people seeking an education. Young men seeking higher education were given employment in the mines and surface departments to earn money for their education. They were also employed during vacation periods. I know of three young men who were advanced funds to attend business college and returned to take clerical positions with Witherbee Sherman and Company. They, of course, repaid the loans. My father was one of them. I was told that at one time a young man working with the underground survey crew correctly figured out a geological twist in the ore structure that had baffled the mining engineers. When company officials learned of this they sent him to college to train as a mining engineer.

Community pride and spirit were demonstrated in many ways by families of company officials and employees. Mrs. Frank Witherbee donated an ornate concrete bandstand, constructed in the center of the village of Port Henry. I recall the Wednesday night weekly concerts by the Port Henry Citizen's Band during the twenties and thirties. How sad that, in the name of progress, the bandstand was removed, for it gave the village square a unique character. Mrs. Witherbee also arranged for the original layout of the golf course at Port Henry.

Nowhere was community pride more evident than in the baseball teams. Teams included office workers, miners, furnacemen, local merchants and others. The mining companies furnished equipment and built an athletic field at Mineville. Joe Gilbo, dean of area baseball for many years, always fielded a Port Henry team to contest arch-rival Mineville. Mineville baseball teams played all over northern New York. On a pre-World War I Mineville team, my father played center field and was manager. In this period before easy distant travel, attendance at baseball games drew large crowds. Joe Gilbo told me that a three-game series between Mineville and Port Henry at the Westport Fair drew such crowds that is was difficult to keep the infield clear of spectators. Betting was heavy and he recalled holding $2,100 of one man's money bet on a single game.

11

As America drew closer to direct involvement in World War I, the expansion program of Witherbee Sherman and Company became most vital as the nation girded for war. The one million ton plus production years beginning in 1916 established Mineville as an important producer. Commencing in 1906 the company had set aside for a Mine Extinguishment Fund a royalty of fifteen cents for every ton of crude ore mined. Through 1916 this totalled $980,923 and had financed the improved facilities completed during that period.

In 1915 Witherbee Sherman and Port Henry Iron Ore Company had leased their dock properties at Port Henry to the Lake Champlain and Moriah Railroad Company for that company to construct a modern wharf for storing ore and pig iron for shipment by barge or rail. This was timed to coincide with completion of work on the Champlain Division of the New York State Barge Canal, providing a channel approximately twelve feet deep from Port Henry to New York Harbor. Company owned barges and tugs would transport the ore to the Albany-New York market during the lake shipping season at a cost saving over rail shipment. Of equal importance, storage of various ore grades on the ore dock rather than at Mineville eliminated a storage and re-handling cost at the mines. The completed dock featured a traveling ore bridge covering an area 200 feet wide by 500 feet long, capable of loading to rail cars or barges. (The ore bridge was dismantled in the 1950's.)

In anticipation of the completed navigation channel, in 1915 Witherbee Sherman purchased three fleets of canal boats; two fleets each composed of a power boat and four barges and one fleet of one power boat and five barges. These boats operated during the summer of 1915 between Albany and New York harbor; ore being rail shipped from Port Henry to Albany where it was transferred to the boats, carried to Elizabethport, unloaded and shipped by rail to customers at a through rate from Port Henry to destination slightly less than the all rail rate.

In the spring of 1917, Witherbee Sherman and Company formed a wholly-owned subsidiary company called the Ore Carrying Corporation to take over the boats purchased for use in the canal. The fleet then consisted of three cargo-carrying steamers and fifteen barges. The company advanced money to the Ore Carrying Corporation for construction of a fleet of four specially designed wood boats consisting of a steamer and three barges. The boats were about 150 feet in length by 33 feet beam, and the fleet was designed to carry 2,500 to 2,800 tons per trip.

Although dock facilities at Port Henry were not completed during 1917 and the ore had to be transshipped to Albany by rail, the company was able to move 118,000 tons of ore with the fleet which could not have been moved otherwise due to a severe shortage of railroad cars to handle the production from the mines. During 1917 ore shipped from Port Henry was 1,046,605 tons, including 812,683 tons by Witherbee Sherman, 192,332 tons by Port Henry Iron Ore Company and 41,590 tons by Cheever Iron Ore Company. Due to the severe rail car shortage, every effort was made to load rail cars to maximum carrying capacity, with an average of 67 cars shipped per working day. With this effort, the load per car increased 22 percent over the previous year.

The historical ups and downs of ore sales and the costly storage and re-handling problem at the mines resulted in layoffs and rehiring to meet sales demand. This made it difficult to maintain a uniform force. When layoffs occurred men had to leave and seek employment elsewhere as there were no unemployment benefits nor insurance benefits in those times to protect the family from destitution. Good workers, finding steady secure jobs in a less hazardous work place, did not return when the mines resumed full operation. New men had to be hired and trained.

In the years prior to 1920 Witherbee Sherman and Company had spent vast sums for plant and housing. In 1914 the company owned 282 dwellings and by 1920 this had increased to 505. Park Street in Mineville was laid out with wood frame and stucco houses built there and along the plank road during 1917-19. Company overhead costs for housing were high.

The companies hoped efficient storage facilities at the ore dock would permit them to plan uniform mining operations to reduce the impact of surges in demand. In theory this was fine, but the demand cycles were too severe for the companies to tie up necessary funds in stocked products.

Increased mine production produced a similar increase in iron ore tailings. Attempts were made to develop markets for these waste products. Tailings sand and crushed rock made strong concrete. Crushed rock was used as ballast on railroad track beds. Apatite in Old Bed ore tailings had been used in small amounts for agricultural fertilizer for more than fifty years.

Recovery of apatite was mentioned earlier in describing No. 2 Mill as it was operated during 1905; see Appendix F. Studies continued to improve the quality of apatite. During 1913 equipment changes in No. 2 Mill for apatite recovery were successful. A new larger apatite mill was built at Mineville and operated until destroyed by fire in 1919. See Appendix L.

While improvements of surface milling and transportation facilities were occurring in the second decade of this century, there was an expanded concurrent mine development program underway to insure a continuous flow of crude ore from underground to these facilities. Witherbee Sherman and Company kept abreast of the latest mining methods. Company engineers modified those methods to suit changing local conditions.

New improvements in mining equipment were tried at Mineville in a continual effort to improve mine operations and reduce costs. Equipment tested under various operating conditions frequently resulted in improved design changes by the manufacturer. In 1913-14 experiments were made with hammer drills and these drills were selected to replace all piston drills. The drill adopted for sinking decline slopes and for driving level drifts was the Ingersoll Water Leyner drill. For stope mining and all other mining work, the Ingersoll one-man jackhammer was chosen. The introduction of these machines produced substantial cost savings in development and stope mining.

Broken ore in the stope areas was mostly hand shoveled by two-man crews into one-ton cars and hand trammed to dumping points on hoisting slopes. Labor shortages before and during World War I led to the introduction of electric powered mechanical shovels in large stopes. Myers-Whaley, Halby and Thew 5/8 yard shovels of this type were used, resulting in increased production at reduced cost. Electric locomotives and four-ton capacity cars, all built in the company shops at Mineville, transported ore from the shovels to the dumping points. In 1919 there were one Myers-Whaley, one Halby and five Thew shovels operating in Harmony Mine. In that year those shovels handled 47 percent of the mine production. This equipment could only be used in large stopes. Hand loading and tramming with one-ton cars continued in stopes in the thinner ore seams.

Remoteness of the mines from equipment manufacturers and suppliers forced the mining companies to carry large inventories of spares and to maintain shop facilities for repair and often complete rebuilding of mine and mill equipment. In 1910-11 Witherbee Sherman had constructed a large complex of connected concrete block buildings consisting of a three-story warehouse, cement and wire rope storage areas, machine shop, blacksmith shop and, in separate adjacent buildings, an electric shop and foundry.

*Witherbee Sherman and Company Office and Staff Force
at Mineville Office in 1918.*

Back Row: Bill Vogan, Neil Weldon, J. Navin, W. Bartlett, B. Towser, W. Comstock and S. Nason.

Middle Row: Pat Farrell, Sr., John Shea, Ed Dudley, Frank Waite, C. Myers, V. Hanna, Fields, L. Jackson, John Brennan, Sr. and S. LaMountain.

Front Row: Unknown with dog, Francis Myers, Murray, E. Henry, Silas Witherbee, A. Flack, H. Pigg, H. Comstock, George Foote and W. Kelley.

Central Power Plant, Barton Hill and No. 4 Mill, circa 1918.

New Bed Mine, shops, tunnel and Thomas Shaft, circa 1918.

In an emergency everything could be fabricated locally to keep the plant in operation. Patterns were made in the carpenter shop; castings made in the foundry; gears and car wheels finished in the machine shop and motors built and re-wound in the electric shop. Magnetic separators, ore skips, mine cars and steel structures were all fabricated in the shops. Skilled machinists, foundrymen, electricians, carpenters, masons and a pattern maker were all on the company payroll. Company engineers furnished specifications and drawings.

The rapid increase in Witherbee Sherman and Company production goals created increased demands on mines, mills and support facilities. An addition was built on No. 1 Power House for a new 500 H.P. electric-driven double-drum Wellman Seaver Morgan hoist to service Joker Shaft, replacing the steam-driven hoist. The Bonanza Shaft hoist was converted from steam to electric drive. Additional air compressors were installed to supply air to drills and other mine equipment. Following a fire, a new and larger sawmill, carpenter shop and dry kiln were built near Roe Pond. Additional company housing was built to accommodate the increased employment.

Power contracts were negotiated with Hortonia Power Company in Vermont to supply additional hydroelectric power from Lake Dunmore and other stations. The company continued to purchase power from Kingdom and Wadhams hydroelectric plants, but these latter plants were not dependable in dry periods. The coal-fired steam plant at Port Henry and Central at Mineville furnished reserve power when needed but were more expensive to operate.

Power furnished to the mine and mill plants and to the hamlets of Mineville and Witherbee was 25 cycle. Witherbee Sherman distributed power from their substations through a wholly-owned utility company called Mineville Light Heat and Power Company. This was operated on a cost basis with yearly income barely exceeding operating costs. I recall during the 1930's power was converted from 25 to 60 cycle, requiring all plant motors and domestic motors in homes and small business places to be rewound for 60 cycle power. The noticeable change to residents was a steady light from 60 cycle versus a slightly flickering light from 25 cycle power.

Witherbee Sherman and Company had raised their productive capacity at Mineville to 1,500,000 annual tons. The nearest they came to that figure was in 1917 with 1,320,217 tons mined. The low production year in the 1911 through 1920 period was 1914 with 441,459 tons mined.

The yearly variation in iron and steel demand was detrimental to cost efficient operations. In this decade skilled labor was scarce. The company spent large sums to recruit foreign workers and bring them to Mineville and Port Henry. Housing was constantly in short supply and even the company boarding houses were crowded. Many families living in company houses took in boarders. The foreign languages still created problems, and severe occupational injuries were frequent. The wage scale was constantly adjusted to reflect both market demands and availability of labor. When ore sales were down the work force was reduced to conserve cash, and orders were filled from stocked ore on the dock.

Work force, wages and accident statistics for the ten-year period for Witherbee Sherman and Company are as follows:

Year	Men Employed	Daily Wage	Lost Time Injuries	Fatal Accidents
1911	913	$2.10	239	3
1912	847	2.17	243	8
1913	1,178	2.36	343	7
1914	757	2.43	250	2
1915	896	2.31	325	5
1916	1,454	2.64	828	7
1917	1,603	3.16	542	3
1918	1,347	3.80	380	3
1919	984	4.27	452	2
1920	878	4.94	445	3
Total			4,047	43

These statistics show that during the ten-year period, in which Witherbee Sherman mined 8,271,944 tons, there was on average a lost-time accident for every 2,044 tons mined, and a fatal accident for every 192,371 tons mined. Major causes of severe accidents were falls of ground, improper handling of explosives, careless use of haulage equipment, and lack of guards on equipment and in dangerous areas. In 1911 one man fell into Joker Shaft and another man into Bonanza Shaft. In 1914 a company police officer, attempting to settle a disturbance in Witherbee, was fatally stabbed. His assailant escaped town and was never brought to trial.

The New York State Workmen's Compensation laws were enacted in 1915-16. John Shea told me that some company officials thought the cost would soon break the companies, but they found out it was the best thing that could have happened for it not only protected the injured employee, but benefited the companies. This spurred development of safety programs with training of workers and foremen.

The company doctor and hospital were central to the health needs of the mining communities. A nurse-welfare worker, on the company payroll, visited homes to monitor conditions within families. She conducted classes in health care. Family illness, surgery and maternity cases were treated at the hospital. Company officials maintained a close watch on sanitary conditions and health of employees. The influx of labor was a potential source of epidemics.

Dr. Thomas J. Cummins, who succeeded Dr. W. F. Brown as Mines Surgeon and Physician on December 1, 1917, discussed the handling of two serious health problems.

From the Medical and Surgical Report, 1917:

"Early in December two men but lately arrived from New York came down with Diphtheria of the black, malignant form, at one of the company boarding houses. They were promptly isolated and a pest house built to receive them. Fast and thorough work on the part of the Mines Physician and Hospital Staff, ample fumigation, etc., blocked what at one time promised to be a serious situation. Both cases are now ready for discharge and no others have developed."

From the Medical and Surgical Report, 1918:

"On September 28, 1918 seven men were brought in from Boston. Shortly after coming four of them became ill; these four working in Harmony Mine. A diagnosis of influenza was made, they were placed in the pest house and a male nurse supplied. All recovered. From this point of infection a virulent form of influenza was started throughout the community. At first the cases were noted among the employees of Harmony, next their families and later the whole community became involved. A notice was issued October 7th regarding the disease and advising those who had it how to care for themselves, also stating that the epidemic was prevalent all over the country. This was printed in several languages. A few days later a large placard was placed on bill boards around town advising care and stating the numerous cases of pneumonia that followed the influenza epidemic, and the fatal character of the pneumonia.

"The epidemic was raging, and about October 14 the Volunteer Firemen, 12 in number, were placed in different sections of the town and a complete census of those ill was taken. Those unable to care for themselves were looked after by them and by eleven Volunteer Nurses. The hospital was used as a central point to bring those severely infected. By centralizing the very sick, they no longer became a source of infection. The epidemic began to wane soon after these measures were put in force and cleared up very rapidly.

"The number of cases during the epidemic reached approximately one thousand. The mortality during the entire epidemic was forty-three. At one time as many as thirty-three cases were in the hospital. The mortality among those brought to the hospital was necessarily very high on account of the malignant form of the disease of those brought there. An orderly became ill with pneumonia and one nurse became infected with influenza. Recovery, however, was complete."

Following construction of the Witherbee Memorial Building and prior to 1918, part of that building served as an emergency hospital. With mine and plant expansion and an influx of labor, it was not adequate. Following construction of a new shops complex in 1910-11, Witherbee Sherman converted a former blacksmith shop building, near the office, to a hospital. The building was one story, brick construction, with plans arranged for expansion when needed. Initially it consisted of a doctor's office, operating room, recovery room, supply room and bathroom.

In 1916 the hospital building was completely remodeled and enlarged. A maternity ward was added with equipment donated by Mrs. W. C. Witherbee. Renovations provided two wards, an operating room, surgery, baby room, kitchen, four private rooms for patients and supply storage areas. A large porch was built over the entire front of the building for patient use during warm weather. Capacity of the hospital was nineteen patients. In 1918 the porch was glassed and screened so it could be used all year to give patients fresh air without exposing them to bitter winter cold. X-ray equipment was installed to aid in diagnosis. The company also built a horse-drawn ambulance.

Dr. Cummins reorganized the hospital and medical services, and developed a program for first aid treatment. The hospital staff, in addition to Dr. Cummins, consisted of two trained nurses on day shift and one trained nurse on night shift, and two orderlies, one on each shift. Foremen and mine captains were instructed in first aid treatment and proper handling of the injured, the necessity of cleanliness in dealing with wounds and resuscitation from electric shock and gas poisoning. First aid equipment was placed in the mines and on surface near work areas. Emphasis was given to reporting injuries immediately to avoid infection and other complications.

Training the work force to readily accept changes in work habits was not an easy matter due to the language barrier. For example, a Witherbee Sherman nationality report at the beginning of 1912 showed 14.2 percent of the work force classed as Americans with the remainder classified as Poles, Hungarians, Italians, Swedes, French and Irish. The largest groups in the work force were Poles 44 percent and Hungarians 18 percent.

In the spring of 1920, Witherbee Sherman and the Port Henry Iron Ore Company by joint agreement created a special department to handle all welfare and community work which each company had previously administered independently. Their goal was to broaden these activities to provide increased civic, social, recreational, and educational activities for employees and their families. The plan was accomplished by formation of a three-member committee called the Mineville and Witherbee Community Committee. The members were chosen one from each company and the third, a resident of the district but not connected with either company, selected by the other two. Their activities were carried out through a director chosen for the work. He only reported to the companies directly on matters involving relations between the employees and the company employing them.

Committee members were A. M. Cummings, general superintendent of Witherbee Sherman and Company; F. E. Clonan, superintendent of Port Henry Iron Ore Company and Rev. A. C. Kenny, pastor of Sts. Peter and Paul's Catholic Church. The committee appointed Rev. C. C. St. Clare, a former pastor of the Presbyterian Church at Port Henry as director. The social center of activities was the Memorial Building equipped with bowling alleys, billiard room, reading room, lunch counter and auditorium that served as ballroom, theater and meeting room. The program was successful and operated for several years supported by the mining companies and the financial success they had enjoyed since the turn of the century.

Company organized social and recreational programs were a necessary part of community life in the early part of the century. Communication with and transportation to even nearby places was not a simple matter. For example, during the summer months occasional excursions were made from Mineville to Lake Champlain with a day-long steamboat trip and return in the evening. This required the L. C. & M. Railroad to bring Delaware and Hudson passenger cars to Mineville to transport employees and their families to the steamboat dock at Port Henry and then return them to Mineville in the evening. The excursions were popular events and the band participated, providing entertainment. The mining companies encouraged employees to go on the excursions as they believed it was beneficial for them to get away occasionally. It was not worthwhile to operate the mines for the few who remained.

Holiday events were also well planned activities for community participation. Independence Day celebration was a special two-day event for many years. The 1916 program could be considered typical. There were contests in machine rock drilling, double-jack hand drilling, hand mucking, drill sharpening and a tug-of-war in which miners representing Witherbee Sherman and Company, Port Henry Iron Ore Company and Cheever Iron Ore Company competed for cash prizes equal to several days' wages. There were foot races for adults and children; a parade of local and visiting organizations with floats; dinner on the grounds; and at Memorial Hall a contest of bands; a ball game with Mineville versus Port Henry one day and Mineville versus Ticonderoga on the second day; supper at Memorial Hall and a concert by the winning band; dancing in the evening at Memorial Hall on both evenings, followed by distribution of prizes on the second evening.

With over 2,000 men employed by the three mining companies, plus Northern Iron Company furnace employees, small business employees, farmers, etc. and their families, it was necessary for the companies to take a leadership role in organization and financial support for community affairs. It was also important that control of these matters be delegated whenever possible to capable members of the community who were not company officials. However, it was generally accepted that the companies ran things as they saw fit and people were satisfied. This led to a lasting over-dependence on the companies.

In describing mining activities during the first two decades of the twentieth century, I have concentrated on the development and expansion of Witherbee Sherman and Company because of the remarkable advances made by the company. However, Port Henry Iron Ore Company achieved substantial profits during those years producing only crude lump and fine ore for the market. The following paragraphs describe that company's development and mining operations from 1900 to 1920.

In 1908-09 Clonan Shaft was sunk 560 feet and bottomed in ore. A steel headframe was erected in 1909 and a connection made from the shaft to the "21" Mine workings. The Clonan Shaft hoisting plant featured boilers, air compressors, a steam driven hoisting engine and the required electrical equipment. Regular mine production through the shaft began in August 1910. During this same period the company expanded development in Welsh Mine, a shallow underground mine north of "21" Mine. Port Henry Iron Ore Company crude ore production in 1910 was 231,634 tons, with 51 percent hoisted through "21" Mine, 42 percent hoisted through Welch Mine and 7 percent hoisted through Clonan Shaft. Mining down the "21" ore structure had progressed deeper underground and by 1915 ore hoisted through Clonan Shaft was 55 percent of the total. In 1920, 74 percent of Port Henry Iron Ore Company production was hoisted through Clonan Shaft.

The underground workings mined through Clonan Shaft were massive with high pillars in solid ore to support the roof. Intermediate floors were left in ore to cut down stope height and suit the mining method. Mules were used at one time in the mine to haul ore cars. I remember seeing some of the mule stalls in the upper Clonan levels many years ago. A special harness was devised for lowering mules in vertical mine shafts such as Clonan. The harness was placed on the mule and the animal led to the shaft. The cage was raised above surface and planks laid over the shaft beneath the cage. A chain was fastened from the bottom of the cage to a hook ring on the top of the mule harness. The cage was raised and the mule led onto the planks over the shaft. As the cage continued to raise, the mule was lifted in the harness into a position similar to a dog sitting up begging. The planks were then removed and the cage, with the mule suspended beneath was lowered into the mine. Unloading at a mine level was the reverse of the loading procedure. The mules were fed and stalled in the mine and only brought to surface when no longer needed underground.

In 1916 the company installed two electric shovels underground and developed further use of electric power, including locomotive haulage, to reduce costs. The daily wage rate in December of that year was $2.90. Eventually Clonan Shaft, 10 feet by 20 feet in rectangular cross section, was extended to 1,132 feet vertical distance below surface and bottomed below the 170 level. On that level a connection was made with the Joker workings of Witherbee Sherman and Company.

There were accidents in the Port Henry Iron Ore Company mines but statistics comparable to those for Witherbee Sherman are not available. On March 2, 1914 a fall of ore underground injured two men. E. P. Clonan, company superintendent for 18 years, went to the accident scene to investigate and was killed by a further fall of ground. His son, Frank E. Clonan, who had worked closely with his father, was appointed superintendent and served in that capacity for many years.

Port Henry Iron Ore Company, although smaller in plant size and capacity than Witherbee Sherman, was similarly affected by the cyclical nature of the iron ore trade. In times of low demand they continued to mine limited tonnage to keep the work force together, stocking the ore at Mineville or on the dock at Port Henry. Funds were borrowed to maintain a cash flow and were repaid when business picked up and the stocked ore sold. Their general overhead cost was much lower than Witherbee Sherman and Company. Their lump ore found a ready market in good times but the fine ore, not being concentrated to raise the grade, did not sell unless at a reduced cost or in a period of high demand. Company engineers designed a concentrating mill to process "21" Mine fine ore and possibly Fisher Hill Mine ore. The mill was to be located on the Waite farm at Mineville but it was not approved for construction.

Top management of Port Henry Iron Ore Company, during the first two decades of the twentieth century, continued to rest with the secretary-treasurer as in the past since 1864. From 1900 through 1920 the position was held successively by A. E. Tower, Henry Brinsmade and S. S. Freeman.

During the twenty-year period between 1900-1920 development and growth of Witherbee Sherman was due to the continuity of successful management that implemented the plans of the directors and President Frank S. Witherbee. Charles Cady was succeeded by Sheldon Norton who served as general manager until 1910, continuing thereafter as a consultant. Norton was followed by Solomon LeFevre in 1910; H. Comstock in 1914; and George C. Foote in 1917.

In 1914 A. J. Cummings was superintendent of mines, A. M. Cummings, foreman in Old Bed Mine; and E. C. Henry, foreman in Harmony Mine. A. M. Cummings, son of A. J. Cummings, became assistant superintendent of mines and then superintendent of mines following the death of his father in 1918. He became general superintendent following the resignation of Mr. Comstock in 1919, and held that position until 1937.

There was depth in the operating management of the mines and mills. Superintendents and managers had all held previous operating positions and were backed up by capable men for replacement when necessary. H. Comstock had advanced from assistant general manager; H. F. Pigg, electrical engineer (later with the Chateaugay Ore and Iron Company); A. K. McClellan, assistant chief clerk, eventually became controller and E. L. Dudley, paymaster in 1912, served in accounting at Mineville into the 1950's. E. C. Henry became mill superintendent; then assistant general superintendent in charge of mines, and later chief engineer.

As mentioned earlier, Frank S. Witherbee joined the company following the death of his father in 1875, becoming president when the company was incorporated in 1900. Mr. Witherbee was a member of the American Institute of Mining Engineers, a charter member of the American Iron and Steel Institute, vice president of Tennessee Coal and Iron Company, vice president of Cheever Iron Ore Company, president of Lake Champlain and Moriah Railroad Company, and a director of several banks.

Possessed with a strong sense of history, Mr. Witherbee was deeply disturbed that the Crown Point fortress was being destroyed to furnish building stones for houses and barns. He purchased the property in 1910 for $10,000 and donated it to the State of New York that it be preserved for future generations. In a letter to Mr. Witherbee, Governor Charles Evans Hughes expressed the gratitude of the state and nation for his generous act. The state legislature enacted bills of acceptance for the property to remain in perpetuity as the Crown Point Reservation. Of further historical interest, the French government made Mr. Witherbee Knight of the Legion of Honor in recognition of his services in behalf of the Champlain tercentenary.

Frank Witherbee was an astute businessman who understood the cyclical nature of the iron and steel industry on a national and world basis. For a few years he was instrumental in developing interest in the exportation of Lake Champlain iron ore to Europe. He applied sound geological and engineering principles to decisions in development of company-owned mineral lands and to the production and beneficiation of magnetic iron ores. He hired consultants but his decisions were based on his own intuitive nature.

With all of his personal achievements of wealth, political and social status, Mr. Witherbee was not without personal tragedy. The death of his only son, age 21, in his senior year of college, was a blow from which he never fully recovered. Frank S. Witherbee died at his New York City residence on April 13, 1917 at the age of 64.

I believe Frank Witherbee's death was a tragic event for Witherbee Sherman and Company as decisions and events in the ensuing five years brought the company to the brink of ruin. Factions on the board of directors squared off to determine the future direction of the company—to increase ore production or expand blast furnace operations. However, the second decade of the twentieth century was a prosperous time for the mining companies, their employees and the communities in the Town of Moriah.

12

From 1913 on, while mining and transportation facilities of Witherbee Sherman and Company were being improved, there was occasional interest expressed by the directors to increase production of pig iron. The Company-owned Cedar Point blast furnace at Port Henry, built by Thomas Witherbee, had been leased for several years to Pilling and Crane of Philadelphia.

Capacity of the furnace had been raised to about 200 tons per day using Mineville ore. The operation netted Witherbee Sherman about $30,000 per year. Some studies showed that company shipments of pig iron would bring a much larger net return per ton than ore sold only as lump ore or concentrates. In 1919 the lease on the furnace to Pilling and Crane expired and, not wishing to renew it, the company took over the furnace plant in April of that year. Large sums were spent to upgrade the furnace, including purchase of a pig casting machine to eliminate casting pig iron in sand molds as heretofore.

Changes in Witherbee Sherman and Company top management in 1917, following the death of Frank S. Witherbee, seemed to initiate a shift in policy from emphasis on specialty iron ore products to increased production of pig iron. Lewis Francis succeeded Frank Witherbee as president. Walter C. Witherbee, son of one of the founders of the company, was chairman of the board. His son, Silas Witherbee, had been active in the company but was in military service in France. George C. Foote was general manager. To the management group the one million ton per year plant ore capacity seemed adequate to meet future demands. There was no capital debt and the company had enjoyed several years of substantial profits.

An independent consulting engineer's study in 1916 showed the company to be in a sound financial position. Tons shipped and net profit figures for the ten-year period 1906 through 1915 are shown below.

	Total	Av./Yr.	High Yr.	Low Yr.
Tons shipped	4,748,698	474,870	602,521	300,374
Net earnings	$5,998,329	$599,330	$966,056	$212,014
Earnings per ton		$1.26	$1.60	$ .68
Approp. fr. net earnings	$1,862,498	$186,250	$307,721	$49,739

During this period the company appropriated 31 percent of net earnings for improvements. Average net earnings per year, after deducting all appropriations, were $413,583. The high and low year figures indicate the uneven market due to fluctuations in the national economy and the impact of foreign imports at east coast ports.

The ore dock facilities at Port Henry had been designed to stock large tonnages of the various ores when necessary to keep the mines operating. Through completed improvements in the Lake Champlain Barge Canal, the Ore Carrying Corporation's fleet of steamers and barges could now transport iron ore products to the Hudson Valley and New York harbor at a low seasonal cost. With this productive and financial capability the timing was right for proponents of expanded blast furnace operations to take steps and for the company to seek a larger share of the lucrative pig iron market.

Past interest by other companies in securing iron and steel facilities in the eastern area tended to support expanded blast furnace operations. In 1910 Standard Oil Company, requiring 50,000 tons of steel annually to supply its business needs, determined it should erect a steel plant near New York, figuring that through the sale of excess steel to eastern consumers it could satisfy its own requirements at a very low cost. Discussions were held between Standard Oil Company and Witherbee Sherman, and Standard Oil engineers visited the property. Witherbee Sherman established a sale price for all its assets at $12,500,000. A sale at that time would have undoubtedly been concluded but for the fact that a suit in federal court resulted in the breakup of the giant Standard Oil Company. The oil company dropped its plans for a steel plant.

Following the end of negotiations with Standard Oil, discussions were held in 1912 between officials of Witherbee Sherman, the Tahawus property, and Corrigan McKinney and Company of Cleveland. They explored the possibility of forming a company with the Adirondack ore properties and some of the Corrigan McKinney Lake Superior iron ore properties. The purpose of this combination would be to build two blast furnaces and a pipe plant or steel works at New York harbor.

At this same time Witherbee Sherman held discussions with officials of Bethlehem Steel Company concerning Bethlehem's possible purchase of the company. Frank Witherbee and Charles Schwab of Bethlehem had discussed the matter many times. Mr. Schwab was interested in acquiring Witherbee Sherman and offered to pay $9,000,000 for the property. Mr. Witherbee informed other stockholders with controlling interest that he believed Bethlehem would pay $10,000,000, but Witherbee Sherman would not reduce their price below $12,500,000 and the deal fell through.

Mr. Witherbee reported that Mr. Schwab seemed very much impressed that there might be competition in New York harbor and urged Mr. Witherbee not to join any concern which would erect a steel plant there, saying he could sell steel at a loss if necessary in competition. These events occurred before Bethlehem Steel purchased Lackawanna Steel Company, owner of a one-third interest in Witherbee Sherman and Company.

Belthlehem Steel Company, desiring to acquire magnetic iron ore, had purchased 51.4 percent of the Cheever Iron Ore Company stock in 1909 and with Witherbee Sherman became co-owner of the Cheever property, previously described in Chapter 9. Mr. A. E. Hodgkins, general manager of the Cheever Iron Ore Company, had urged Bethlehem in 1911, again in 1915 and in 1917 to purchase the Witherbee Sherman Mineville and AuSable holdings. An acceptable sale price was never negotiated despite the continued interest of Bethlehem Steel in the property for several years.

Witherbee Sherman and Company management hired John V. W. Reynders as consultant to evaluate the company; its position in the eastern pig iron market area, and the feasibility of expanding its blast furnace operations. In a preliminary report prepared for a meeting of the board of directors in March 1922, the consultant pointed out, among other things, that the company had a distribution advantage over competitors and the probability of seasonal cheap water transportation.

The consultant reviewed Witherbee Sherman production, cost and profit history, noting that the average earnings realized per ton of concentrate during the period 1908-20 would have been 4.0 times greater had those tons of concentrate been converted and sold as pig iron. He recommended construction of an additional blast furnace to permit the company to convert one half of the yearly concentrate produced to pig iron. He assumed mine production of 80 percent of the 1,000,000-ton annual capacity. He recommended a vigorous marketing program among pig iron users rather than depending on the changeable ore requirements of a restricted number of blast furnaces, many of which drew first upon their own mines then purchased "peak ore" requirements in the open market.

There were options available to Witherbee Sherman for increased earnings during improved economic conditions. These were listed as investing in existing furnaces or steel plants; combining with other mining properties in the eastern districts; or building a blast furnace at New York City, Port Henry or an intermediate point. The consultant recommended Port Henry as a site for a new blast furnace based on the following:

a. Lower investment
b. More favorable labor conditions
c. Lower net cost of iron delivered to consumer market
d. Elimination of uncertainties attending the establishment of an enterprise in a new location from the ground up
e. Ample room for future extensions on land available at Port Henry.

It was proposed to erect a new 400-ton per day blast furnace at Port Henry, remodel the existing furnace and build a sinter plant to convert flue dust and ore concentrate fines into sinter for blast furnace feed. To construct these facilities and provide working capital would require a bond issue of $4,000,000.

The financial position of Witherbee Sherman and Company as of December 31, 1921 was stated as follows:

Capital assets	$17,544,535
Other net assets	982,009
Total assets	$18,526,544
Commercial notes payable	$1,375,700
Ore and pig iron in inventory	$1,433,577
Capital Stock - No funded debt	$3,000,000

Tons of ore and pig iron in inventory valued as of December 31, 1921 had increased in value to $1,971,577 by April 1922. This indicates the volatile price nature of these products.

The Reynders Report pointed out that converting 50 percent of ore produced to pig iron would substantially reduce the ore to be sold. One-fourth of the ore to be sold would be open hearth lump ore commanding a special price. The remaining three-fourths would be blast furnace concentrates averaging 65 percent iron. The high content of iron and uniformity of the concentrates would insure a ready market at remunerative prices. On the basis of these projections with an 80 percent rate of operations, there would be for sale each year 264,000 tons of ore and 176,000 tons of pig iron. The rate of production used in estimating the future figures represented a concentrate production of 520,000 tons per year. (In past history that figure had only been exceeded in 1910 and each of the years 1916 through 1920.)

The consultant's tabulation of concentrate production showed 341,540 tons produced in 1921. This was only 65 percent of the projected 528,000-ton yearly production used as a basis for future earnings. This should have been considered a "red flag" to remind the directors of the historical cyclical nature of the iron and steel business and their own operations. The war years and their immediate aftermath, 1916-20, were certainly not typical production years for Witherbee Sherman and Company, nor for any similar operation. The ability of the eastern market area to absorb the increased productive capacity of Witherbee Sherman had yet to be tested in normal peacetime years.

The consultant's report listed the New England States and New York, except for New York harbor, as being the market area tributary to Port Henry. Annual pig iron consumption in this area was 820,000 tons, and he projected Witherbee Sherman to capture about 20 percent of those tons.

This rate of pig iron production would be about three times the tons produced by the company in 1921. The projected increased production would be in competition with furnaces in the market area that were customers for Witherbee Sherman iron ore sales. It seems to me the impact of this competition on iron ore sales and uncertainty of the recommended "vigorous marketing program among pig iron users" would have weighed heavily in the decision to build an additional furnace. With only a couple of years operation since taking over Cedar Point furnace from Pilling and Crane, the company could have operated that furnace at full capacity for an additional year or two to determine if there was a real demand for Port Henry pig iron beyond existing furnace capacity. My opinions have the benefit of history, and hindsight is always clearer than foresight.

General manager George Foote and controller A. E. Hodgkins had worked closely with the consultant, furnishing production and cost data for the report. Mr. Hodgkins became controller of Witherbee Sherman following dissolution of Cheever Iron Ore Company in 1919 when Witherbee Sherman purchased the Cheever stock held by Bethlehem Steel Company. Messrs. Foote and Francis were Witherbee Sherman and Company stockholders as were other individuals who were either heirs or married to heirs of S. H. and J. G. Witherbee representing two-thirds ownership in the company; the remaining one-third interest held by Lackawanna Steel Company.

Witherbee Sherman decided to build the new blast furnace as recommended, including a small sintering plant to be used in agglomerating blast furnace flue dust and fine ore. Sintering is a process whereby the material, in this case fine ore and flue dust, is mixed with a small amount of anthrafine coal and laid on a grate bed. The top of the bed is ignited and air drawn down through the bed by means of a suction fan duct. This causes the coal to be burned off, leaving a hard porous mass that is broken into chunks and fed into the blast furnace. The construction cost of these facilities was estimated at $2,000,000.

I was told many years ago by Dr. Robert Scott, a social acquaintance of many of the stockholders, that this decision was far from unanimous, with some strongly opposed to building an additional blast furnace. He said because of this some of the stockholders who had been lifelong friends became estranged for the remainder of their lives.

Plans for No. 2 Furnace, prepared by Freyn Brassert and Company of Chicago, were approved on June 7, 1922. Work was immediately begun and the furnace completed in one year. The first fire was laid in the new furnace at 3:45 p.m. on June 16, 1923. Sinter plant construction was started on June 5, 1923 and completed and placed in operation on November 19 that same year. For a description of construction, start-up and operation of No. 2 Furnace through 1924, see Appendix M.

Statistics for the five-year period 1920-1924 show a steady decline in ore production. There were large year-end inventories of ore products at a time when necessary new construction expenditures were required. There was a severe drop in iron and steel demand in the market area that was not anticipated, or ignored, in hopes of a short duration. Construction costs at the furnace plant ran higher than expected but had to be continued once underway. Declining ore and pig iron sales created a severe cash flow problem, requiring increased borrowed funds.

On Saturday evening, May 19, 1922, No. 3 Concentrating Mill and Harmony "A" Shaft headframe were destroyed by fire. To maintain production from Harmony Mine, ore handling underground and to No. 5 Mill had to be revised. For details, see Appendix N.

The severe business decline during the early 1920's affected all the eastern blast furnaces and mines. Many furnaces were shut down and those operating either reduced their inventories of ore, or purchased it from the lowest cost sources. Unfortunately for Witherbee Sherman the capital program for a new blast furnace was underway at the time. Also the loss of No. 3 Mill created increased operating costs at a time when attempts were being made to reduce them.

Port Henry Iron Ore Company, although a smaller operation with lower overhead expense, was similarly affected by the business downturn. Crude ore tons mined and shipped by that company for the five year period were as follows:

Year	Tons Crude Mined	Tons Shipped
1920	112,085	81,221
1921	96,078	69,622
1922	90,293	65,430
1923	110,040	79,739
1924	0	0
Total	408,496	296,012

In a report to stockholders for 1921, Port Henry Iron Ore Company reported poor results due to the very small volume of business throughout the country, the low operating rate of furnaces and steel plants, and the large quantities of ore carried over by those plants from the previous year. With little market for their output, the company seriously considered closing down the mines and discharging the force. They were dissuaded from this course by three very forceful reasons: They would lose their efficient organization; with the mines closed down, the men would be out of work; with no jobs available, families would suffer. All the employees, realizing the seriousness of business conditions, offered to accept cuts in wages. The company accepted the offer and continued to operate the mines at a reduced rate. To carry this out it was necessary to borrow money, covered by the value of ore inventory on the dock at Port Henry.

For 1922, the Port Henry Iron Ore Company reported continued poor business. High freight rates during the first half of the year and the large quantity of duty-free imported foreign ore directly affected eastern domestic ore shipments. The company continued to borrow operating money covered by the value of unsold ore on hand.

For 1923 the company reported demand for its ore was small, principally due to increased foreign ore imports. They again considered shutting down the mines. Another reduction in wages was made in December. Ore tons in inventory increased by 44,381 tons for a total value of $715,662. Additional money was borrowed for operations.

The company studied a new concentrating process to make the ore more competitive and began pumping out the old Fisher Hill Mines, idle since 1893, for possible operation to produce Bessemer quality ore for which there was some demand. Mining potential of the company-owned Pilfershire Mines was reviewed by a consulting geologist. John Jacka, a mining engineer for Port Henry Iron Ore Company at the time, told me if operations at Fisher Hill had been resumed and the concentrating mill built, the company would have been able to compete in the market.

Ore shipments continued to decrease during 1924. As the company had accumulated a large inventory of mined ore, mining operations were discontinued on April 4th and the force terminated with only a minimum maintenance crew retained. Orders received for ore were filled from stockpiles at Mineville and on the dock at Port Henry. Mining operations were never resumed. Thus ended the sixty-six year productive mining of the famed "21" Mine begun in 1858 when the Port Henry Iron Ore Company was organized.

The decline in mine production and shipments after 1920 resulted in wage reductions and layoffs by Witherbee Sherman and Company.

No. 1 and 2 blast furnaces at Port Henry, furnace power house is in foreground, circa 1924.

Blast furnaces, sinter plant, and rail yards at Port Henry, circa 1924. Dumping trestle and ore dock are at right.

However, the Mineville and Witherbee Community Committee continued the social programs sponsored by the two mining companies. Activities at Memorial Hall expanded to include movies, card parties, church suppers, dances and educational classes. Baseball and basketball teams were organized with games well attended. The director maintained close contact with families to assist with problems.

In 1924, as depressed business conditions continued, financial support to the Community Committee by the mining companies was drastically reduced, with aid continuing only for programs absolutely necessary for the well-being of the community. No money was spent for sports during the year but the baseball and basketball teams continued with success. Volunteer labor maintained the tennis courts and the ball park.

When Witherbee Sherman suspended mine operations on May 17, 1924, there were 241 families living in company houses. By the end of 1924, the number was reduced to 202. The company considered this remarkable as many men sought and obtained work elsewhere. People were reluctant to leave in the hope operations would resume. The company reduced rents, which enabled the men to work elsewhere and still support their families. Financial support for the fire department was discontinued, but the firemen held their organization together in spite of the fact that many were working out of town. No major fire losses were reported during the year. The services of a uniformed policeman were dispensed with and four men, two from each company, were deputized for emergency purposes. The deputies were not called on during 1924 and Witherbee Sherman reported that during the five years of the Community Committee, Mineville and Witherbee had never been more law-abiding and peaceable.

During the years of low production, mine development was reduced to a minimum. Efforts to reduce mine costs were intensified following the fire that destroyed No. 3 Mill. The use of large mechanical shovels in Harmony ore mining areas was expanded. In 1923 an area was excavated on the plus 200 level for the installation of a liquid oxygen plant. The plant was placed in operation October 1 with Ingersoll-Rand Company and Air Reduction Company experimenting with the use of liquid oxygen as a blasting agent in mining operations. Tests continued until Harmony mining was discontinued in February 1924. The liquid oxygen plant was dismantled in October by Air Reduction Sales Corporation and shipped to Lebanon, Pennsylvania. Liquid oxygen blasting was somewhat successful in tests but not to the extent that it replace dynamite as a low cost blasting agent in mining.

Following the shutdown of Harmony Mine in February and Old Bed

Mine in March of 1924, only mine pumping and necessary plant and housing maintenance were continued by Witherbee Sherman through 1924 and 1925.

13

Severe decline in business conditions coinciding with a new blast furnace construction program placed Witherbee Sherman and Company in a precarious financial position. Funds spent for new construction at the mines and blast furnace during 1921-24 amounted to $1.47 for each ton of ore mined. Borrowed funds to maintain the plants ready for an expected renewed demand for ore and pig iron put the company deeper in debt. In 1924 No. 1 Blast Furnace was shut down February 9th and new No. 2 Blast Furnace was shut down on April 8th. The sinter plant operated all year, except June, to stock sinter so No. 2 Furnace could be burdened with 100 percent sinter when operations resumed, but business conditions worsened.

Witherbee Sherman engaged consulting engineers, H. A.Brassert & Company of Chicago, to study the plant and operations, conditions of competition, cost of mining ore, manufacture of pig iron, and recommendations for operations and product sales. For details, see Appendix O.

The consulting engineers stated the Witherbee Sherman situation in proper perspective. Although some of the recommendations were followed, the company was not able to improve its financial position. The expectation of profit from operation of the new furnace was not realized. The severe depression in the iron trade continued for several years causing large operating losses.

A severe blow to earnings occurred after 1920 when Bethlehem Steel Company, one-third owner of Witherbee Sherman and Company, terminated its purchases of ore except for 200,000 tons of concentrates in 1923. Bethlehem obtained its ore thereafter from its own interests in Chile. The No. 3 Concentrating Mill fire in 1923 caused extra mine development expense to rearrange Harmony ore handling. Mine development expense and a huge cost overrun in blast furnace construction consumed over $800,000 of bond issue funds which were intended for working capital. It was impossible for the company to earn the interest on the bonds and bank loans. No reduction could be made in its indebtedness to the National City Bank of New York, amounting to $1,500,000.

In September 1925 plans were submitted for three levels of operation. The bank reviewed the plans and the general level of business in the market area. It determined only the minimum plan had any chance of success. This called for production and sale of 150,000 tons of pig iron through the new No. 2 Furnace and production and sale of 375,000 tons of concentrated ore per year with the mines operating one shift. If business conditions improved and ore inventories became low, operations would be raised to the other planned levels. Operations were resumed with E. O. Marting in charge as president and general manager.

With continued inability to generate satisfactory sales goals and production output, and burdened with high interest costs on notes payable and funded debt, operations were continued at a deficit for several years, although at a declining rate, as shown below in relation to crude ore production for the years 1924 through 1928.

	Crude Ore Tons Mined	Operating Deficit
1924	174,966	$1,182,000
1925	None	829,000
1926	590,231	568,000
1927	950,867	532,000
1928	813,700	470,000

The financial handicap of the new blast furnace was a load too heavy for Witherbee Sherman and Company to carry. It was an unwise management decision in 1921 to build the furnace at a time when the eastern market was undergoing change. The location of the furnace at Port Henry was far from coke supply, with high freight rates to Port Henry. Barge shipments of ore and pig iron through Lake Champlain and the Barge Canal did not achieve the expected cost savings.

The sintering process proved most successful. Sintered Adirondack ore was a uniform product that worked well in the blast furnace, requiring less fuel per ton of pig iron produced. The single pan sinter plant, expanded to three pans as previously mentioned, was later enlarged to five pans with a daily capacity of 1,800 tons. It was at one time reputed to be the largest capacity sinter plant in the world. The sinter process only came into general acceptance around 1920. If Witherbee Sherman had not built the blast furnace but instead constructed a large sinter plant to produce sintered ore for sale, the capital cost would have been low. The company would no doubt have expanded ore sales to eastern furnaces and continued operating at a profit. Cedar Point No. 1 Furnace would have continued to operate efficiently on sintered ore, producing 225 tons of pig iron per day. Its capacity output would not have posed a strong competitive threat to ore customers.

The failure of Witherbee Sherman to obtain the required volume of pig iron business was not due to lack of effort. The whole eastern blast furnace industry was affected by competition from the Great Lakes furnaces which had the advantage of cheap coal and ore. They could dump excess pig iron production, not required by their own steel plants, into the eastern area at low rates. Pig iron consumption in New England, eastern New York and New Jersey at the time was about 500,000 tons per year, (300,00 tons less than the 1922 projections in the Reynders Report) and there were furnaces of several million tons capacity located within economic shipping distance.

The competitive position of Witherbee Sherman and Company furnaces was further threatened by the construction of a new coke plant and blast furnace complex by the Hudson Valley Coke and Products Corporation at Troy, New York. Iron production from this plant was begun March 29, 1926. The Troy furnace had the advantage of cheap water transportation as far as Delaware River points. It also enjoyed a lower fuel cost than the Port Henry furnaces. Due to its location, the Troy furnace was dependent on Adirondack ores as its source of supply. An arrangement combining the operations of the Port Henry and Troy furnaces might have benefited both companies through an exchange of coke from Troy for ore from Port Henry, both at production cost plus a small profit. However, only a strong demand in the eastern pig iron market could relieve the financial problems of Witherbee Sherman furnaces.

In August 1929 a report was submitted to the National City Bank suggesting the possible consolidation of eastern by-product coke interests and iron furnaces with the Witherbee Sherman ore and iron properties. The combination would include the Troy coke and furnace plant and the Mystic Iron Works furnace near Boston. The report suggested an association of Port Henry, Troy and Mystic furnaces could stabilize the eastern market with an adequate supply of pig iron at low cost and reasonable profit. A profitable operation was the only possible way to liquidate without loss the large indebtedness of Witherbee Sherman and Company to the National City Bank. The plan was not implemented.

Any possibility for Witherbee Sherman to survive rested with the successful volume ton operation of its mines. High quality of the ore with vast reserves, its availability to furnaces in the eastern market, and the metallurgical advantage of its use in the furnaces, either alone or mixed with lower grade ores, indicated a long future mining potential. However, the heavy debt incurred by the decision to build the blast furnace indicated the structure of the company, as it existed since 1900, could not survive.

Following the mine shutdown in 1924-25, Witherbee Sherman and Company operated three mines during the ensuing five years and produced tons as follows:

	Old Bed	Harmony	New Bed	Total
1926	374,300	181,262	34,669	590,231
1927	365,457	327,269	258,141	950,867
1928	447,810	348,225	17,665	813,700
1929	439,315	371,133	25,954	836,402
1930	505,653	439,292	76,094	1,021,039

Smith Mine did not operate after 1919. It had produced high phosphorus iron ore but this type ore was produced at a lower cost from Old Bed Mine.

For a description of the Mineville ore bodies and the mining methods during the 1920's, see Appendix P.

Mine wages during the period were based on an hourly rate. A mine bonus or premium was paid to all classes of labor based on productivity.

Mine Wage Schedule for 1927

Job Title	Hourly Rate
Trammers	$0.32
Drill runners	.36
Hoistmen & locomotive operators	.34
Carpenters and repairmen	.40
Foremen and roofmen	.41
Shift foremen	.45

For tramming, twenty-eight cents per car over the base rate was paid to men who loaded and trammed ten cars per shift; twenty-nine cents for eleven cars, and thirty cents for twelve cars and over. Men tramming less than ten cars per shift received the base rate of thirty-two cents per hour or $2.56 per shift. Loaded cars trammed averaged one ton.

For drilling, an average of thirty tons per man for a period of one month for all men drilling was the basis of the drilling premium. Fourteen cents per ton for the average tons drilled per man was paid to each man engaged in drilling. When the average tons per man drilled fell below 30 tons, the men received the base rate of thirty-six cents per hour or $2.88 per shift.

The difference between the $2.88 per shift for drill runners and the amount earned at fourteen cents per ton was the bonus. With the exception of trammers, this bonus or premium was paid to all mine labor classifications including the mine captains, in addition to their hourly rates.

The average rate for all men at Harmony and Old Bed Mines for the year 1927 was $5.63 per day.

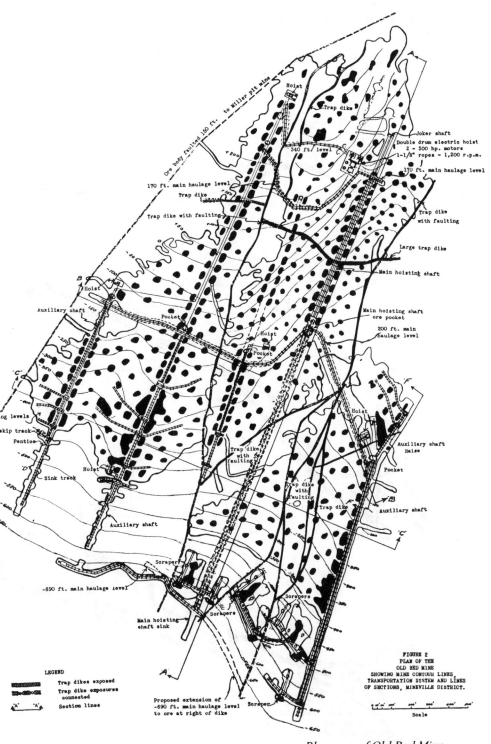

Plan map of Old Bed Mine.
U.S. Bureau of Mines Circular No. 6092, 1928

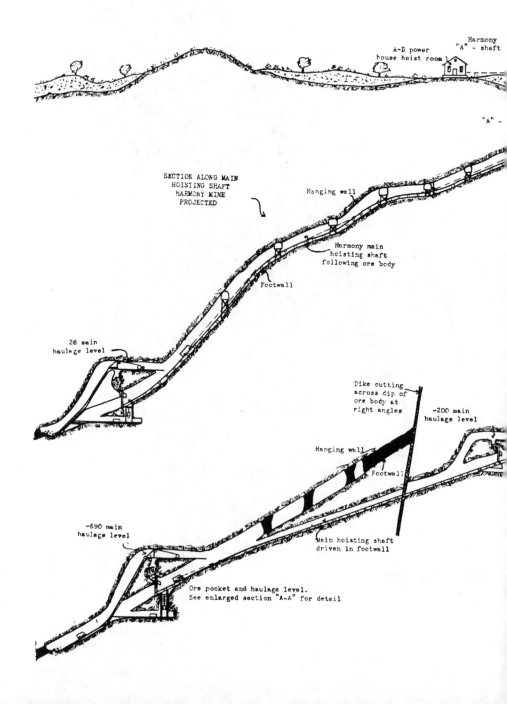

A-B power house hoist room

Harmony "A" - shaft

"A" -

SECTION ALONG MAIN
HOISTING SHAFT
HARMONY MINE
PROJECTED

Hanging wall

Harmony main
hoisting shaft
following ore body

Footwall

26 main
haulage level

Dike cutting
across dip of
ore body at
right angles

-200 main
haulage level

Hanging wall

Footwall

-690 main
haulage level

Main hoisting shaft
driven in footwall

Ore pocket and haulage level.
See enlarged section "A-A" for detail

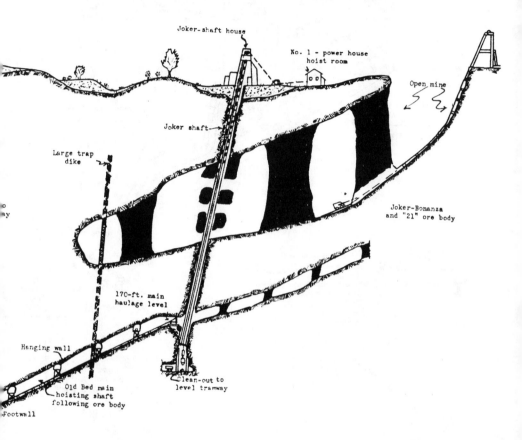

Joker-shaft house

No. 1 - power house
hoist room

Open mine

Joker shaft

Large trap
dike

Joker-Bonanza
and "21" ore body

170-ft. main
haulage level

Hanging wall

Old Bed main
hoisting shaft
following ore body

Clean-out to
level tramway

Footwall

FIGURE 1
SECTION "A-A"
THROUGH MAIN HOISTING SHAFT
IN THE OLD BED MINE,
SHOWING
JOKER-BONANZA AND "21" ORE BODIES
AND HARMONY MINE PROJECTED
SCALE
0' 50' 100' 200'   300'   400'

Section showing Joker, Bonanza and "21" ore
bodies and Harmony Mine projected.
U. S. Bureau of Mines Circular No. 6092, 1928

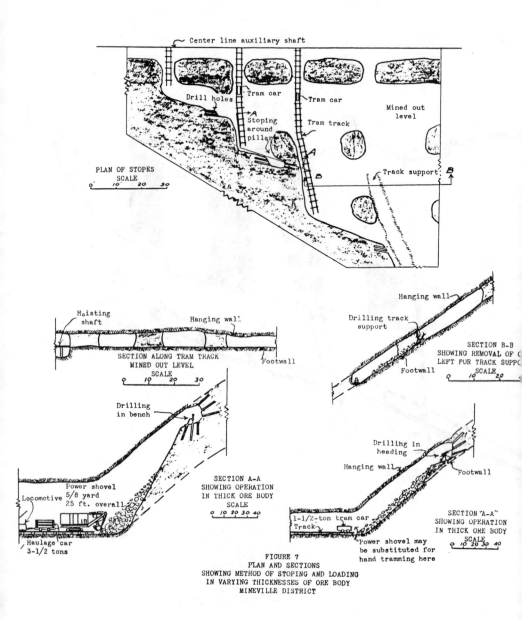

FIGURE 7
PLAN AND SECTIONS
SHOWING METHOD OF STOPING AND LOADING
IN VARYING THICKNESSES OF ORE BODY
MINEVILLE DISTRICT

*Plan and Sections - Open stoping in various thickness
of ore in Mineville Mines.*
U. S. Bureau of Mines Circular No. 6092, 1928

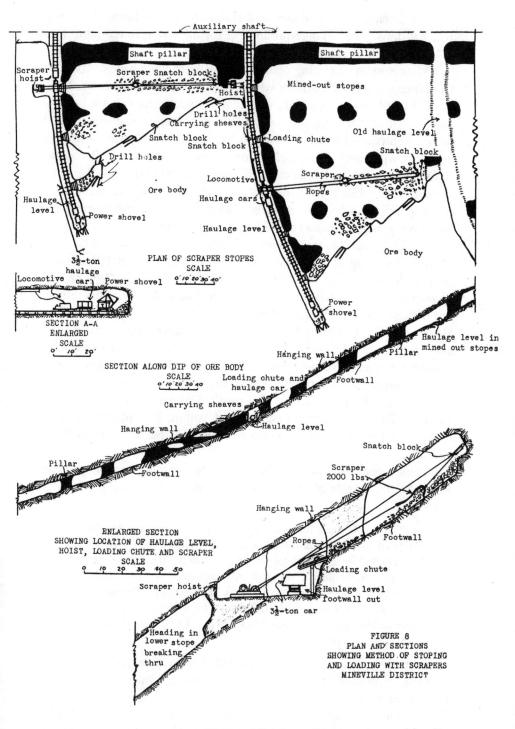

*Plan and Section - Open stoping and loading
with scrapers in Mineville Mines.*
U. S. Bureau of Mines Circular No. 6092, 1928

Ore hoisted from Old Bed and Harmony Mines during 1927 was 692,726 tons. The average production for all underground labor was 7.46 tons per man per day.

Management of mining operations was in capable hands. Alvin M. Cummings, a mining engineer who served as a consultant for the U. S. Bureau of Mines on occasion, was general superintendent. He had advanced within the company having held positions in engineering and mine production. He was backed up by Thomas F. Myners, a mining engineer with mining and milling experience in the Mineville operations. Despite general financial difficulties of the company, the mine management, while conserving costs wherever possible, had maintained development at a level to meet increased production when required. However, general business conditions failed to improve.

Business cycles in the iron ore industry were well known in the long history of mining at Mineville and furnace operations at Port Henry. Serious depressions in 1837-43, 1873-78, 1882-85 and 1892-96 had all damaged local industries, forcing some mining and furnace operations out of business. However, Witherbee Sherman and Company and Port Henry Iron Ore Company had managed to weather each storm. Recessions in the years following World War I did not end as expected with renewed iron and steel demand, as had followed previous major business downturns. In October 1929 there began a series of severe drops in stock prices with panic selling that resulted in the great depression of 1929-32. This was the worst economic downturn in United States history with American productive output dropping 30 percent in those three years.

The depression sealed the fate of the local mining companies. The June 17, 1933 edition of "Skillings Mining Review" carried the following:

> "The two blast furnaces and iron mining and concentrating plants of Witherbee Sherman & Co., Port Henry, N.Y., valued at $20,000,000 were sold at auction May 27 for $530,000 to organization and bondholders' committee. A reorganization will be effected within a few weeks. The two stacks have an annual capacity of 250,000 tons of low phos. malleable and foundry pig iron. The iron mines at Mineville, N. Y. have a capacity of 1,000,000 tons of magnetite and concentrates."

Port Henry Iron Ore Company ended mine production in 1923, thereafter continuing only to sell ore in inventory stocked on surface. The company was reorganized under the name of Port Henry Mining Corporation. On August 21, 1929 its securities were acquired by Witherbee Sherman, a stockholder in the company. Cumulative losses of the

Port Henry Mining Corporation, with no renewed operation in the following few years, finally resulted in the reorganized Witherbee Sherman Corporation acquiring the property.

Mine production by Witherbee Sherman and Company during the five-year period 1926-30 showed a low of 590,231 tons in 1926 and a high of 1,021,039 for 1930. The devastating effect of the depression on the company and its employees is shown by the mine tons produced during the following five years. New Bed Mine did not operate after 1930.

	Old Bed	Harmony	Total
1931	238,405	46,669	285,074
1932	None	None	None
1933	None	None	None
1934	150,958	48,760	199,718
1935	198,708	98,394	297,102

14

Community life in the Town of Moriah during the early decades of the twentieth century was not unlike other rural villages and hamlets in northern New York State. Because travel to the nearest cities fifty to seventy miles distant was difficult, the hamlets developed a self-sufficiency to fill their needs and this condition prevailed even to the late 1930's. Prior to the completion of the Lake Champlain Crown Point Bridge in 1929, a trip to Vermont meant crossing the lake from Port Henry on the steam ferry *G. R. Sherman*, or in winter driving on the frozen lake surface to the Vermont shore.

Mineville and Port Henry continued to field semi-pro baseball teams. The high schools in Mineville, Moriah and Port Henry also had highly competitive athletic teams. Card parties, church suppers and dances were well attended. The annual New Year's Ball, sponsored by the American Legion Post and held in the Port Henry High School gym, was a formal social event. The Wednesday night band concerts drew large crowds that gathered on the village square to enjoy the music, socialize and shop. The stores and ice cream parlors did a brisk business.

In Mineville there were two grocery stores, a drug store and soda fountain, a theater, two gas stations, a garage repair shop, two barber shops and two taverns. Witherbee had four grocery stores, two clothing stores, a restaurant, two barber shops and several taverns. In Port Henry there were seven grocery stores, two drug stores, two ice cream parlors, six clothing stores, four car dealerships, three insurance agencies, three barber shops, a bank, library, several restaurants and taverns, two theaters, a building supply, coal and oil dealers, several gas stations and two hotels. The Lee House Hotel was a popular stopping place for traveling dignitaries.

The company-owned Mineville Hospital continued to serve the communities. There were now five medical doctors, two dentists and several attorneys practicing in the town. There were, and still are, five U. S. Post Offices in the Town of Moriah. There were Presbyterian, Methodist, Episcopal and Catholic churches in the town, and two parochial schools in the village of Port Henry.

There was a certain amount of bigotry in the town that would surface occasionally. One year the Labor Day parade at Port Henry included an open touring car with the five occupants robed in white with a KKK sign in place of the license plate on the rear of the car. Some said it was a joke, but the identity of the robed figures was not revealed. This was not long after a confrontation over an attempted cross burning by the Klan in the town.

Witherbee Sherman and Company top officials were a WASP group but the majority of their employees were Catholic. The company was generous in supporting all of the churches and their activities, including the Catholic churches. There was no religious barrier to foremen positions in the mines, mills or furnaces, but the office positions leading to management of operations or accounting were filled by men with Protestant and Masonic affiliation. In one of the last visits I had with John L. Shea in 1978, we discussed some of the past history of Witherbee Sherman with which he was familiar. Near the end of our discussion he remarked, "In the old days of Witherbee Sherman and Company there would be no way you could ever hold the position you now have with Republic Steel, no matter how hard you worked or what you accomplished."

The communities in northern New York fell upon hard times during the Great Depression, although not to the extent experienced by the cities and dust-belt sections of the country. The mines were completely shut down during 1932-33, except for minimum pumping and maintenance. Single men left to search for work elsewhere. Most of the married men with families remained to wait out the depression. Conditions in other areas were no better and many were worse.

During that period many families planted vegetable gardens, had a cow and raised chickens. Deer hunting, always an Adirondack way of life, became serious to augment the winter food supply. Main meals of vegetable soup and biscuits or baked beans and corn bread are vivid memories. Ice fishing on Lake Champlain became a winter occupation for many, and local merchants purchased the fish for shipment to New York City restaurants. Times may have been tough in the Town of Moriah, but nobody starved or faced the privation that occurred in many sections of the nation.

There was very little home heating by fuel oil in those days, the main fuel being coal or wood. Witherbee Sherman opened their woodland property and allowed the local people to cut their firewood supply on designated lots without charge. Some of the company houses were vacated and boarded up.

As I recall, local residents didn't panic when President Roosevelt closed the banks after taking office in 1933. He initiated federal work projects under the WPA which became available to communities in the North Country. In Port Henry an athletic field was built at the high school. Concrete sidewalks with curbs were built from Mineville to Witherbee. Local men were employed three or four days a week on these projects.

Slowly iron ore demand began to pick up and in 1936-37 the mines produced the highest yearly tonnage since 1930. Frederick Baker, of the banking interest controlling Witherbee Sherman Corporation, was in overall charge of the company. Alvin Cummings was still general superintendent in direct charge of operations. He was also president of the Mineville School Board of Education. Early in 1937 contracts of the capable and highly respected school principal and two excellent teachers were not renewed. This resulted in a student strike that was reported in New York papers. Shortly thereafter Alvin Cummings resigned from Witherbee Sherman Corporation and Thomas Myners became general superintendent.

In the spring of 1937, Witherbee Sherman hired several hundred men for both underground and surface work. Single men were again able to find steady employment. The company sawmill and carpenter shop turned out rough and finished lumber and a large force of carpenters, masons, painters and general labor worked several months to put the plant in shape and rehabilitate houses which had been abandoned for some time. A salvage crew was sent into New Bed Mine to recover equipment and rails for use in Harmony and Old Bed Mines.

In April 1937 I was hired by Witherbee Sherman Corporation in the general surface department and in September transferred to the engineering department under chief engineer John Jacka. The department had a total force of seven for all engineering functions including detailed surveying and mapping, structural and mechanical design, detail drafting, special mill testing and maintenance of records. Everyone had a part in all projects in both office and field work.

We surveyed all stope mining and development headings to prepare a new mine map each month. Contacts of ore and rock were carefully located and geological maps and sections prepared for exploratory diamond drilling and mine layout. We frequently rode the Joker Shaft ore skip into the mine if the morning man cage men and material trips had been completed and the cages removed for ore hoisting. This caused me some concern as four men were dumped in the shaft in 1922 when the skip derailed and inverted. Three of the four men were killed.

By survey the engineers put in center lines for direction in all development headings unless the heading was following an ore and rock contact. Grade lines were put in for raises and declines. The mine captains set the footage bonus rate in headings for the drillers and the engineers measured the footage to determine bonus pay. By 1937 the underground base pay rate was thirty-five cents per hour. In hand mucking, two men were required to load and tram twenty-four cars for their base contract pay of $2.80 per shift. If they loaded and trammed thirty cars, they each earned $3.12. The general mine bonus, previously mentioned in detail for the year 1927, was revised and improved. Average employee earnings were good.

In September 1937, with several hundred men working in the mines, mills and on repairs to plant buildings and company houses, the employees formed the Mineville and Witherbee Employees Independent Bargaining Association of Witherbee Sherman Corporation. Thomas Phelps, acting chairman, and Franklin Carson, secretary of the association, presented to Witherbee Sherman a copy of the constitution and by-laws which had been prepared with the assistance and approval of attorney Thomas McDonald. Thirteen members of the association from the various plant departments, representing 544 signed members of the association, attended a meeting and presented a list of requests to Mr. Myners. They asked that their association be recognized as a bargaining unit.

At this same time an agent of the International Union of Mine, Mill and Smelter Workers of the C.I.O. came to Mineville and attempted to organize the workers but did not succeed. The men preferred their own local union to deal with the company. Job uncertainty at the time was probably a factor, along with general awareness of the poor financial position of the company. The local union later became affiliated with the American Federation of Labor.

In 1937 wages and prices, gasoline was six and sometimes eight gallons for a dollar; choice trimmed T-bone steak at Damian's Market in Mineville was twenty-nine cents a pound; a can of red salmon, fifteen cents. At Tario's Diner in Port Henry a hot sandwich meal was twenty-five cents, and pie and coffee, fifteen cents.

While local business activity was improving during late 1936 and early 1937, Witherbee Sherman Corporation was quietly involved in negotiations that would have a profound and lasting effect on mining in the Town of Moriah and the economic well-being of northern New York.

The economic importance and decline of Mineville ores as a domestic source in the 1930's can be evaluated by the following: In 1875 Mineville ore mines produced 8.8 percent of a total 2.5 million tons mined in the United States. By 1905 production from these mines had increased three times the 1875 rate but this amounted to only 1.3 percent

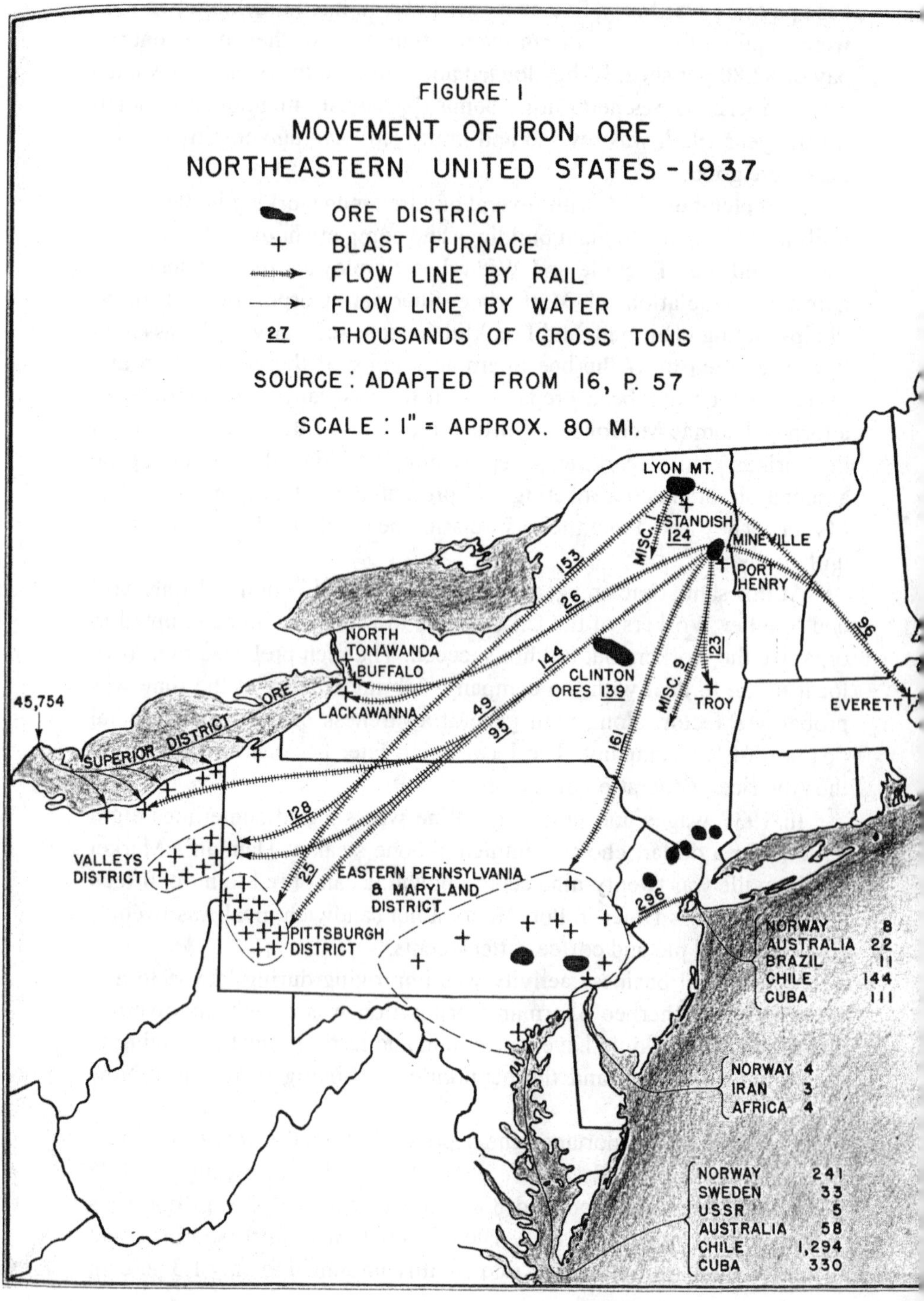

FIGURE I

MOVEMENT OF IRON ORE
NORTHEASTERN UNITED STATES - 1937

🝈	ORE DISTRICT
+	BLAST FURNACE
⇒	FLOW LINE BY RAIL
→	FLOW LINE BY WATER
27	THOUSANDS OF GROSS TONS

SOURCE : ADAPTED FROM 16, P. 57

SCALE : I" = APPROX. 80 MI.

LYON MT.

STANDISH
124

MINEVILLE

PORT
HENRY

153

MISC.

26

NORTH
TONAWANDA
BUFFALO

144

123

CLINTON
ORES 139

MISC. 9

TROY

96

EVERETT

45,754

ORE

LACKAWANNA

49

95

161

SUPERIOR DISTRICT

128

VALLEYS
DISTRICT

22

EASTERN PENNSYLVANIA
& MARYLAND
DISTRICT

296

PITTSBURGH
DISTRICT

NORWAY	8
AUSTRALIA	22
BRAZIL	11
CHILE	144
CUBA	111

NORWAY	4
IRAN	3
AFRICA	4

NORWAY	241
SWEDEN	33
USSR	5
AUSTRALIA	58
CHILE	1,294
CUBA	330

of the total 50 million tons of U.S. ore mined. The great Mesabi iron range in Minnesota was, by this time, the major domestic producer, and the steel industry was growing rapidly with the industrial development of the nation.

By the mid-1930's, two factors bearing on the future of the American steel industry commanded the attention of executives in several large steel companies. Studies indicated that deposits of high grade ore in the Lake Superior region might soon become depleted, and war clouds gathering over Europe would force new demands on the steel industry if the United States were to become involved. No new major ore discoveries had occurred in the United States in the past four decades. Some studies projected that increased demand without developing additional ore might deplete known reserves by the mid-1950's.

Republic Steel Corporation operated several hematite iron mines in the Michigan and Minnesota iron ranges. Company management considered it wise to secure another source of high quality ore with sufficient reserves to insure a long life. Donald B. Gillies, vice president of Republic Steel and former president of Corrigan McKinney Steel Company, was familiar with the Adirondack high grade ores and urged Republic to acquire the Witherbee Sherman properties.

Discussions held between Republic Steel and Witherbee Sherman resulted in an agreement for Republic Steel to lease the Witherbee Sherman properties for a period of twenty-five years commencing on May 1, 1938. It was also agreed that Republic Steel would assume control and operate the plant on November 1, 1937, acting as agent for Witherbee Sherman until the effective date of the lease. During the interim period property title work, maps, and other details would be completed to finalize the lease.

The major share of providing the necessary material fell to the local engineering group. To get the job done, mine survey work and other engineering duties were reduced to a minimum. I recall we worked during a one-month period not only every day, but every other day came back in the evening and worked until 3:00 a.m. There were nearly 100,000 acres of land and/or mineral ownership in three northern New York State counties with titles on some parcels going back to the 1820's. All had to be searched and verified. Small scale maps of the entire property were made with enlarged section maps to show detail. Ownership of surface land and minerals or land only or minerals only was indicated by parcel colors. Tabulation sheets with title data were prepared and checked. Photostat copies of maps were made with data hand-lettered and colored. All of this material was bound in a folder. Twelve copies were prepared in this manner. Every property description was read, re-read, and checked. We all learned a lot about the property that would be helpful in later years.

Despite past financial difficulties suffered by Witherbee Sherman and Company, the local organization had a group of key men running the plant at the time of the lease. This group included Thomas Myners, general superintendent; Alec McClellan, controller; Francis Myers, purchasing agent; John Jacka, chief engineer; Lowell Henry, plant civil engineer; Spencer LaMountain, chief surveyor; John L. Shea, employment and compensation supervisor; Dr. Thomas Cummins, physician in charge of the hospital; Howard Gehret, chief chemist; Leon Jackson, paymaster, and Edward Dudley, accounting and employee dwellings.

Leaders involved in the actual operations of the mining departments included Louis Bouchard, master mechanic, in charge of the foundry, blacksmith, machine and welding shops; Arthur Carlson, chief electrician, electric shop; Frank Waite, general surface foreman in charge of mobile equipment, dwelling maintenance and overall surface labor; John Brennan, Sr., mine captain, Harmony Mine; Charles Begor, Sr., mine captain, Old Bed Mine (Joker); John Genier, foreman on plant construction projects; Frank Chea, general foreman, No. 5 mill, and Edward Greenwood, superintendent of L. C. & M. Railroad.

Depending on demand, the mines and concentrating mill operated three shifts. Some of the foremen I recall at the time were Matthew Ward, Albert Moskwik and Perley McLean in the Joker; Leo Sharrow, Stanley Vitkoski and Francis Hammond in Harmony; Norris Chappell and Charles Drinkwine in No. 5 Mill; Curt Warner, Paul Fountain and Charles Carson on surface; Levi Myers at the carpenter shop and Richard Patten at the foundry.

Beginning with the renewed demand for ore in 1936, to May 1, 1938, the effective date of the lease to Republic Steel, the mines produced these tonnages:

	Old Bed	Harmony	Total
1936	411,500	281,735	693,235
1937	531,007	384,269	915,276
1938	79,204	32,012	111,216

Old Bed Mine tons produced during 1937 set an all-time single year production record.

Ore mined by the Witherbee Sherman and Port Henry Iron Ore Companies from January 1, 1870 to May 1, 1938 totalled 31,510,644 gross tons, including the 217,282 tons of Fisher Hill ore mined by Port Henry Iron Ore Company from 1872 to 1893 inclusive.

I estimate total crude ore tons mined from mines in the Town of

Moriah from discovery through the Witherbee Sherman-Port Henry Iron Ore era, ending on April 30, 1937, as follows:

Period	Mining Company	Total
Discovery to 1870	All Mines	1,250,000
1870 to 1893	Cheever Iron Ore Co.	340,000
1911 to 1918	Cheever Iron Ore Co.	763,290
1870 to May 1, 1938	Witherbee Sherman & Port Henry Iron Ore	31,510,644
Total		33,863,934

One hundred years of mining in the Town of Moriah, dominated by Witherbee Sherman and Port Henry Iron Ore Company interests had been a positive economic force in northern New York State and had contributed to the early industrial development of the nation. Employment occupations in the mines, mills and furnaces passed from fathers to sons and to succeeding generations. Depressions and business cycle downturns had been the nature of the iron industry and these were usually followed by periods of steady employment.

When news of the long-term lease of Witherbee Sherman properties to Republic Steel Corporation became known there was naturally considerable speculation. Generally people looked forward to a long period of steady employment. However, one old-timer remarked at the gas station in Mineville, "A Democrat's life won't be worth a plug nickel now that the Republican Steel is in here."

15

When Republic Steel Corporation leased the Mineville operations in 1938, Rufus J. Wysor was president and Charles M. White vice president of the company. Republic had weathered a severe and somewhat violent strike at the steel plants in 1937, and after things settled down was ready for increased production indicated by the ominous military signals from Europe. For a description of the formation of Republic Steel Corporation in 1930, see Appendix Q.

During the five month period prior to May 1, 1938, while Republic was acting as agent for Witherbee Sherman, a close review of the plant and operations began. Staff engineers, accountants and personnel men from Republic's general office spent several weeks at the Mineville and Port Henry operations. Every operating department and office function was carefully reviewed. Industrial engineers, temporarily assigned from other Republic plants, time studied flow of material and evaluated the size of the work force and wage rate schedules. One industrial engineer remarked, "The ore is handled so many times underground that it is worn out by the time it gets to the surface."

Arthur C. Hansen, a mining engineer with twenty-eight years experience in the Michigan and Minnesota iron ranges, was transferred to Mineville in December 1937 as assistant superintendent, second in command to Tom Myners who was named district manager of the Port Henry District. Frank Blackwell, a Republic geologist and former chief engineer and geologist for Corrigan McKinney Steel Company, was assigned to the district. Paul R. Steffe was transferred from a Republic southern district to install Republic's safety and other industrial relations programs.

There were areas of concern that required immediate attention to conform with Republic's policies and production goals. The underground mining method and ore handling system required change to improve costs. Most of the mining and milling equipment was obsolete and required extensive repair or replacement for efficient operation. No. 5 Concentrating Mill at Mineville used a dry, dusty process which was a severe health hazard. The safety program and accident record were far below standards acceptable to Republic Steel.

Early in 1938 Mineville plant operations were reduced to a bare minimum while reorganizational plans were reviewed. Some of the office clerical and engineering force was placed on layoff or put in temporary plant labor positions. I was on layoff from mid-March through mid-September, when I was recalled to work in No. 5 Mill before transferring back to the engineering department in November. During the reduced operating period, employment records were carefully reviewed and converted to Republic's standards. When operations picked up and the work force recalled, everyone was given a thorough physical examination. Former Witherbee Sherman employees were rehired, even though some had physical impairments that might not be acceptable in a new employment application.

The greatest health hazard in Mineville at that time, other than accidental physical injury, was dust exposure in the mining and milling operations. Employees' x-rays revealed progressive lung damage due to long, continuous, non-protective exposure to mine and mill dust resulting in silicosis. In earlier days it was labeled "miners consumption." My grandfather, who immigrated from Ireland in the 1870's and worked underground at Fisher Hill, died of miners consumption in 1899.

Silica rock was present within and adjacent to the ore veins. It was more prominent in Harmony, New Bed and Fisher Hill Mines than in Old Bed Mine. In drilling, blasting, and ore handling underground, the mine air became dusty, particularly where ventilation air movement was slow. Crushing, screening, grinding, conveying and dumping of ore and waste rock in the dry process No. 5 Concentrating Mill created a very dusty atmosphere. Exhaust fans were in use but completely inadequate. I recall when I worked in the mill in the cellar and over the shipping bin, a 200-watt light bulb four feet distant in some locations was only visible as a faint glow. While hiking in the Adirondack wilderness area in 1939 I saw, on a clear day from the summit of Gothic Mountain, what I thought was smoke from a fire some thirty miles distant toward Lake Champlain. Meeting a forest ranger a couple of days later on the trail, I asked about the fire. He told me that was not fire, but dust from the iron ore mill at Mineville.

Mill workers were given and urged to use protective respirators although the rule was not strongly enforced. The respirators were not comfortable and, due to the volume of dust, the filters had to be changed every hour or two. I always wore a respirator in the mill, not due to pressure from the foreman but because I realized the danger to my health. Some men wore them as little as possible because of the discomfort. In one twelve-hour shift in the mill, three or four inches of dust would accumulate on the floor if not swept up by assigned cleaners.

Dust in underground mining was raised by dry drilling, blasting, scraper or hand loading ore, dumping ore cars and failure to wet down the work area. Insufficient natural or fan-forced ventilation contributed to a dusty atmosphere. Although strict attention was given to maintaining good natural and fan-forced ventilation to mine work areas, a dusty atmosphere would remain in the miner's work area as long as dry drilling and failure to wet down the work area continued.

All ore mined in the 1930's was raised to surface through Harmony "A" Shaft and Joker Shaft. Underground, a series of main and auxiliary slopes and haulage levels transferred ore from the work areas to these two surface shafts. There were over 35,000 feet of hoisting cable used on the various hoisting engines. Each ton of ore was handled many times by many men to bring it to surface.

The accident record, poor by Republic's standards, demanded immediate attention. In 1937, the last year of Witherbee Sherman Corporation operations, there were 386 lost time accidents including four fatalities. There were 2,581,540 hours worked that year and 915,276 tons of crude ore mined. Thus there was a lost time accident for each 2,371 tons and a fatal accident for each 228, 819 tons of crude ore produced. As bad as the accident record was, it would have been far worse but for the outstanding skill of Dr. Thomas J. Cummins, company physician and surgeon, and his Mineville hospital staff in treating the injured. The workers had great confidence in Dr. Cummins and that contributed to his phenomenal success.

Improving the safety record, eliminating the dust hazard, revising the mining method and retraining plant supervision became critical Republic Steel Corporation goals. Some of these could be attacked immediately and others would require time and planning.

Robert H. Ferguson was safety director of Republic Steel Corporation. He was a self-driven, fast-talking, hard worker who knew safety fundamentals and details, and how to implement them in any situation. He had no qualms in head-to-head dealings with foremen, superintendents or plant managers in matters of safety. He could spot the safety aspect of any occupation and make recommendations for improvement. He made a thorough study of the employee injury record, frequency, severity and stated causes. He inspected underground and surface departments with Paul Steffe and held safety meetings with department heads and foremen.

Foot injuries were a frequent source of severe injury that often resulted in partial amputation. Republic immediately required steel safety-toe shoes or boots worn in all operating departments. Arrangements were made with local merchants to sell them at a few cents above cost, and just about everyone, including myself, objected to the "hard-boiled" footwear. We thought the shoes were too heavy, but actually, they were comfortable. A deadline was set for everyone to wear hard-toe shoes, and Paul Steffe stood at the door of the change house at the beginning of the day shift and checked to see that every man was properly equipped. There were a lot of complaints about Steffe, even from foremen, but that didn't bother him as long as the safety rules were observed.

Eye injuries were frequent and sometimes severe. Republic furnished safety glasses and ruled they should be worn at all times in certain occupations and wherever there was exposure to eye injury. This rule was also resisted, but general compliance showed a sharp reduction in eye injuries. The first safety glasses or "goggles" furnished were tight fitting with side shields allowing little ventilation in the warm humid mine atmosphere. They were later replaced by steel frame safety glasses that won general acceptance.

Improved guards around machinery and dangerous work areas, safety ropes for men working where there was danger of falling, and safe handling of explosives became immediate safety goals. Frequent safety meetings in all departments stressed the little things that contributed to accidents. Nails in the top of opened bolt kegs and general poor housekeeping were stressed as examples. One department head said, "What the hell does a sharp nail in the top of a nail keg have to do with broken arms, legs or head injuries?"

When I worked in No. 5 Mill the machinery was belt-driven from line shafting. Pulley bearings had short tubes with grease cups that had to be filled or turned down several times during the shift. It was necessary to reach in near the open, fast-revolving pulley to the grease cups. Access to some of them was by way of a narrow plank catwalk. I used to remove my jacket and roll up my shirt sleeves so there would be no danger of getting my clothing caught. Eight years earlier an eighteen-year-old mill worker doing this same job in No. 4 Mill had his coat caught between the belt and pulley. He was thrown against the roof and killed. I often wondered in later years why, after that accident, no one thought to make the grease tubes longer so they could be serviced from a safe position.

To tackle the dust problem in the mines, all drills were equipped for wet drilling. Water pipe and hose lines were laid to the working faces. Men were instructed to hose down the drill face, roof and muck piles in the work area before drilling or loading ore into cars. This not only settled dust in the mine air, but reduced the lingering explosives fumes that caused headaches. Washing the heading or drill face more clearly exposed any unexploded dynamite that remained from the previous blast. Republic contracted with the Saranac Laboratory for a study of mine and mill dust control with recommendations for improvement. The contract continued through the end of plant operations in 1971.

Slowly it seemed the safety program was begun. Although accidents continued, frequency and severity were reduced. This is shown below by a comparison of Witherbee Sherman Corporation figures for 1937 with Republic Steel Corporation figures for 1938 and 1939.

	1937	1938	1939
Tons mined	915,276	232,422	787,328
Lost time accidents	386	45	53
Fatal accidents	4	0	1
Tons per lost time accidents	2,371	5,165	14,855
Tons per fatal accident	228,819	-	787,328

16

At Mineville, No. 5 Concentrating Mill was one of the more serious problems Republic Steel Corporation faced in taking over the Witherbee Sherman property. This dusty, dry milling operation, located within one-quarter mile of the Mineville-Witherbee 700-student elementary and high school buildings and playground, was an environmental and health hazard that had to be corrected. Witherbee Sherman had done some wet concentration tests in recent years but lack of sufficient capital funds and a dependable on-site water supply were probable reasons a wet mill was not built.

Oscar Lee, a Republic Steel metallurgical and beneficiation engineer, came to Mineville and studied the milling operation. He determined if the ore was crushed finer and the milling process converted to wet separation, the ore grade would be improved and the dust problem abated. He arranged to have two carloads of ore shipped from Mineville to the University of Minnesota Mines Experiment Station Laboratory. Here fine grinding and wet magnetic concentration tests were made with excellent results. The completed report was submitted in May 1939 by Dr. E. W. Davis, Director of the Mines Experiment Station, to Republic Steel Vice President, Donald B. Gillies. This report became the basis for fine grinding and wet magnetic concentration methods developed for Mineville and the entire North American iron ore industry during later years.

Republic decided to build a wet concentration mill which would be a pilot plant to try the new process on a commercial scale. Republic beneficiation engineers Murray Riddell and Dave McKay came to Mineville and laid out a flow sheet and preliminary plant layout. The new facilities were designed so that production of concentrates could continue through No. 5 Mill until the new facilities became operable. For details, see Appendix R.

The shift in the eastern pig iron market which had proved disastrous to Witherbee Sherman and Company gave no indication of improvement. Village and town taxes on the blast furnaces were a costly burden with no schedule for blast furnace operation. Republic's Buffalo, New York and Ohio furnaces could use the Mineville ore products to advantage. In view of these conditions, discussions were held with town and village officials to see if taxes on the furnaces could be drastically reduced until such time as the furnaces could be operable. If this could not be done, the furnaces would be dismantled. The requested tax relief was not granted.

The talk around town at the time was that in no way would Republic dismantle the modern blast furnace that Witherbee Sherman had built fifteen years earlier. Well, they were wrong. The company removed some of the furnace parts and shipped them to other furnace plants and sold the remainder to a scrap dealer for $40,000. Had the furnaces remained, it is more than likely furnace operations would have resumed during World War II and possibly continued for a few additional years.

At Port Henry the concrete block power house building, formerly used in connection with the blast furnaces, was planned as the new No. 6 Concentrating Mill. With the ample available water supply, contiguous rail trestle, storage dock and sinter plant, processing of crushed ore through concentrates or sinter would be an efficient product flow. Tailings generated by ore concentration would be discharged at the lakeshore under water on land owned by the company.

Organizational changes occurred rapidly during the early years of Republic's entry into Adirondack mining. In 1939 Republic leased the Chateaugay Ore & Iron Company with mining, milling and blast furnace operations at Lyon Mountain, New York. The lease was for a period similar to the Witherbee Sherman lease. The Lyon Mountain property became the Chateaugay District of Republic Steel Corporation. Joseph R. Linney, vice president of Chateaugay Ore and Iron Company was named district manager. His eldest son, Robert J. Linney, became mill and sinter plant superintendent. His younger son, William J. Linney, became blast furnace superintendent.

Arthur C. Hansen, assistant to Tom Myners at the Mineville operations, died suddenly while attending a mining meeting in New York City on November 12, 1939. In the short time Mr. Hansen had been in the Port Henry District he had demonstrated a strong mining capability and was highly respected in the plant and in the community. Republic Steel corporate management thereafter combined the Port Henry and Chateaugay Districts and formed the Adirondack District. Joseph R. Linney was named district manager.

The Mineville office building was open on a twenty-four hour basis as its central switchboard furnished telephone communications with the underground mining operations. One morning in December when Tom Myners came to the office, he found J. R. Linney sitting at his desk. Mr. Linney told him that he was taking over the Port Henry operations as

Lyon Mountain Mine, main ore hoisting shaft, change house and mine office. The Linney men managed all Republic Steel Corporation operations in the Adirondacks from December 1939 through September 1956.

J. R. (Joe) Linney   *Robert J. (Bob) Linney*   *W. J. (Bill) Linney*

district manager; that Robert J. Linney would be general superintendent of the Port Henry division and Tom Myners would be assistant general superintendent. Tom asked him by what authority. Mr. Linney pushed the phone across the desk and told him he could call Cleveland for verification.

The Linneys were take-charge men who lost no time establishing their management style. That first morning J. R. ordered a staff meeting for 11 a.m. When the eight or nine regular staff members showed up for the meeting, he told Tom Myners that wasn't an appropriate staff for the size of the plant and to get some people in for a meeting at 1:30 p.m. Ten or twelve more department heads were quickly assembled from the operating departments in what were the quickest staff promotions in the history of Mineville operations. Among other things, J. R. told the group he intended to double mine production, reduce costs and improve the safety record. He emphasized it by saying, "You men are either going to produce or else."

This was pretty tough talk, in sharp contrast to the Witherbee Sherman management style. Loud phone talk and cussing in the management offices became commonplace; one secretary remarked that she didn't know if she could work around those people. After the third weekly staff meeting, Frank Blackwell, the company geologist who abhorred swearing, asked to be excused from attending staff meetings unless geological matters were to be discussed.

Robert J. (Bob) Linney plunged right into the mining and milling operations, evaluating them against his experience in the Lyon Mountain mine and mill. He studied the geology, development and mining plans, and became immediately involved in the new wet concentrating mill under construction at Port Henry. His experience in fine ore wet magnetic separation at Lyon Mountain had resulted in his invention and patent of the Linney Magnetic Separator.

Organizational changes were made in keeping with the expanding activity. Armand H. Engel, industrial engineer transferred by Republic from midwest mines, was given the additional position of chief engineer, replacing John Jacka. William Blomstran was transferred from Lyon Mountain to Mineville and became chief mining engineer. Bill had worked at Witherbee Sherman Mineville mines for a short period following graduation from the Michigan School of Mines. He was familiar with the mining method and geology, and had left Mineville during a shut-down period. John Murphy, an experienced mine foreman and safety supervisor at Lyon Mountain, was transferred to the Mineville mines as shift foreman, replacing Jim Butler who had been brought to Mineville from Michigan mines by Art Hansen. Malcolm

Dezendorf, an electrical, mechanical and maintenance supervisor with broad experience in mine and plant installations was transferred by Republic from Michigan mines to the Mineville operations.

With these organizational changes in place, plans with detailed capital cost estimates for revising the mining method and ore handling system to achieve production goals were carefully prepared and submitted to Cleveland for approval. Expecting speedy approval, J. R. Linney was chagrined when he received a phone call from the Cleveland office advising him that the board of directors had turned the project down and failed to appropriate any funds.

J. R. called his superiors in Cleveland and told them he could not accept that decision without a personal hearing as the local organization had spent a lot of time and hard work developing a plan that was bound to be successful. See Appendix S, "Ore Handling Plan for Single Shaft Hoisting."

He asked to appear before the board to present the program and bring a couple of men with him who would be able to answer any detailed questions to their satisfaction. He was granted permission to attend the next monthly board meeting, but was told that it wouldn't do any good as the directors had been emphatic in their refusal.

With the directors meeting scheduled in about three weeks, J. R. planned a documented presentation that was complete in every detail. Geological maps, development and mining plans, power requirements, operating cost savings, construction schedule and project cash flow were carefully reviewed and the presentation rehearsed. He assembled a few of us in the office and told us to interrupt him and ask questions. He said if we did not understand some parts of the project, the directors knew a lot less about it than any of us. To each question asked, he would delegate the answer to one of the men who would accompany him to the Cleveland meeting. He told them if the answer was satisfactory and accepted to say nothing more—even if it meant stopping in the middle of a sentence.

A few weeks later one of the local men who attended the Cleveland meeting told me what transpired. Mr. Linney took six or more people with him to Cleveland for the meeting, which surprised his supervisors. He was told he could have ten minutes with the directors. J. R. had done his homework well, he had learned who had led the opposition to the project and in the meeting he carefully observed that member's reaction and invited questions. As the meeting progressed he noted increasing interest among the members. Finally, after nearly an hour, the former leading opposing board member said, "We might as well give him his project, he brought his whole gang out here to fight for it." At this point, without any further reference to the project, J. R. said, "Thank you gentlemen, for your time. Come on men, let's go home."

17

While development and equipment installation plans were under-way for the new ore handling systems in Old Bed and Harmony Mines, production continued at an increasing rate through Harmony "A" and Joker Shafts. See Appendix T.

This was a period of full employment for Mineville and surrounding areas. Young men, new to the labor market, easily found work in the mines, mills and surface construction at Mineville and Port Henry. A steady flow of sales engineers and technicians from companies such as Ingersoll-Rand, Gardner-Denver, DuPont and Hercules came to the mines to assist in the transition to new and improved drilling and blast-ing methods. Staff engineers and operating executives from Republic's Cleveland headquarters shuttled back and forth for consultation. The Delaware and Hudson Railroad was the main avenue of transportation with its several passenger trains that stopped at Port Henry daily. The Lee House Hotel in Port Henry was usually filled to capacity during this period and local restaurants and stores did a flourishing business.

On April 9, 1941, the Joker Shaft headframe caught fire. Although the building, built in 1907, was a steel structure, wood platforms and other inflammables fanned by the upcast air from the mine shaft turned the upper section of the headframe into a twisted mass of beams, sheet-ing and ruined equipment. It was no longer possible to hoist ore through Joker Shaft.

At the time of the fire, sinking Don B Shaft by Dravo had not holed through to Harmony Mine workings. Therefore, only Harmony "A" Shaft was equipped to deliver ore to surface, and Harmony ore produc-tion required its full capacity. With the great demand for ore by the steel plants it was imperative to get Old Bed Mine back in production without delay. J. R. Linney and his staff reviewed mine maps showing access from underground to surface and determined not to repair or renew Joker Shaft nor rebuild the headframe.

Clonan Shaft, completed twenty-five years earlier to a vertical depth of 1,132 feet by Port Henry Iron Ore Company, had been idle for seven-teen years. The bottom operating level at elevation plus 170 was con-nected by a crosscut drift to the Joker Shaft area. It was decided to reopen Clonan Shaft to deliver Old Bed ore to surface. A slusher drift was driven from the crosscut drift to the underground skip dump that delivered ore from lower levels to Joker Shaft. The crosscut drift to Clonan Shaft was re-railed and equipped with a trolley locomotive and ten-ton capacity ore cars. A 50-H.P. Ingersoll-Rand slusher hoist with a five-foot scraper drag was installed over the crosscut to load ore from the slusher drift to the transfer train delivering ore to Clonan Shaft. Shaft timbering, skip and cage guides, and the skip loading pocket below 170 level in Clonan Shaft were refurbished. Hoisting, dumping and primary crushing equipment for Clonan Shaft headframe was repaired or replaced.

To transport Old Bed ore from Clonan Shaft to the crushing plant a wood-framed conveyor gallery was constructed from Clonan Shaft to the Joker Shaft bins. This required fabricating and erecting a steel conveyor trestle high above main line and siding railroad tracks north of Joker Shaft. A large force of men in all crafts worked double shifts and longer when necessary to keep all parts of the project moving on a three shift, seven day week schedule.

In determining cause of the Joker Shaft fire, it was found that a nearby fire hydrant was inoperative and may have contributed to the complete destruction of the headframe. One day during construction work on surface at Clonan Shaft, in the presence of the work crew, Bob Linney berated Tom Myners, blaming him for the failed hydrant and lack of water to fight the fire. The language was very abusive. Tom, always a soft-spoken gentleman, asked Bob Linney if he would care to step out on the highway off the property and repeat some of those remarks. Bob looked at him and walked away. Thereafter, Tom Myners was to be transferred to Republic's Northern Coal Mines District on May 1, 1941. However, he left Republic Steel to accept employment with a consulting engineering firm.

Clonan Shaft ore hoisting with lower Old Bed mine production resumed three weeks after the fire destroyed Joker Shaft headframe. The following week the company hosted a dinner party in Ticonderoga and invited every man who had worked to get Old Bed Mine back in production.

With Old Bed Mine again in operation producing ore to surface through Clonan Shaft, Harmony Mine producing to the full capacity of "A" Shaft and development of Don B central hoisting shaft underway, changes in underground development and mining operations were implemented. See Appendix U.

Organizational changes continued at Mineville in response to increased construction and production. While shaft sinking was underway, Frank Kane, who had been the on-site superintendent of a shaft sinking contract at Lyon Mountain, was hired by J. R. Linney as mine superintendent. John Murphy was placed in charge of Old Bed Mine and John Brennan, Sr. continued in charge of Harmony Mine. During 1940-41 there was a nationwide demand for equipment and supplies for new and expanded industrial operations. Al Meacham was transferred by Republic from an Ohio plant to Mineville to take charge of purchasing. Most all material and supplies were regulated by U.S. government priority allocation system.

The portal house and headframe constructed on surface for Don B Shaft included an area under the overhead skipway, and adjacent to the portal house, for a central drill shop to serve all underground requirements. Here rock drills would be serviced and repaired, drill steel fabricated and detachable drill bits supplied and resharpened daily. To assist in design and installation of the new drill shop, Ingersoll-Rand sent Howard "Scrubby" Morrow, a drill equipment service engineer from their Phillipsburg, New Jersey plant. He was to lay out the drill shop and determine equipment needs. Following the hole-through of the new shaft, I was assigned to work with Scrubby and prepare drawings, based on his designs, and follow through construction in the local shops.

Improved efficiency in both development and stope drilling was necessary for increased mine production. Good drill steel and bit performance were target areas for improvement. In past practice Harmony Mine had a central drill shop on plus 26 level and Old Bed Mine had a similar shop on minus 680 level. In these shops the crew, using forge furnaces and pneumatic drill sharpeners, prepared new drill rods and repaired worn and broken drill steel returned by the drillers. One end of each drill rod was heated and shanked to fit the chuck on the rock drill. The other end was heated, upset and a bit forged and sharpened using proper dies in the drill sharpener. Both ends of the rod were quenched for hardening. This required a lot of drill steel handling between the drill shops and work areas. Frequently only the drill bit on the drill rod required sharpening.

Converting the drilling operations to 100 percent detachable bits required the new shop to operate a production-line product flow. Development drifts used 1-1/4-inch round steel in Ingersoll-Rand DA35 column-mounted drifter drills. Stopes used 7/8 and 1-inch hex steel, shanked for use in tripod-mounted and hand-held jackhammers. The 7/8-inch size was soon eliminated and stope drills converted to use 1-inch steel.

Oil-fired 27F furnaces were used in heating drill steel for shanking on IR-54 drill sharpeners. The opposite end of the steel was annealed so that it could be easily threaded. Threading was done on a 16-inch lathe with a cutting-off slide and a geometric expanding die head. After being threaded and shanked, the ends of the drill rod were tempered by again heating them in a furnace and immersing the heated end in a bath of quenching oil. The quenching tank was designed with a water jacket to maintain a constant temperature in the oil bath. Broken, worn and used rods returned to the shop were put though the same process. Finished drill steel was stored by size and length in bins in a manner to rotate the steel so that rods in each size would have equal service. This reduced steel breakage from fatigue failure. With the introduction of detachable bits, the miners no longer had to carry a supply of drill rods daily to and from their work area. Drill steel was delivered to each level by the supply crew and placed on racks.

Each driller received his daily supply of sharp bits going on shift and returned his dull bits to a dull bit cart in the portal house at the end of his shift. The cart was hauled into the shop and the dull bits taken to a sorting table and put into bins according to type and size. Type 1 bits were used for jackhammers and stopers. Type 2 bits were for drifter drills. The bits were reconditioned by heating them in pyrometer-controlled furnaces, then ground to gauge and sharpened on a IRJB Hot-mill. At each resharpening the bits were reduced 1/16 inch in gauge. They were then allowed to cool at atmospheric temperature prior to hardening.

For hardening, bits were placed in a pyrometer-controlled furnace and heated to 1420 to 1440 degrees F. They were then removed one at a time and placed on quenching fountains. Water rising around the cutting edge and center hole of the bit hardened it to the exact height desired. The bit was then picked off with tongs and dropped into a temperature-controlled hot water bath, the effect of the hot water being to normalize the steel. Hand-picking the bits off the quenching fountains was based on the visible degree of redness showing on the skirt of the bit as it was being water-cooled. This caused a problem maintaining uniformity, some bits being soft and easily dulled, and others being too hard and breaking. We found in addition to human judgment error, that on a bright day the bit skirts looked less red and were removed too soon, while on a dark day the skirts seemed more red and the bits were left on the quenching fountains.

Bob Linney asked me to design an automatic quenching machine that would allow a bit to be quenched for a controlled time, then picked off automatically by a magnet and dropped into the hot water bath. With Scrubby Morrow, we enlisted the assistance of Malcolm Dezendorf, the maintenance-electrical engineer and Louis Bouchard, the shop's master mechanic. They reviewed the designs and I prepared detailed drawings of all the components. The machine was built in the company shops from material we were able to salvage within the plant.

The automatic tempering machine was a rotary type with eighteen individual quenching fountains. When a bit was placed on one of these, water rising around the bit hardened it to the exact height desired. The rotation speed was controlled so that the proper chilling was obtained in one revolution. After a bit completed its travel it was automatically picked off its fountain by an electromagnet, then dropped onto a slide from which it fell into the hot water bath below floor level. The impact of the bit hitting the magnet then falling on the chute removed scale that might have clung to the bit. After the bits cooled following quenching, they were put into individual bins according to size, then strung on wires, placed on a hand truck and moved to the portal house to be picked up by the drillers going on shift.

With the tempering machine the hardening process was automatically controlled with no errors in human judgment involved. Bits produced were uniform and the drill footage per bit showed a marked increase. The machine eliminated one man's labor and increased the output of this operation from 100 to 1,000 bits per hour. Bob Linney was later granted a patent for the tempering machine. Subsequently four more of these units were built in the Mineville shops for other Republic Steel mines.

A section of the drill shop was designed and equipped to repair and recondition all types of rock drills in use without interfering with other drill shop functions. All drills to be repaired were brought to the surface shop, dismantled and inspected. Replacement parts were available in the nearby storehouse. Drills were thoroughly spray cleaned in a special booth with fan suction exhaust. The surface repair shop improved control over spare drill machine parts.

It is difficult today to visualize the problems in obtaining machinery and supplies in the early 1940's. Scrubby Morrow designed placement of equipment in the drill shop. All of the necessary support items such as carts, sorting bins, cooling tanks, etc. were custom-designed by him for the required task. Frequently he would bring in a sketch on a paper bag or restaurant place mat showing an idea. I would prepare drawings and our machine shop would build the item. If a gear required replacement and a spare was not available, our shops manufactured one. Our shops fabricated ore cars, skip cars, conveyor galleries and numerous other items not available for purchase.

Scrubby redesigned the spare drill parts section of the storehouse and determined the amounts required to keep equipment operating. At one time when drill steel was difficult to purchase and deliveries uncertain, Scrubby learned that a contractor at the Delaware Aqueduct in the Catskills was finishing a tunnel section and had several tons of good used drill steel on hand. He arranged for Republic to purchase the steel thus avoiding a possible production delay for lack of drill steel.

All scraper scram drift and open stope locations were equipped with Ingersoll-Rand 50-H.P. scraper or slusher hoists. These units were ideally suited to the Mineville mining layout. Handling Old Bed ore, they were frequently operating on a high overload condition, held up well and could be serviced in place. When necessary, they were completely dismantled in the surface machine shop, rebuilt with necessary new parts and returned to the mine in as-new condition. These hoists were still in use performing well when mining operations ceased in 1971.

The hoe-type scraper drag, developed at Mineville in the 1920's for use with shop-fabricated scraper hoists, consisted of a 60-inch curved manganese steel plate with reinforced scraping edges so the blade could be reversed. The blade was bolted to two side arms that were curved and bolted together at the ends with a clevis attached for fastening the 3/4-inch pull rope. A 300-pound cast iron weight was bolted to the back of the blade to aid in digging. A chain with a ring and two clevis was attached to the backplate; the 5/8-inch back pull rope was attached to the ring. This type scraper, with some modification, was in service for many years.

For driving 9 by 12-foot drifts the drill crew consisted of two men with a flatcar to carry their equipment. Arriving at the drift heading they tested the roof and side walls, scaling down any loose ground. They then attached the water hoses to the water line and washed down the heading, roof and side walls to improve ventilation and expose any unexploded blasting powder remaining from the previous blast. Each man set up an 8-foot long by 3-1/2-inch diameter column bar with a 30-inch long column arm and saddle mount for an Ingersoll-Rand DA35 drifter drill. The column bar was screw-jacked against a foot block on the floor of the drift and wood wedges at the roof. The drifter drills had a 36-inch power feed, therefore the steel change was three feet. Drill rods 3 feet 8 inches, 6 feet 8 inches and 9 feet 8 inches were used to drill each hole deep enough to advance the heading eight feet per blast.

Twenty-six to twenty-eight holes were drilled per round, then loaded with 60 percent dynamite in 1 by 8-inch cartridges with a primer cartridge and capped fuse at the bottom of each hole. Two hundred-fifty pounds of dynamite were used for each round. Fuses were trimmed for proper firing sequence and were lit for the blast at the end of the shift. Exhaust ventilation was supplied by a fan piping close to the heading.

Cleaning or mucking a development drift was normally done on the night shift by a two-man crew consisting of a shovel operator and helper. First they scaled down loose ground and wet down the roof and side walls. An Eimco 21 rocker shovel was used for shoveling up the broken muck. The machine was air-operated with a long hose connected to the compressed air line. A battery locomotive with one to five cars served the shovel. One car was link-and-pin coupled to the shovel and the shovel discharged its load overhead into the end of the car. When the car became full it was uncoupled from the shovel, coupled to the locomotive and hauled to the ore pocket and dumped. If hauling a great distance, the car would be switched to a siding and an empty car brought to the shovel. When all cars were loaded, the train would haul them to the storage pocket.

As the heading was cleaned, the shovel crew advanced the rails on temporary track. The shovel crew fired any misfired holes encountered so that the heading would be ready for the drill crew on the day shift. After four or five drill-muck cycles were completed the day shift repair crew installed and graded permanent track and advanced air and water lines as necessary.

A drill carriage, or jumbo, was built in the shops to speed up driving a drift through hard rock between Old Bed and Harmony Mines on 1185 level. It featured a flatcar with a frame on the front with four mounted drills. The jumbo was successful and became the forerunner of drill jumbos built in later years.

18

New facilities for Old Bed and Harmony Mines were still in the construction stage when the war in Europe, after the fall of France in 1940, suggested the possibility of a ten-year conflict. England was ill-equipped following the evacuation of its army from Dunkirk, and Hitler's forces were advancing unchecked all through Europe. If America was to become the arsenal for democracy, an adequate supply of iron ore would be required. Urged and financed in whole or part by the United States Government, additional Adirondack mining operations were planned by several companies.

Jones and Laughlin Ore Company developed and opened the Benson Mines open pit iron ore mine at Star Lake in St. Lawrence County, idle since 1919. The Hanna Ore Company reopened and developed the Clifton underground ore mine, about ten miles north of Benson Mines, idle since about 1890. At Tahawus, in the remote Adirondack forest, at the foot of the High Peaks region, National Lead Company developed the MacIntyre Iron Company's Lake Sanford open pit mine, idle since 1855 except for an unsuccessful attempt to reopen it in 1913. The Lake Sanford Mine was reopened to primarily produce ilmenite, with iron ore as a by-product.

Republic Steel Corporation, with its vast Adirondack mineral lands, was urged to develop additional sources of iron ore. Maps, drill core and ore reserves records were carefully evaluated. The choice for development lay between reopening the AuSable Mines in Clinton County and the Fisher Hill Mines north of Mineville.

During 1910 Witherbee Sherman had completed extensive geological studies of AuSable lands that the company had acquired, including several former operating mines. Substantial ore reserves had been tabulated. Following World War I some consideration was given to resuming operations at AuSable Mines but business conditions in the iron industry were not favorable.

The Fisher Hill Mines, located two miles north of Mineville, were last operated in 1893 by the Port Henry Iron Ore Company. The Burt Lot mine property, adjoining and north of the Fisher Hill group, had lain idle since the mid-1800's. These properties, with an estimated 40 million tons of crude ore, were selected for developing a new mine. They were sufficiently situated for mining through a central shaft. The abandoned roadbed of the L. C. & M. Railroad Smith-Sherman Mine branch reached the site and Fisher Hill was reasonably close to established operations. Republic submitted a plan for developing the Fisher Hill ore body to the U.S. Defense Plant Corporation and approval of the project was granted in September 1941.

The Fisher Hill plan included development of a mine with an annual capacity of 2,500,000 tons of crude ore from which 1,000,000 tons of concentrate and/or sinter would be produced. The plan at the mine site included a portal house, headframe with primary crusher, secondary crushing plant, hoist-compressor house, change house, storehouse, shops, ore bins, railroad tracks, offices and utilities. In conjunction with the Fisher Hill plant, a new concentrating mill and sinter plant were planned to be located along the main line of the L. C. & M. Railroad south of Mineville.

An engineering force was assembled to design and prepare detailed drawings of the Fisher Hill mine plant and the concentrating mill and sinter plant. The idle former Witherbee Sherman corporate office building at Port Henry became the project engineering office under supervision of Armand Engel as chief engineer and Lowell Henry as assistant. Alec McClellan, Jr., an electrical engineer, was in charge of electrical design. Alvin W. Inman, a well-known architect, led the building design crew. Sixty engineers and draftsmen were hired for the project and came from all sections of the eastern part of the country. Six of the engineers were transferred temporarily from other Republic districts to aid in the project.

Field survey crews were hired to make detailed topographic and boundary maps of the Fisher Hill and concentrating mill plant sites, tying all work into the established Mineville plant survey and map system. The mining engineering group, familiar with all plant survey work, established the original control points by running surveys from Mineville plant control points to the new construction sites. They prepared maps and descriptions for purchase options to acquire land from several individual landowners in the concentrating mill site area. However, with the expanded on-going operations at Mineville and the underground planning for Fisher Hill, further survey and mapping for the plant sites was handled by the surface field group.

The selected mill site along the Lake Champlain and Moriah Railroad was at the upper and lower "Y"s where back-switching was required to overcome the steep grade. This easterly sloping topography favored gravity-assisted product flow in plant design. This 370-acre plant site included thirty-one acres of our family farm.

The field survey crews worked from the engineering offices at the Mineville office building. Two engineers spent full time on map work. The field men completed detailed topographic surveys from which building locations were planned. Main line railroad relocations and new plant rail sidings were designed and located at both Fisher Hill and the concentrating mill. The mill site was named No. 7 Concentrating Mill and No. 7 Sinter Plant.

A section on the ground floor of Harmony change house building had been converted to a mining engineering office for efficient coordination of engineering and operating activities. Bill Blomstran, chief mining engineer, hired several mining engineers and helpers and purchased additional survey and geological equipment to meet requirements for expanded operations. He assigned F. S. LaMountain and J. T. Finkbeiner to the Fisher Hill engineering office.

With all the defense plant expansion nationwide it was difficult to get and retain engineers and draftsmen. One morning Paul Steffe, industrial relations superintendent, came to our Mineville engineering office and said he had a difficult problem. There was an anti-discrimination rule in Republic and in agreements governing the new government-financed plants to be built. Steffe hired engineers based on the best qualified applications. One highly qualified engineer appearing at the office in response to an offer of employment was black.

Steffe said the Port Henry engineering office force was composed of many engineers with southern backgrounds. Having heard a black engineer was to be hired, a large number said they would quit if he was assigned to their group. The company had been fortunate in getting engineers but could not stand to lose any if the work was to be done on schedule. He asked us how we felt about having a black engineer in our office. The leader of the field survey group, although from Maryland, had no prejudices. We told Steffe we had no objection and the engineer came to work in our office. He did excellent map work, was congenial and I don't think anyone ever gave much thought to the color of his skin.

A few months later the Port Henry engineering office group participated in a stage show at the high school featuring local talent. They all had a lot of fun and the show was a great success. The star of the show was the black engineer singing "Deep In The Heart Of Texas."

The Austin Company, engineers and builders, became the prime contractor for construction of all surface facilities at No. 7 and Fisher Hill plant sites. They constructed temporary wood frame offices, shops, storehouses and other necessary buildings at both sites. They had a 700-employee force of superintendents, engineers, foremen, heavy equipment operators, building trades craftsmen, accountants, clerks and laborers. Construction of all the surface facilities at both sites was completed in late summer 1943, within two years after approval of the project.

After initial mine pumping and development at Fisher Hill, sinking the main shaft was let to E. J. Longyear Company for part of the distance and then to Stiefel Construction Corporation for completion to a few feet below the sixth level station. The shaft roadbed construction was similar to Don B Shaft at Mineville except the Fisher Hill Shaft featured three tracks, two for handling ore and one for men and material. On the south side of the shaft, adjacent to the man-material track, utility lines for power, compressed air, water and pumping and a concrete stairway ran the full length of the shaft.

The ore hoist was a double drum Nordberg, formerly at the Ironton Mine in Michigan, rebuilt with new drums by Nordberg and designed to wind 5,000 feet of 1-3/4-inch diameter wire rope. The hoist was driven by two 1,000 horsepower direct current motors. Fisher Hill ore skips, the largest ever used in the Adirondacks, were seventeen feet long, weighed twelve tons, and carried an average load of seventeen and one-half long tons of ore. Skips were hoisted in balance with a top hoisting speed of 2,800 feet per minute.

The man and material hoist was a 500 horsepower single drum Nordberg winding 1-1/8-inch diameter wire rope. It had a top speed of 1,850 feet per minute but was operated for men and material at 800 feet per minute. It was equipped with automatic safety controls for overspeed and travel distance at surface. A standard 48-man capacity cage was used for handling men, or for material that would fit in the cage. Larger and longer material was loaded on a flatcar attached to the lower end of the cage.

Not long after the shaft was completed below the fifth level, blasting in one of the stopes on the first level opened into an old unmapped flooded mine. Fortunately the blast occurred at the end of the shift when all the men were out of the mine. Water from the opened old mine cascaded five feet high through the first level and down the shaft, tearing out timber platforms on the level and washing shaft track ballast to the heading. I went into the mine after the flood and photographed some of the damage. The force of the rushing water on the first level had torn the rail reinforced door from a steel five-cubic-yard mine car and bent it into a horseshoe shape.

The Fisher Hill - Burt Lot ore structure was somewhat similar to the New Bed and Harmony Mines, although low in phosphorus similar to New Bed. The ore was lenticular in shape along the strike and dipped

Tandem cages lowering seventy-two men in Don B. Shaft, 1943.

Looking down Don B Shaft at 550 level.

about thirty degrees to the southwest. The structure was folded and, while the ore was continuous along the strike, it was thicker on the anticlines and synclines than on the flanks. In previous mining, slopes or shafts were sunk from the outcrop at surface in the thick zones of ore and several of them were not interconnected. They had been mined individually and bore such names as Star Pit, Sweeney Pit, Nigger Pit, Big Pit, 9 Slope, etc.

All available engineering data was reviewed and it was decided to begin dewatering the mine through Sweeney Pit. A single drum electric hoist, formerly at the Odgers Mine in Michigan, and an air compressor and a temporary timber headframe were installed on surface to service preliminary development and pumping operations. Temporary track was laid on the footwall of Sweeney Pit as pumping lowered the mine water. This temporary arrangement was used to develop the first, second and third levels as Sweeney Pit was over 1,000 feet deep along the slope. The three upper haulage levels were spaced 300 feet along the slope and were driven to the projection of the permanent shaft. This allowed excavation of the shaft to be done by raising. The line of the main shaft from surface followed one of the old pits that ended below the second level.

As the levels were driven north and south from Sweeney Pit, advance diamond drill holes were bored to known old pits and to test ahead of drifting for unmapped mine workings. Water from these pits drained through the diamond drill holes and was pumped to surface from a single pump station at Sweeney Pit.

Support facilities for the temporary operations included a wood frame change house, drill shop, office and storehouse buildings. Charles Dewey, who had been associated with Frank Kane in contract work at the Continental Divide Tunnel, was in charge of developing the underground workings. Others associated with Kane and Dewey plus some men transferred from Harmony and Old Bed mines formed the development force. This was a difficult period for hiring men as there were abundant employment opportunities nationwide.

Fisher Hill ore mining, hoisting and primary crushing was similar in flow sheet to Mineville operations except the equipment was generally larger capacity. See Appendix V.

19

In the early months of 1944 the war in Europe was raging. The British and American Air Forces were pounding German controlled industrial centers and at the same time trying to shield England from Hitler's relentless bombing. Hundreds of planes were destroyed and American industry continued to turn out replacements and spare parts —always in short supply. The mines of America supplied the necessary raw materials.

At 7:03 p.m. on May 29, 1944, a strong earthquake was recorded by the Dominion Observatory at Ottawa, Canada. The center was placed in the vicinity of Massena, New York, about fifty miles northwest of Lyon Mountain. At that same time eleven men were underground at the Lyon Mountain Mine, some of whom were assumed to be at the 1226 shaft ore pocket engaged in repair work. Efforts to contact them failed and a rescue squad was organized. Fortunately the man cage was at the surface and the rescue crew was lowered into the mine. The cage stopped at the 900-foot level where it became wedged between shattered shaft divider walls. Continuing down ladders to a point 75 feet above the pocket, the rescue crew found the shaft completely blocked. The cage compartment was cleared down to the 963 level which was open. They continued down a raise to the 1263 level and back to the shaft. From here they climbed the shaft ladderway to the caved area at the 1226 level pocket, where three men were known to be trapped. Two were rescued and the body of the third recovered.

Inspection of the caving revealed that the shaft had been severely damaged for 500 feet. Power cables were cut and pump lines broken. By the time damage was determined the mine had been without power for 23 hours and rising water had flooded the 2313 level pump station. Power was restored, pumping resumed and repairs organized to get the mine back in production as soon as possible. The shaft was repaired in eleven days, a noteworthy accomplishment.

Chateaugay low-phosphorus ore was vitally needed for the war effort. Fortunately Fisher Hill Mine at Mineville was in production and 30,000 tons of Fisher Hill low-phosphorus concentrates were diverted to replace the flow of Chateaugay ore interrupted by damage to the Lyon

Mountain mine shaft.

It is an interesting footnote to history that some months later, at a supervisory force dinner meeting at the Lee House in Port Henry, J. R. Linney commented on that shipment. He was discussing the $14,000,000 that Fisher Hill and No. 7 Plant had cost to construct and place in operation. He noted that at the time the Lyon Mountain shaft was damaged and out of production, Chateaugay low-phosphorous ore was being used to make aircraft engine parts for the war. He said he was told by a War Production Board representative that it would be impossible to place a value on the 30,000 tons of Fisher Hill low-phosphorous ore used to keep the production line intact. Mr. Linney further stated he was told, "If the Fisher Hill Mine and Plant never produces another ton of ore we should consider its cost paid in full."

With ten million men and women in military service, industry was hard-pressed to staff plants, even though military deferments were granted to men in industries vital to the war effort. There was strong competition among companies for available manpower.

Some employees urged by family members, or for other reasons, left to work in other industries considered less hazardous than underground mining. With all defense industries short of labor, it was an opportune time to change occupations. Republic paid good wages, provided insurance benefits, had a good safety program, and general working conditions were probably the best in the mining industry. However, mining was subject to more physical risks than many other industries.

Republic initiated a program at Mineville to counter apprehensive feelings of miners' families and other residents of the area. Tours of the underground mine and surface plant were conducted for local businessmen and clergy. Groups of women were given the same tour. They were taken underground to minus 550 Level. Here they rode an ore train to a stope mining location where they observed drilling and loading ore. A few in each group operated a jackhammer. The safety program, including use of explosives, was explained. Returning to surface they observed the hoisting and crushing operations, followed by lunch at the Lee House in Port Henry. Each member of the group was given a booklet describing plant operations, and later received a copy of their group photograph. I photographed the groups and over 300 women visited the mining operations.

The tours were a public relations success. I recall an incident in John Murphy's office one morning before the start of the day shift when one of the drillers came in and said, "John, I don't think it was a good idea to take all those women underground. You showed them the cleanest, safest and best looking working place in the mine. My wife said, 'Don't tell me how hard you work in the mine when I ask you to do something. I've been there and I don't think you work half as hard as you say.' I told her she didn't see the place where I work." He laughed, but I know the miners were pleased that women were invited to take the mine tour.

There was quite a staff turnover in those wartime years. Some supervisors left either through Republic corporate transfer or voluntary choice.

Superintendent of Mines Frank Kane was transferred from Mineville to be general superintendent of Republic's Southern Ore Mines District. Charles Dewey left Fisher Hill and went with Kane. Armand Engel was appointed superintendent of Fisher Hill and Smith Mines, but left shortly thereafter to accept a position with National Lead Company at Tahawus. Lowell Henry became chief engineer and William Coghill, district industrial engineer.

John Jacka was appointed chief chemist. William Blomstran, chief mining engineer, divided his work force between the Mineville and Fisher Hill mine offices. John Murphy and John Brennan, Sr. were named superintendents of Old Bed and Harmony Mines. Thomas Catanzarita was appointed superintendent of primary crushing plants at Mineville and Fisher Hill.

Francis Myers became superintendent of concentrating and sintering operations at No. 7 Plant. Paul Steffe, superintendent of industrial relations, was transferred by Republic to a southern steel plant. Ray Munson, safety supervisor, replaced Steffe. William Thiesen was later appointed safety supervisor.

Following the death of Alec McClellan, Sr., Vernon Slater was named district accountant. Louis Dufrane was placed in charge of shops at Fisher Hill. Walter Habert was transferred from Cleveland to Mineville in charge of plant security.

The company owned 470 employee dwellings in Mineville and Port Henry with an average rental, in 1942, of ten dollars per month. Frank Waite had a large force of carpenters, painters and plumbers continually working on house repairs as well as plant buildings. Employee housing was always a large red figure on the district cost sheet.

In conjunction with the wartime expansion in Mineville, the Federal Housing Authority erected five dormitories with a capacity of 300 men. Republic Steel converted a large building nearby into an independently managed restaurant. The Housing Authority also built an elementary school and 207 houses with a capacity of 430 families. The housing site was along the Plank Road south of Mineville and was named Grover Hills in honor of Oscar J. Grover, the first Town of Moriah soldier to be killed in World War II.

The Mineville office building built by Witherbee Sherman and Company in 1906-07 was enlarged by a two-story concrete block addition on the east end. Accounting offices were provided on the first floor addition and management offices on the second floor. The attic space on the third floor was converted to an office for the geologist. During the major wartime construction period, district accounting was done in the Port Henry office building and Defense Plant Corporation accounting was done in the Mineville office.

The sixteen-bed company hospital at Mineville continued to serve employees, their families and the general public under the direction of Dr. Thomas J. Cummins.

The hospital was a necessity for the mining operations and was not intended to operate as a profit-making facility. It was equipped with the latest X-ray and surgical equipment. In 1942, eighty percent of the hospital patients were non-employees. The employee rate, which included family members, was $2.50 per day including meals, with a $6.50 charge for the operating room. The hospital also served as a monthly clinic for visiting physicians from the New York State Hospital for Tuberculosis. Complete physical examinations, including chest X-rays, were given yearly to all employees. A south wing was added to the hospital and included a laboratory with special equipment for treatment of employees who in past years had contracted silicosis. The hospital and staff provided all medical care for the communities during those years when major medical centers were distant and ambulance squads non-existent.

Company emphasis on production with safety, employee training, regular safety inspections of work places and work habits were stressed at weekly safety meetings. Republic's company-wide safety program was augmented with inspections by safety supervisors from other Republic plants. These safety measures, improved mining and milling methods, and employee cooperation produced a marked improvement in the safety record.

Ore concentration and sintering and L. C. & M. Railroad operations made a smooth transition from No. 5 Mill at Mineville and No. 6 Mill and sinter plant at Port Henry to No. 7 Mill and sinter plant. See Appendix W for detail.

Those war years were a time of full employment and government-issued ration cards for meat, gasoline and tires. With gasoline in short supply, the company purchased two cars and hired drivers to take engineers and office personnel to the various work locations as required. Belden and Edwards in Port Henry ran a bus service from Ticonderoga to Fisher Hill with stops at Crown Point, Port Henry, Moriah, Switchback (No. 7 Plant), Witherbee, Mineville and Fisher Hill. Trips coincided with the work shift change.

The mines were a defense industry and everyone was issued an identification number and badge. Civil defense was organized. Fully equipped emergency first aid rooms were installed at various plant locations for use in a disaster situation. Blackouts were scheduled on a test basis. One clear night I was over at the Crown Point Fort to observe the blackout. On schedule, all lights from the lake shore at Port Henry inland and north and south along the lake were doused. There was only one light visible in the entire area and it was the headlight on the L. C. & M. train bringing ore from the mines down to Port Henry.

General Electric Company, American Locomotive Company and the U.S. Watervliet Arsenal were vital defense facilities heavily concentrated in the Albany Capital District area. Many other defense industries were equally concentrated in the Northeast. U.S. military maneuvers in 1936 had demonstrated the difficulty in moving a large force from New England and New York to Camp Drum near Watertown, New York. Northern New York highways at that time were not suited for heavy traffic and became clogged, particularly through hamlets, during the military movement.

If the war in Europe ended badly for Allied Forces, a probable invasion route to America would be through the St. Lawrence River and down the Champlain and Hudson Valleys to cut off the industrial northeast. The U.S. Coast Guard studied the area for possible defense measures. In later years, although some of the major industries in the northeast were decentralized, the lack of adequate highways for military movement to the north was probably a major factor in federal government support for construction of the Adirondack Northway.

There were over one thousand men and women from the Town of Moriah in military service. Many men from the mines enlisted after the attack on Pearl Harbor and the younger age group was later drafted as the war in Europe and the Pacific intensified. Gold stars began to appear on the honor rolls in the village square at Port Henry and in the change house at Mineville. The local Western Union office had the too-frequent, unpleasant task of delivering War Department telegrams.

20

Reopening Clonan Shaft following the Joker Shaft headframe fire in 1941 furnished access to the "21"-Joker-Bonanza ore body last mined by the Port Henry Iron Ore Company in 1924. Examination of the mine workings and a review of mine maps and sections revealed a potential for recovery of a substantial tonnage of Old Bed ore at little mine development expense.

The "21"-Joker-Bonanza ore body probably resulted from intense geological folding and pinching. The ore body pitches downward at approximately 30 degrees along an axis striking south 30 degrees west. It totally encloses a "horse" of rock, and in cross section resembles a doughnut. From the original outcrop at surface downward, the structure became progressively smaller in cross section until the "horse" of rock, and finally the ore, disappeared in the surrounding wall rock.

Former mining by Port Henry Iron Ore Company in the underground section of "21" Mine above the bottom of the open pit followed the room and pillar method. In this massive ore body, pillars of solid ore were left standing above and below the "horse" of rock to the adjacent rock above and below. On either side of the "horse" of rock the ore had a vertical thickness of 200 to 450 feet. A decline "21" Shaft was sunk from the bottom of the open pit underground extending the skipway from the tipple at surface along the floor of the open pit to the underground mining areas below.

In 1909 Port Henry Iron Ore Company sunk Clonan Shaft, a vertical shaft from surface, to improve ore handling and mining in the underground mining areas. Electric shovels and locomotive haulage were introduced in 1916 to further improve the mining system and reduce costs. However, these measures did not forestall final shutdown of operations in 1924.

In 1941, following the Joker Shaft headframe fire, the refurbished Clonan Shaft provided access to the unmined Port Henry Iron Ore Company ore reserves for mining by Republic Steel during a period of high ore demand. Thirteen vertical holes blasted in one of these pillars yielded over 16,000 gross tons of ore.

For a detailed description of mining methods used by Port Henry

Iron Ore Company and Republic Steel Corporation in this large ore structure, see Appendix X.

The U.S. Bureau of Mines, at the request of the company, conducted a geophysical program to determine if there were any unusual stresses occurring in the roof and wall rock as pillars were removed. The test method used by U.S.B.M. engineers featured around-the-clock micro-seismic recording of sub-audible rock noises. Results of the tests, conducted over a period of a year and a half, indicated the pillar recovery had not created any detectable rock strain. The test program further indicated that the roof over the entire ore body formed a natural arch which, with the supporting pillars above and below the "horse," furnished a strong roof support over the limbs on either side.

Access to some of the areas to be reclaimed required driving raises to mined areas nearer to surface in "21" Mine. Drilling equipment, explosives and other materials had to be carried or hoisted to these areas from operating levels below. To alleviate this problem 170 feet of joined ladder sections, reinforced with wire rope, were installed at the face of the "21" open pit down to the entrance to the upper pillar area. A stiff-legged derrick with an air tugger hoist was installed on surface to lower supplies to the bottom of the ladderway. Underground, a cable bridge consisting of planks bolted to cables securely anchored on either side of a large deep mine opening provided easy access for miners to the reclaiming areas.

A small headframe with hoist was installed at Bonanza Shaft to lower equipment and supplies from surface to the upper Bonanza area to be reclaimed. The day the timber work at surface was completed, John Murphy and I rode down the shaft on top of the small cage to inspect the shaft sets. About eighty feet from surface the cage travel became blocked by a piece of timber in the guides. Our safety ropes were tied to the cage and while we were attempting to remove the piece of timber, an old cable and two timber sets from the sidewalls above loosened and fell down the shaft, striking the cage but hitting neither of us. However, that was a close one and John and I recalled it many times in later years.

With safe access to the "21"-Joker-Bonanza old mine workings and safe methods of pillar recovery, over one million tons of very high grade magnetite ore were recovered. Only skilled miners worked in those areas, men who knew how to work safely in very high places under abnormal conditions.

In the late 1970's I went down Clonan Shaft to the 430 Level to a stope area where one of the large pillars had been removed many years earlier. I noted the catwalk still intact on the high roof. There was no broken fall rock material on the floor of the stope. This proved to me the soundness of the geophysical test program conducted when pillar recovery began.

During a peak period of wartime production from Clonan Shaft, the ten-inch diameter, twenty-two-foot long main shaft on the Clonan ore hoist sheared. There was no available spare and to get Clonan shaft ore hoisting quickly back in production appeared remote. All steel manufacture and finishing was on a national priority basis. Republic Steel's Chicago plant could produce a billet for the shaft in three weeks but could not machine the finished shaft. The only known nearby facility that could turn the billet into a finished shaft was the Watervliet Arsenal, and that plant was on full production of guns for the United States Navy.

Shop foreman Louis Bouchard determined that a large old lathe seldom used in the shop could machine a shaft for the hoist. He also recalled that the old steam hoist, still in place at "21" open pit hoist house, had a wrought iron shaft larger in diameter and longer than the broken shaft. Drawings of both shafts were checked and only a couple of keyways in the wrought iron shaft would require building up to prepare it for machining to fit the Clonan ore hoist.

The old "21" steam hoist was dismantled and its shaft brought to the shop, cut to length and placed in the lathe. Bill Hunt and Adam Zelinsky worked around the clock welding a buildup in the keyways. This was a critical operation as the welds had to be carefully and slowly applied to prevent fracture to the shaft. With the welding completed the shaft was machined to the required specifications and installed in the Clonan ore hoist. Clonan shaft ore hoisting was back in operation within four days. The steel shaft billet produced at Chicago arrived three weeks later, and was machined at the Mineville shops. It was installed in the hoist during a planned maintenance period the following year.

There were numerous times, particularly during the war years, that demonstrated the resourcefulness of the plant force. If a required piece of equipment could not be purchased, the engineers and shops would design and build it. The slusher drag bucket or scraper, as it was called, was an example.

The original plant-designed Witherbee Sherman scraper drag had performed well but tended to tip over and lose its load if not handled properly. It was also a high-maintenance item.

In the 1940's Bill Blomstran conceived a semi-box type design scraper with an exchangeable manganese steel blade tip. The digging angle in relation to the pull on the drag was designed to dig and lift the load. The drag had a low center of gravity and resisted turning over. The side arms were curved to accommodate more load. I made several drawings of this unit, modifying the digging angle and making other minor revisions based on its performance. This unit, weighing 2,300 pounds, was far superior to any on the market, was one-fourth the cost of machinery company manufactured units, and remained in use until the end of mining operations in 1971. Several hundred of these scrapers were completely built in the Mineville plant shops.

The Linney management style was as resourceful as the rest of the organization. One day I was in Bob's office discussing a machine drawing when he received a phone call from the secretary of Republic's vice president, Charles White. She said Mr. White wanted to rent a choice suite at the Westport Inn overlooking Lake Champlain for two weeks in August. Bob assured her there would be no problem and he would arrange it.

The Westport Inn was generally booked to capacity as were all Adirondack hotels during the war years, due to restricted foreign travel. Bob knew the inn manager and called him to reserve the best suite for Mr. White. The manager replied, "Bob, I would like to help you but there is no way I can let you have that suite. It has been reserved for over a year for the chairman of one of New York's largest banks." Bob hung up the phone and said to me, "I'll have to get that suite somehow. It's most important to our operations to keep Charlie White happy."

At a lunch meeting the following day Malcolm Dezendorf, superintendent of maintenance, said, "Bob, the manager of the Westport Inn called me with a serious problem. He has a large dinner dance crowd every evening and finds that the floor under the ballroom should be reinforced. He has tried from Montreal to Albany to get a couple of steel beams but none are available. He would like to buy a couple of new or used beams and columns from Republic, if possible."

Bob thought a minute and then said, "I know him well and we ought to help him out. Tell him this is what we will do: We'll send the engineers up to the inn, have them design the support structure, have the beams made up in our shops and send your rigger crew up to install them. Tell him we understand the trouble he is in and are glad to help out and it will cost him nothing."

Dezendorf said, "You mean we are going to do all that and charge him nothing?" Bob replied, "Yes, and you can remind him that I appreciate a favor he is in the process of granting Republic." The next morning on my way underground, I met Dezendorf and he asked me what I knew about the Westport Inn deal. He suspected I knew something. I said nothing, and he continued, "I went up there full of enthusiasm for Republic's generous offer and the inn manager said to me, 'That no good so-and-so.' "

The Westport Inn had its floor support structure designed, fabricated and installed by Republic; and Mr. White had his choice suite without ever knowing how it was arranged.

21

The invasion of Europe in June 1944 and Allied success in North Africa, the Mediterranean and the Pacific marked a turning point in the war. American war industries were in high gear supplying the necessary ships, tanks, guns and planes. The nation's mines were suppling the copper, iron and other raw materials in increasing volume. Many Republic plants were awarded the Army-Navy "E" banner for excellence. It was conservatively estimated that one million Allied casualties would result from a land invasion of Japan. This no longer was a concern after President Truman authorized the use of the atomic bomb to bring a quick end to the war.

The companies moved rapidly in the transition from wartime to peacetime production. The steel industry was the basic producer for civilian goods. No new model cars had been built for nearly four years as steel and auto plants had been on full military production. Appliances, electrical equipment, homes and many other civilian needs were in short supply. There was no labor shortage with ten million returning service men and women joining the work force.

U.S. government policy also took the lead in rebuilding the basic European industries that had been ravaged by war. Rufus Wysor, president of Republic Steel, was sent to Europe to coordinate rebuilding the steel industry. Charles White succeeded Wysor as president.

Republic's production record at Mineville, after the plant acquisition from Witherbee Sherman Corporation in 1938, had been impressive. Mine production was as follows:

Gross Tons Crude Ore Mined

Year	Old Bed	Harmony	Fisher Hill	Total
1938	107,286	125,136		232,422
1939	453,674	333,654		787,328
1940	555,249	275,164		830,413
1941	614,093	488,306		1,102,399
1942	675,763	502,213		1,177,976
1943	719,751	514,956	2,851	1,237,558
1944	868,207	491,640	252,367	1,612,214
1945	788,765	331,026	356,580	1,476,371
Total	4,782,788	3,062,095	611,798	8,456,681

From the 8,456,681 gross tons of crude ore mined, 5,004,582 gross tons of shipping product were shipped to Republic's furnaces. This was one ton of shipping product produced for each 1.7 tons of crude ore mined. The tabulation shows that by the end of the war all three mines were at a high production level. Harmony and Old Bed Mines were operated by Republic Steel, and Fisher Hill underground mine production was by contract with Stiefel Construction Corporation.

Joseph R. Linney resigned on April 1, 1945, having completed twenty-eight years of active management of Adirondack iron ore mines. Robert J. Linney succeeded him as district manager of the Port Henry district and William J. Linney was named district manager of Lyon Mountain operations. J. R. Linney served as a mining consultant for the next few years until his death at age 64 while on a tour of mining operations in Peru, South America.

Following the end of World War II in 1945, American labor renewed demands for increased wages and benefits. The American Federation of Labor represented the workers at Mineville. However, the C.I.O. sent organizers to Mineville to ostensibly organize plant foremen in a union, but the real goal was to replace the A.F. of L. as the plant bargaining unit. There was a lot of rhetoric extoling the virtues of each union, but there did not seem to be any strong feelings among the workers. Adron Coldiron was the C.I.O. organizer and his group put out a paper labeling the A.F. of L. the "All for Linney Union." The A.F. of L. countered with a fact sheet labeled "Hot Rivets for Coldiron."

A National Labor Relations Board election was scheduled to determine which union would represent the workers. I was an inspector during the ballot voting. The C.I.O. won the election by a margin of better than two to one and also won the right to represent the workers at Lyon Mountain.

In 1946 the mines at Mineville and Lyon Mountain were on a rather lengthy strike, demanding an eighteen and one-half cents per hour wage increase. J. R. Linney was engaged by Republic to try to reach a satisfactory settlement, but the union stood firm and its demands were finally met.

With operations resumed, Bob Linney made some organizational changes. Francis Myers was promoted to assistant district manager; Tom Catanzarita, concentrating mill superintendent; Paul Gebo, sinter plant superintendent; and Bill Hunt, superintendent of crushing plants at Mineville and Fisher Hill.

At the time of the 1946 strike, Stiefel Construction Corporation was notified by Republic that their mining contract at Fisher Hill was terminating and would not be renewed. The company would pay Stiefel for any broken ore mined by them and left in the stopes based on tons agreed by Stiefel and the company engineers.

In March of 1947 Republic resumed operations at Fisher Hill with plans to develop the Smith Mine Old Bed type ore. John Murphy was named superintendent and I was sent to Fisher Hill to help him get the mine equipped and in production. Walter Nels became a foreman at Fisher Hill as he had worked there for Stiefel following his return from military service. We were limited in transferring men from Mineville to Fisher Hill as the Mineville and Fisher Hill mines were separate seniority units. We could only move exempt foremen and supervisors freely.

Walt Nels and I spent one full day in the Westport, Crown Point and Ticonderoga areas contacting men who had formerly worked in the mines. We recruited eighteen-year-olds who had never worked in a mine. I made a recap sheet showing that of 125 men working in the mine, only seventeen had previously worked underground, and of these, only eleven had ever operated a rock drill. The potential for serious injury to these men was of great concern. Some experienced miners from Old Bed and Harmony Mines were given non-bargaining unit status to serve as drill and mining instructors to train new men. Technicians from explosives and rock drill companies visited the work places underground to instruct the new miners.

The worst problem was the condition in which Stiefel workers had left the stopes. There was a lot of loose rock and ore hanging on stope roofs. Stiefel had used electric blasting and misfired holes were found everywhere. Sticks of powder were found stored under slusher motors. Drift ditches had not been cleaned and most track rails were under water. These problems were quickly recognized and corrected. Republic Steel always emphasized good housekeeping and Fisher Hill Mine was to become a model. Somehow it all fell together and within three weeks of start-up the mine was producing 1,000 tons per day.

One afternoon John Jacka, chief chemist and former chief engineer, stopped in my office to give me some advice on mining Fisher Hill. Pointing to the mine map on the wall, he said, "The stopes as laid out with loading platforms built by Stiefel, are not aligned properly to mine the ore at an acceptable ratio. If you mine in the direction these are laid out, you will end up mining rock and leaving the ore in pillars. These stopes are all lined up at right angles to the drift and you can see that the folds of ore are northeast from the drift. Now is the time to make a change. You will have to rebuild some of the stope loading platforms but that will mean a big saving in the long run."

I discussed Jacka's suggestions with John Murphy. He told me to go ahead and change the stopes the way Jacka suggested as we should take advantage of his knowledge of Fisher Hill ore trends. Jacka had been mining engineer for the Port Henry Iron Ore Company in the 1920's, when that company unwatered some of the mine pits and made extensive geological studies for possible operation. Murphy was always willing to listen and open to suggestions. I was associated with John Murphy for many years and never knew a superintendent or foreman who could get better cooperation, performance and respect from the work force.

A large timber repair crew began rebuilding loading platforms at several new stope locations on four mine levels. This proved beneficial in getting new stopes started and following the trends of the thicker ore in the synclines and anticlines rather than crossing into thin ore sections in the flanks of the ore structure. The mining engineers thereafter determined stope locations and direction, following study of the projected trends balanced with data from short diamond drill holes.

At the time of renewed operations in 1947 the Fisher Hill shaft heading was thirty feet below the sixth level shaft station, and the heading for the sixth level drift was thirty feet south of the shaft station. A two-man drill crew advanced the sixth level drift heading on day shift and a shovel operator and helper cleaned the drift on night shift. The Eimco Model 21 air shovel was used to clean the drift and later replaced by the new larger Model 40 when it became available. When the drift heading reached a planned branch, the drill and muck crews were able to get extra cycles by mining an alternate heading while repairmen were extending permanent track, air and water lines.

There was an advantage to the development crew in Fisher Hill Mine. Travel time at Fisher Hill from surface to any underground work location was ten to fifteen minutes. In Old Bed Mine travel time was thirty-five to forty minutes with the same travel time at the end of the shift. Work schedules had to be arranged so that men could pass by the time clock on surface within their eight-hour shift.

Bob Linney had been spending a lot of time underground on minus 1500 level in Old Bed Mine as development of ore stopes was behind schedule. One evening at a social gathering, Bob remarked that the 1500 level drift crew had made forty-eight feet of advance the previous week. I remarked that the sixth level drift crew at Fisher Hill had made sixty-six feet of advance that same week. The Old Bed development foreman, who was in the group, said it was not possible for a single drift crew to make sixty-six feet.

The next morning John Murphy called me into his office and asked, "What went on last evening about development drifting? Bob Linney called and said for you to stay on surface until he comes to Fisher Hill.

He wants to look at the sixth level development footage." I showed Murphy the footage sheet and he said with a grin, "We're right this time and I think he expects to find some mistake." Bob came in shortly after and asked to see the development footage sheet. He studied it and said, "That's pretty good performance by the Fisher Hill drift crew."

Republic appropriated funds to sink the Fisher Hill Shaft from the sixth to below the twelfth level. This would provide six additional mine production levels to mine the ore structure to the limit of its hoisting facilities. Crosscuts were planned from two of these levels back through the footwall to ore projected from Smith Mine.

For detail on development drifting and shaft sinking in Fisher Hill and Smith Mines, see Appendix Y.

In the original shaft sinking at Fisher Hill, contractors used as many as twenty-five men in the crew. In shaft sinking below the sixth level we used a five-man drill crew and two men on an alternate shift cleaning the heading with the scraper slide. In the mucking operation the center track ore skip was removed at surface and a small skip, designed for use with the scraper slide, attached to the center hoist rope. This equipment change usually only required ten minutes at the beginning and end of the shift. Ore hoisting was confined to one shift with shaft sinking operations on the two idle shifts.

When shaft sinking had advanced sufficiently below the sixth level, heavy doors that could be raised and lowered were constructed at the sixth level station. These featured steel beams hinged to the sixth level station main beam and covered with six by eight-inch creosoted timbers. The doors were designed to stop any loose rock or material that might go down the shaft while men were working below. Touch wires were installed outside all shaft rails that would sound an alarm in the hoist room if a derailed skip, cage, or any metal object came in contact with the wire. At the alarm, all hoisting would stop until the cause was investigated.

A large section of loose roof was encountered between the sixth and seventh levels, requiring steel and concrete support. Otherwise, no steel roof supports were necessary. By the end of 1948 the shaft heading had been advanced below the seventh level and drift development started on that level.

Republic placed a high priority on safety, but serious accidents did occur. On January 5, 1949, a loaded ore skip being hoisted to surface from the Fisher Hill fifth level ore pocket was struck by the descending empty ore skip that jumped the track below the first level pocket. Ore hoisting was in balance in that when one skip was being hoisted the other was lowered. The skip passing point was near the second level just below where the collision occurred. The impact of the colliding skips tore the cross bail away from the side straps on the center track skip. The touch wires which signaled the hoistman if a skip derailed rang and immediately the hoistman felt the impact of the skip collision at the hoist. The hoist rope did not break and the skip cross bail was still attached to it.

The runaway loaded ore skip, with a total weight of twenty-nine tons, went unrestrained on the center track down the shaft, demolishing the center track bulkhead door at the sixth level without touching the north or south bulkhead doors. Lowell Henry later estimated that the loaded skip on the track was traveling over 350 miles per hour when it crashed through the sixth level bulkhead. About a hundred feet below the bulkhead the center track rails spread and the skip tumbled on its side down to the shaft heading.

Four men were working below the sixth level bulkhead doors preparing forms for pouring concrete track support piers below the seventh level. Three of the four men were struck by flying debris, fatally injuring two and slightly injuring the third man. This was a tragic accident and morale was low. When an accident occurred it touched all miners and their families.

22

In the spring of 1949 there was an unexpected drop in demand for alloy steel that idled ten electric and six open hearth Republic furnaces. Officials in Cleveland ordered Fisher Hill Mine shut down by May 1. This came as a surprise for in the month of March the three mines had established a production record of 230,773 tons of crude ore mined. During that month Fisher Hill Mine had produced 62,602 tons, exceeding its previous monthly record by 7,270 tons. However, Fisher Hill Mine was a high cost mine due to a high ratio of crude ore to concentrate. Bob Linney had a tough time convincing Charlie White to keep Harmony Mine operating. He successfully argued that Harmony shared hoisting and crushing facilities at Mineville with Old Bed Mine and the combined tons from the two mines would benefit product cost.

Under an agreement with the U.S. government, Fisher Hill Mine had to be maintained on standby condition should an emergency require its operation. Equipment, including rock drills and slusher hoist motors, was brought to surface for storage. Mine pumping was automatic, but a hoistman and two maintenance men checked the pumps and locomotive storage batteries regularly.

Following shutdown of Fisher Hill, mine superintendent John Murphy again took charge of Old Bed Mine. I returned to the engineering department at the main office to work on projects assigned by the district manager. One of these involved force shuffles required by the layoff of 160 Fisher Hill employees out of a total plant force of 1,100. In later years I was involved with the Industrial Relations Department and the Union in all plant force shuffles.

Fisher Hill Mine production tons from March 1947 through April 30, 1949 were:

Year	Crude Ore Mined	Concentrate Produced
1947	372,318	112,510
1948	523,304	135,094
1949	195,163	49,347
Total	1,090,785	296,951

These production figures resulted in a ratio of 3.67 tons of crude ore mined per ton of concentrate produced. However, the figures do not tell the complete story. Twenty-seven percent of the ore in Fisher Hill Mine was non-magnetic crystalline hematite. In the Fisher Hill crushing plant, the hematite was not recovered by the magnetic separators but passed to the waste rock storage pile. Had this twenty-seven percent of the crude ore been recovered, the total concentrate figure above would have been 377, 135 tons with a resulting ratio of 2.89 tons of crude ore per ton of concentrate produced. The development program of rock crosscut drifting and shaft sinking produced no ore. This inflated the ratio figure. It became obvious if Fisher Hill were to operate, the non-magnetic ore would have to be recovered. However, with the 1949 shutdown, plans for continued mine development of Fisher Hill and Smith Mine ore were cancelled.

At the same time, other developments underway in the American iron ore industry would have a lasting influence on the long term future of Adirondack iron mining operations. In the 1940's several large American steel companies had studied possible development of iron ore projects in Labrador, South America and Africa.

Republic Steel acquired a major interest in Liberia Mining Company which owned a large iron ore deposit in Liberia, West Africa, and also a one-half interest in Reserve Mining Company, a large taconite magnetite property in Minnesota. For details, see Appendix Z.

Increased ore demand for Republic furnaces in 1950 placed pressure on Mineville mines to increase production. Fisher Hill Mine was re-opened in September with workers on layoff recalled and new men hired. Old Bed Mine was the main producing mine and John Murphy remained there to expand development and production. John Brennan, Sr., superintendent of Harmony Mine, was placed in overall charge of Fisher Hill Mine along with the Harmony operations. Bob Linney sent me to Fisher Hill to operate the mine as Brennan would spend nearly all his time at Harmony Mine.

It was easier to get the mine back in production in the fall of 1950 than in 1947 as the mine had been left in good condition. Shortly after resuming production, a group of Republic Steel, Armco and Reserve Mining Company officials visited the Mineville and Fisher Hill plant operations. Their particular interest was in the flow of ore from primary crushing at the mines through the secondary crushing, concentrating and sintering process.

In October 1950, Bob Linney resigned as district manager of Republic's Port Henry District to become general manager of Reserve Mining Company. One afternoon before he left Bob came to my office

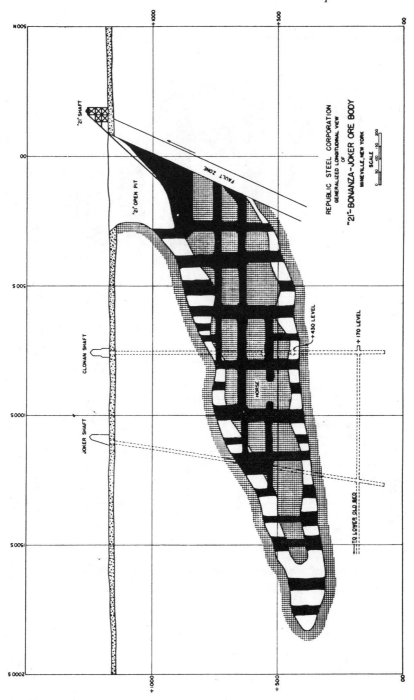

Longitudinal view of Mineville's "21"-Bonanza-Joker ore body in the 1940's.

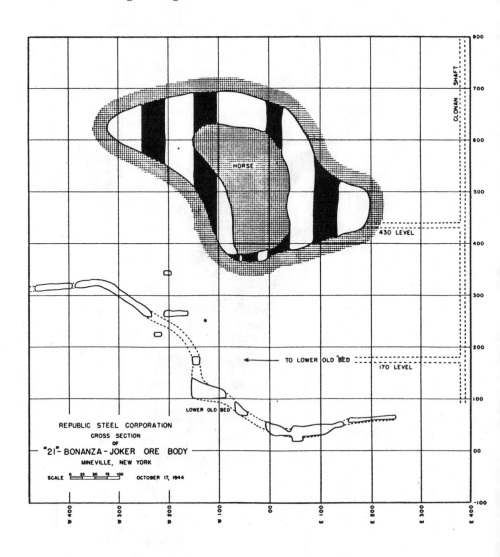

Cross section of Mineville's "21"-Bonaza-Joker ore body in the 1940's.

Extending a suspended catwalk to the high pillars in Clonan Shaft in "21" Mine for pillar recovery during the 1940's.

Working from a catwalk, miners cut the pillar away from the roof prior to drilling and blasting the pillar down to the floor below.

at Fisher Hill and we discussed the Reserve plant. His immediate task would be to develop an operating pilot plant to refine the concentration process for final design of the Silver Bay production plant. He said, "When Reserve reaches full production, pellets will be the desired blast furnace feed. You and I are about the only ones who believed in the long-range future of Fisher Hill, but Fisher Hill Mine will not be able to compete and I think the competition for Harmony, Lyon Mountain and even Old Bed mine ores will place their future in doubt."

Bob Linney recruited experienced men from Republic and other companies to fill key positions. While the inland Babbitt pilot plant and townsite were being built, the railroad and Silver Bay townsite and plant were also under construction. In 1951, Dr. Davis, know as Mr. Taconite, took a leave of absence from the University of Minnesota to join the Reserve organization.

In 1960 the Silver Bay plant of Reserve, appropriately named the E. W. Davis Works, went into production—the world's first full production iron taconite plant. In that same year Bob Linney became president of Reserve Mining Company, succeeding W. M. (Doc) Kelley.

In 1964 Bob Linney resigned as president of Reserve to become executive vice president of Hanna Mining Company. He led Hanna through the planning, construction, and start-up of new American and Canadian facilities capable of producing ten million annual tons of iron ore pellets. In 1968 he resigned as executive vice president of Hanna, and remained as a consultant. Robert J. Linney died at his home in Cleveland in 1971 at age 63.

When Bob Linney left Mineville in 1950, Republic's Adirondack operations were again combined into one district under the management of William J. Linney, who then moved to Port Henry to be near the larger division of the Adirondack operations. Walter Crusberg was assistant manager at Lyon Mountain and Francis Myers assistant manager at Mineville. Bill Linney's management style differed from that of his brother, Bob. Bill let his assistant managers run the operations, getting involved only when a problem developed, whereas Bob had maintained a hands-on contact with all departments and their superintendents. However, Bill Linney became more involved in labor relations.

The mines met the renewed demand for Mineville ore in 1950. At Fisher Hill the martite non-magnetic ore was still being lost in the crushing plant and concentrating mill tailings. In 1953 a martite recovery system, featuring an eight by eight-foot ball mill, classifiers and Diester tables, was designed and installed in the Fisher Hill unit at No. 7 Mill. Magnetic separation in the secondary crushing plant at Fisher Hill was discontinued and all crude ore was ground to crushed ore with no rock discarded. Tailings from the Fisher Hill magnetic concentrating mill unit were passed to the martite section where the non-magnetic ore was recovered on the Diester concentrating tables. The non-magnetic concentrate, containing some apatite, was passed to the Old Bed concentrate bin in order not to raise the phosphorus content of Fisher Hill magnetic concentrate.

Underground mine development was expanded in both Fisher Hill and Old Bed Mines to meet the demand for increased production. See Appendix AA for details.

Ore produced from the three mines following the end of World War II through 1950 was as follows:

Gross Tons Crude Ore Produced

Year	Old Bed	Harmony	Fisher Hill	Total
1946	459,016	205,394	93,012	757,422
1947	878,505	400,632	372,318	1,651,455
1948	951,153	409,948	523,304	1,884,405
1949	850,575	435,686	195,163	1,481,424
1950	917,750	455,139	101,535	1,474,424
Total	4,056,999	1,906,799	1,285,332	7,249,130

23

The 1950's were a period of consolidation of the Mineville facilities for a more cost-effective operation. The machine, blacksmith, welding and electric shops at the Mineville plant were abandoned and their functions moved to the newer more productive shops at Fisher Hill. Continued staff changes were made during this period.

In September 1951, Dr. Thomas J. Cummins died at his home in Mineville at the age of seventy-four. He had been physician-surgeon in charge of the company hospital at Mineville since 1917, having served thirty-four years. His passing was a loss to the people of the Town of Moriah and surrounding areas. His treatment of mining accident cases earned him the respect and confidence of miners, their families and the entire township. He served as confidant and advisor to many in their personal matters.

Doctor Cummins had delivered a whole generation of the adult population. In the early days he was a familiar figure riding horseback to his daily house calls. He performed all types of major surgery in the company hospital.

The general sadness and respect for Dr. Cummins at his death were manifest in several ways. For the first time since the funeral of Jonathan G. Witherbee in 1875 all mining operations ceased so the miners, many whose lives he had saved, could attend his funeral. The Mineville-Witherbee schools were closed, and a special early funeral mass was held for the children. Six miners served as pallbearers, and members of the Essex County Medical Society and Knights of Columbus served as honorary bearers. Six uniformed student nurses from Champlain Valley Hospital in Plattsburgh and the nursing staff at the Mineville Hospital attended in a group.

After the church service, I overheard a physician and colleague who had come from Albany remark, "Today we pay tribute to one of the last great country doctors who was a specialist in all fields." This brought to mind the community celebration held several years earlier to honor Dr. Cummins for twenty-five years of service. On that occasion George C. Foote, former Witherbee Sherman manager who hired Dr. Cummins in 1917, referred to him in an academic way as "Doctor of Humanity." A framed parchment scroll presented to him by the people of the community read: "The worth of a man is measured by the loyalty, love, and devotion of his fellow men. Thomas J. Cummins, eminent Physician and skilled Surgeon. He lives to serve."

There was concern shared by company officials, the labor union and townspeople to find a competent surgeon to replace Dr. Cummins. The hospital was a vital part of the community. Although improved transportation in recent years brought hospitals in Ticonderoga, Plattsburgh and Burlington within reach, everyone was accustomed to first-class emergency medical and surgical service close at hand. The company recognized this in its search for a physician-surgeon. No doctor could be expected to give to the people as unselfishly as Dr. Cummins who was available twenty-four hours a day, seven days a week and rarely took a vacation. One surgeon was hired and proved unsatisfactory. Finally Dr. Oscar Greene was hired and served as company surgeon until he resigned in the late 1960's.

In the ensuing years the plant safety record improved resulting in less frequent severe accidents. With access to major medical centers there was far less demand for local major surgery than in prior years. The hospital, with its low rates, continued to operate at a loss and was a red figure on the district cost sheet. However, it served as a source of very low cost medical care for the area.

Republic Steel Corporation was generous to the Township. The Witherbee Memorial Hall in Mineville was maintained and utilities furnished by the company. The building with its auditorium and classroom space was leased to the school district for $100 per month, and that did not begin to cover the operating and maintenance costs. When the Federal Housing Project with its four-grade elementary school, was built at Grover Hills in 1943, classrooms in the basement of Memorial Hall were abandoned. Republic later installed six bowling alleys in that space.

Perhaps more than anyone else, Bill Blomstran was responsible for Republic installing the bowling alleys. He had formed a Republic Miners Bowling League a few years earlier and more than fifty men from all departments traveled to Ticonderoga each week to bowl. This gave Bob Linney strong support in getting funds appropriated for the alleys.

A short time after the bowling alleys were built, Company President, Charles White, visited the Adirondack district. During his tour of Mineville plant facilities, Bill Linney, at that time manager at Lyon Mountain, accompanied the group and hoped for an opportunity to ask for bowling alleys for Lyon Mountain. When the group visited the Mineville alleys, Mr. White anticipated Bill Linney's request, for he said to Bob Linney, "This is a nice installation and these are the first and last bowling alleys that Republic is going to build." The alleys were opened to the public and operated by the Mineville and Witherbee Community Association.

The Memorial Building was later donated by Republic Steel to the Veterans of Foreign Wars, who still maintain and operate the bowling alleys.

The company purchased land adjoining the Grover Hills school and constructed an athletic field complete with lights for night baseball and football games. At the time it was hoped that semi-pro baseball would expand to northern New York communities. The athletic field was named for J. R. Linney and continues in use by the Moriah Central School District.

The Witherbee Sherman corporate office building at Port Henry had served as engineering headquarters during World War II for the design and construction of plant facilities. This classic 1875 building was donated by Republic to the Town of Moriah and serves as the present town office building.

There was a demand for Adirondack ore for Republic furnaces during the 1950's. Ore shipments from Reserve Mining Company were a few years in the future. Development in Old Bed Mine was scheduled to insure a long range supply. Harmony development of mining areas above minus 1185 Level would augment the Old Bed Mine production. The long range development of Fisher Hill Mine, discontinued in the 1949 shutdown, would not be renewed but completion of mining above the eighth level was planned.

In the late 1940's and early 50's, Republic's chief geologist, E. Fitzhugh was headquartered at Mineville with a staff of field geologists to make an in-depth study of the company-controlled Adirondack mineral lands. The AuSable area, last mined in the 1880's and acquired by Witherbee Sherman in 1910, was considered as an additional source of ore. There was a sizeable deposit of lean ore that could be mined as an open pit. Republic successfully negotiated with Witherbee Sherman to reduce the royalty Republic would pay on tons mined at AuSable. The ore was lower grade than Mineville ores, and a large plant investment would be required. However, Republic did not proceed with the AuSable development. This was the fourth time in the twentieth century renewed mining operations at AuSable were considered and rejected.

As part of Fitzhugh's program, deep diamond drill holes, some over 4,000 feet, were drilled ahead of the main Mineville ore structure. Drill holes penetrated the ore and the ore horizon but, due to their depth, it was difficult to pinpoint their locations as the holes tended to wander. It was possible for a vertical hole to wander to any point on a circle several hundred feet in diameter around the target center. In addition, the tightly folded syncline narrowed the width of the target area down plunge. Extreme care was taken to control the drill holes, and acid tests were made to determine the angle of each hole at depth. Valuable geological information was obtained, but full confidence in the deep hole drill program was lacking.

Ed Fitzhugh's group studied all ore prospects on Republic's Adirondack leased mineral lands and other northern New York properties. Some prospects outside the United States were also reviewed. However, no mining developments on these lands occurred. Following completion of this work, Ed Fitzhugh returned to Republic's Cleveland office. Not one ton of ore was produced as a result of these studies.

Old Bed crude ore was the highest grade of Adirondack District ores. The ore structure was larger, yielding more tons per foot of development drifting and stope preparation than the other mines. Less tons of crude ore were required to produce a ton of shipping product. Old Bed ore required less fine grinding to concentrate. Witherbee Sherman officials and mine reports referred to Old Bed Mine as the "Joker," named after the hoisting shaft. Shortly after J. R. Linney came to Mineville in 1939, he said, "Old Bed is by far the best mine Republic Steel has anywhere and I don't want to hear anyone calling it the 'Joker.' "

Harmony crude ore was lower grade than Old Bed ore, but the mine could operate in periods of low demand as it shared hoisting and crushing facilities with Old Bed. In contrast, Fisher Hill Mine absorbed all its hoisting and crushing plant operating costs. However, capacity of the Fisher Hill ore handling facilities, shorter hauling distance and reduced employee travel time were all cost benefits. Ore handling distance from mining areas to surface was less than half the average distance for Old Bed and Harmony mines. Travel time for men from surface to and from their underground work areas was about an hour less in an eight-hour shift at Fisher Hill.

Daily ore output from Fisher Hill Mine could be hoisted and crushed in less than one full operating shift. It became practice to hoist ore on the 11-7 night shift. This furnished 1,400 tons in the headframe hopper and crude ore bin on surface at the start of the day shift crushing plant operation. When necessary, extra crude ore was hoisted during a couple of hours on the day shift. On some of those days 3,000 tons of crude ore were put through the crushing plant on a single day shift.

With all its plant productive advantages, Fisher Hill was a high finished product cost operation due to the ratio of crude ore mined to concentrate. I always felt Republic's Cleveland office Raw Materials

Fisher Hill Mine hoist and compressor room.

Fisher Hill Mine 2,000 horsepower Nordberg double drum hoist.

No. 7 tailings pile, concentrating mill and sinter plant in 1944.

Fisher Hill sheave towers, headframe, drill shop and portal house in 1944. Shops in right background, looking west.

Department monitored Fisher Hill costs more closely than any other Republic iron ore mine. During periods of moderate demand, the mine was ordered shut down if other sources could produce the required tons. If ore was in short supply Fisher Hill Mine resumed production.

Ratio of crude ore tons mined to tons of concentrate produced was the key to acceptable costs. Stope mining areas were sampled to maintain a balance between lean ore and rich ore stopes. Development drifting and raising for new stope areas was controlled to limit the amount of rock in the crude ore hoisted. Bill Linney had orders from Cleveland not to do any development work at Fisher Hill. He noted some drifting and raising figures on the weekly mine development report. I explained we were preparing replacement stopes for those being mined out and it was necessary to do some drifting and raising to open areas for mining. He commented, "Then you are not developing, only preparing stopes for mining. I think that will satisfy anyone who asks."

No. 7 Mill was designed with three separate milling units, one for each mine. The mill design permitted ore from any of the mines to run on a single unit or on all three units. At times, when plant railroad cars were in short supply and the Fisher Hill crushed ore bins at No. 7 Mill full, Fisher Hill crushed ore was dumped into the Harmony bins. Concentrates produced from this ore were credited to Harmony, and lost to Fisher Hill. This happened only when the bins were full or in freezing weather when the cars had to be dumped to prevent the ore from freezing. However, the mill had strict orders to keep Fisher Hill ore separated to obtain a true cost. I tried to get a weightometer installed ahead of the Fisher Hill No. 7 Mill unit but was turned down as management said Fisher Hill crushed ore was weighed before it left Fisher Hill. I was able to make my point with Bill Linney when Fisher Hill concentrates produced from crushed ore gave the mine a ratio of nearly five tons crude to one ton concentrate. On that same mill run, Harmony figures showed more tons of concentrate produced than crude ore mined.

Following a downturn in ore demand, Fisher Hill Mine was shut down on March 12, 1954, ending its longest period of continuous operation. During this time from September 1950 to shutdown, the mine operated 986 days. Crude ore produced was 1,622,308 gross tons for a daily average of 1,645 tons from which 554 tons of concentrate were produced at a ratio of 2.96. One hundred sixty men were placed on layoff in the resulting force shuffle. Mine pumping and maintenance were continued.

In September 1956, William J. Linney died suddenly at his home in Port Henry at the age of 44. His death brought to an end a thirty-seven-year era of family management of Adirondack ore mines during which a father and two sons accumulated a total service of 74 years.

Following the death of Bill Linney, Republic's Adirondack mines were divided into two districts. Walter Crusberg was named district manager of Lyon Mountain operations and Francis J. Myers became district manager of Mineville operations. Both Crusberg and Myers had been assistant district managers under Bill Linney.

Francis Myers had been associated with Mineville mines continuously since 1913. His expertise was in ore concentration, but he had broad knowledge of the operations, having held various positions with Witherbee Sherman and Republic Steel. In June 1958 Francis Myers retired and was succeeded as district manager by William A. Blomstran.

Bill Blomstran had been employed in Adirondack iron mining since 1934. He understood the complexities of the Lyon Mountain and Mineville ore bodies. His concern was for future long-range planning of new facilities to improve ore handling from Old Bed and Harmony mines to surface.

Following the Fisher Hill shutdown in March 1954, the mine remained idle for nineteen and one-half months. It was again reopened on November 2, 1955 in response to a demand for Adirondack ore. Our local goal had been for an orderly completion of mining through the eighth level with continuous operation. Each time operations were resumed, we were assured we would complete the mining schedule. Yet, when downturns in the steel industry occurred, Fisher Hill was always the first mine to close. During this period, Fisher Hill operated 458 days and mined 886,291 gross tons of crude ore from which 326,110 tons of concentrate were produced at a ratio of 2.71 tons mined per ton of concentrate.

Fisher Hill Mine was again shut down in October 1957, remained idle for twenty-five and one-half months, then reopened in November 1959. Bill Blomstran told officials in Cleveland the mine should not be reopened unless it would be mined to completion as formerly planned. Shutdowns were costly and disruptive to the entire plant force. Experienced miners on layoff found other employment and new men had to be hired and trained to replace those who did not accept recall. Bill was assured this time Fisher Hill would be mined to completion as the company had use for the ore. This was good news for I had been in charge of operations at Fisher Hill and responsible for start-up and shutdown since 1949, and had assisted John Murphy in the 1947-49 period.

We had good rapport with the miners and good relations with the labor union. Everyone was concerned with safety, costs and production goals. Without these conditions it would not have been possible to mine Fisher Hill.

On June 30, 1960 all mines at Mineville and Lyon Mountain were shut down for a vacation period. An unexpected business downturn extended the idle period fifteen months until November 13, 1961 when mining operations were resumed. However, Fisher Hill Mine never reopened and the promised completion of mining at Fisher Hill did not occur.

During its final short period of operation Fisher Hill Mine was in production 153 days, mining 228,969 tons of crude ore from which 83,735 tons of concentrate were produced at a ratio of 2.73. In its seventeen-year operating history, beginning in 1943, Fisher Hill Mine was a victim of the cyclical nature of the American steel industry.

John Brennan, Sr. retired in June 1959. In the spring of 1960, John Murphy transferred to the L. C. & M. Railroad and I became superintendent in charge of the three mines.

Old Bed and Harmony mines produced substantial tonnages during the 1950's. During each of three of those years Old Bed alone mined over one million tons of crude ore. For the ten-year period, 1951 through 1960, production from the three Mineville mines was as follows:

Gross Tons Crude Ore Mined

Year	Old Bed	Harmony	Fisher Hill	Total
1951	1,042,203	436,953	425,517	1,904,673
1952	948,701	332,873	438,715	1,720,289
1953	1,086,849	362,846	557,171	2,006,866
1954	998,544	277,734	99,370	1,375,648
1955	1,104,635	285,498	47,159	1,437,292
1956	971,472	249,104	454,976	1,675,552
1957	884,594	239,132	384,156	1,507,882
1958	349,534	122,124	None	471,658
1959	567,706	186,017	31,725	785,448
1960	408,716	144,986	197,244	750,946
Total	8,362,954	2,637,267	2,636,033	13,636,254

24

In the early 1950's, Old Bed Mine continued to be the major producer in the district. Harmony production was on a decline, but the mine continued to operate as long as Old Bed was in production. As mining down plunge reached 1035 and 1185 Levels, a change in the geological structure was encountered. The Old Bed and Harmony ore bodies, lenticular in shape with minor faults and folds, folded into a deep syncline and turned sharply to the south. This changed the quality of Harmony ore. There was less concentration of rich ore in mining areas, and more lean ore. Old Bed ore structure, underlying Harmony by several hundred feet, continued to have a sharp contact between rich ore and rock in the geological folds. However, with Harmony ore tapering off from rich to lean in the adjacent rock, mining lean ore areas was determined by the engineers with regard to an acceptable ratio of crude ore to concentrate.

Don B Shaft from surface to below 1185 Level and No. 9 Slope in Old Bed Mine, connected by crosscut drifts, were the transportation arteries for bringing mined ore to the surface. In 1940, decisions for the direction of Don B Shaft and No. 9 Slope were based on the historical configuration of the ore structure as mined for decades. The geological change to the south would require long crosscut drifts to be driven on each level to bring mined ore to the hoisting shafts. Disposal of waste rock from crosscut drift development, and additional travel distances for men and material to mining areas would be costly. However, the high quality of Old Bed ore would justify these additional costs.

It was obvious that within a few years a new mine shaft would have to be sunk from surface to eliminate the excessive long distance multiple ore handling and personnel travel time. Don B Shaft and No. 9 Slope had been designed to serve the twenty-five year term of the original Republic mining lease from Witherbee Sherman ending in 1963. In 1941 the lease was extended an additional fifteen years to 1978. Although Fitzhugh's drill program confirmed previous projections by our mining engineering department of the continuation of the ore structure, these data were not deemed adequate for the company to commit several million dollars for a new mine shaft. Fitzhugh would not accept the mining engineering department estimates of total projected ore reserves. In subsequent years our mining engineers' estimates proved valid.

In 1956 Ed Winning, Republic's assistant vice president for mining, retired. He was replaced by Charles Dewey who became general manager of Republic's Ore and Limestone operations with his office in Cleveland. Dewey was employed by Republic at Mineville in the early 1940's and was familiar with the mining operations.

Following the June 30, 1960 shutdown at Mineville, we soon realized the plant would remain idle for a long time. Reserve Mining Company was in production and supplied much of the ore required by Republic's furnaces. The interest cost alone on the debt to build Reserve Mining Company was a continuing cost that required owners Republic and Armco to keep that plant in operation even during periods of low demand. There was no major capital debt on the Mineville plant and the idle plant expense could be absorbed until demand for ore improved.

In view of the idle plant status at Mineville, staff reductions were made. Some department heads were transferred to Liberia Mining Company and others to Republic's Cleveland office. Several in the non-union clerical force were placed on layoff.

Bill Blomstran used this idle period to formulate a plan for a new vertical mine shaft from surface that would reduce multiple ore handling, increase production and improve costs. He had full confidence in the continuation of the major Old Bed ore body at depth. It disturbed Bill and those of us involved in the plan that our projected ore reserve estimates were ignored whenever a new deep shaft project was reviewed in Cleveland.

During the 1960 shutdown period, the mining engineering department was directed to start from scratch and review all available data to make an independent new ore reserve estimate for the shaft project study. As superintendent of mines, I was to be involved with the new ore reserve calculations and other aspects of the deep shaft project. Art Hughes computed the reserves from known and projected geological data including the day-to-day drilling and mapping underground that had been recorded by the mining engineers.

Based on the completed ore reserve study, it was calculated there was sufficient ore for the mine to produce 1.3 million tons of shipping product per year for nearly forty years to the end of the twentieth century. With this annual tonnage established, plant force requirements, mine development and operating cost estimates were made for a shipping product cost per ton.

The more immediate concern in 1960-61 was to get the mine back in production. Although the work force on layoff drew unemployment

Fisher Hill Mine surface plant in 1944, looking east.

Scraper slide used to clean heading of 33½-degree Fisher Hill Shaft in 1948-49. Slide designed by P. Farrell. Charles DuFrane is operator shown in this 1948 photo.

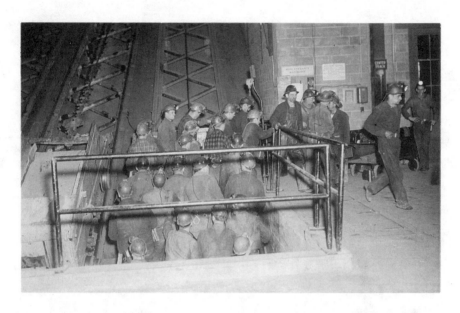

Miners coming off shift at Fisher Hill Mine in the 1940's.

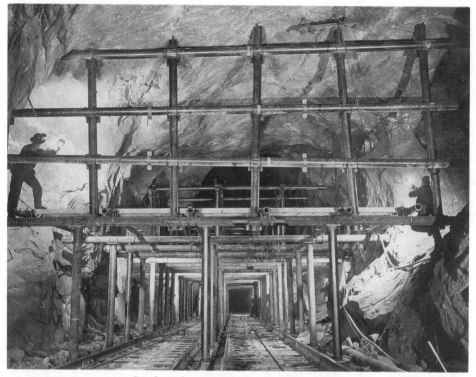

Steel roof support in Don B Shaft, 1950.

Cedar lagging in roof support in Don B. Shaft, 1950.

Don B Shaft, September 18, 1963. From left: W. Coghill, C. Dewey, T. Patton, Chairman and CEO Republic Steel, W. Blomstran, P. Farrell.

Mineville Plant, 1974.

benefits, a long shutdown would lose many good men to other industries. Conditions in the mine and plant would deteriorate. The local economy would suffer. A prolonged shutdown would adversely affect the entire area and its people.

During 1960-61 the U.S. government built twelve Atlas Missile sites in northern New York. This was an urgent $125,000,000 military project in the international arms race. Each of the twelve sites was to be thirty-six feet in diameter and one hundred seventy-six feet deep, excavated in the Adirondack North Country hard rock. Miners from Mineville and Lyon Mountain, on layoff from Republic Steel, were hired by the contractor to mine the sites.

As program chairman of the Adirondack section of the Society of Mining Engineers of AIME, I arranged for a meeting and tour of the missile sites for our AIME group and seventy-five members of the Canadian Institute of Mining. At a dinner meeting at the Lewis Hotel, the engineer in charge of the project for the U.S. Corps of Engineers told us that the missile sites could not have been completed on schedule without the skilled miners from Mineville and Lyon Mountain.

In efforts to get Mineville mines back in operation, competitive product cost studies were made with Mineville versus other iron ore mines. Rail freight rates and incentive bonus wage rates were high Mineville cost items. Nothing could be done about the established rail freight rates. A ton of ore could be loaded on a boat in West Africa or South America and unloaded at a U.S. east coast port cheaper than a ton of ore could be rail shipped 350 miles from Port Henry to Buffalo, New York. The incentive rates in the mines were based on crude ore. Our shipping product cost was per ton of concentrate or sinter produced. The crude ore cost multiplied by the ratio of crude ore to concentrate inflated the shipping product cost.

After several months of idle plant in 1960-61, a revised lower incentive schedule was prepared which would make the mine competitive. This was presented in detail to the union committee and Adron Coldiron, the union area representative. Coldiron was a hard bargainer and could be tough, but he was fair. After lengthy discussions of the revised incentive plan, Coldiron said, "As I understand it we have a dead horse here and if we agree to these revisions, we just might get that horse up and running." Shortly thereafter the union committee agreed to accept the revised incentives. This was a major factor in resuming mining operations in Harmony and Old Bed Mines on November 13, 1961. I believe had the union committee not accepted the revised incentives in 1961, Mineville would have experienced a final plant shutdown.

By 1962, with three-quarters of all ore mined on the lowest operating levels, ore handling problems from source to surface increased. For details, see Appendix BB.

Long range plans were always kept on the front burner, but in the early 1960's achieving good production with acceptable costs through existing plant facilities was a continuing challenge. Only the high quality of the shipping product and its metallurgical advantage in the blast furnace kept the mine in operation when many others failed.

In the continuing development of 2100 Level it became apparent that, if we were to meet costs, revisions in mining and developing methods would be necessary. For details of these methods, see Appendix CC.

Large tonnage from newly developed open pit iron ore mines in the United States, Canada, Africa and South America posed a severe threat for the survival of underground iron ore mines. Mining machinery companies met the challenge and new equipment designs prolonged the life of many mines. These developments were carefully monitored at Mineville and we made on-site observations of new prototype equipment being tested in other mines.

At Mineville we were faced with numerous problems in meeting competitive delivery prices at the furnaces, but the fact that the mine was an underground operation was not the major impediment. One of the men in Republic's Cleveland office, enamored with high tonnage open pit iron ore mines, said, "You can no longer mine anything underground." I responded, "You can mine underground anywhere, even on the moon, if you deliver the product to the market at an acceptable cost." The point is we had an excellent high grade iron ore product and were delivering it at a competitive cost.

The ore structure at Mineville had been mined down plunge to and beyond the original design limits of the existing facilities. Ore was being handled five times from its mined source to surface and thirty men were involved in moving the ore through the hoisting shafts, pockets and ore transfer drifts. Men were paid on a portal to portal basis, permitting them to punch their daily time cards in and out on surface within eight hours. Moving the mine force through the shafts and drifts to their work areas meant high "travel time." This and the allowable lunch period limited men in Old Bed Mine to approximately five and one-half hours production time per day in their work areas. Freight rates were high, yet we had the advantage of year-round rail shipping to the furnaces.

In the 1960's our most pressing problem was to keep the mines operating regardless of freight rate, travel time and ore handling problems. Everyone was aware of problems facing iron ore mines and the impact foreign ore imports would have on Mineville operations. However, the bottom line was, without sinking a deep shaft from surface, mine operations at Mineville could not long survive.

In the early 1960's it was evident the major portion of crude ore mining would be concentrated on 2100 Level in Old Bed Mine. New mining areas had to be rapidly developed to furnish enough crude ore to keep the plant operating during the latter part of the decade. As this work was charged directly to operating cost, it was essential to keep labor within an acceptable figure on the cost sheet. Revised mining methods with new efficient labor-saving equipment were studied.

We asked the machinery companies to furnish a two-drill jumbo for a two-man operation featuring more powerful drills and mountings, with power feeds designed to use a single ten-foot drill rod. Ingersoll-Rand engineers studied the drifting operation and arranged for Molten Engineering Company to design and build a rail-mounted jumbo with two Ingersoll-Rand hydraulic-operated booms and D-475 drills with ten-foot chain feed shells.

The jumbo was placed in operation on 2100 Level with a two-man drill crew. Drifting was a safer operation with the new jumbo. Drillers operated the drills from a cab with a protective roof. With a single drill rod and tungsten carbide insert button bit, it was no longer necessary for the driller to be at the heading to change drill rods as with the former jumbos. This unit, with one less man in the drill crew, improved drifting performance and cost.

Driving long steep raises from one mine level to another was a slow process. It was a one-man operation using a Gardner-Denver stoper drill.

Boring of steep raises had been tried successfully and we observed two new prototype raise boring machines operating in northern Michigan mines. For details on the introduction of raise boring at Mineville and its successful operation, see Appendix DD.

There were intangible benefits in raise boring that would not appear on a cost sheet. The most important, in addition to expediting mine development, was a far safer operation. Raises were bored from a single safe location and the perimeter of the raise was not fractured by blasting as were conventional drilled raises. The smooth wall interior of bored raises enhanced the free flow of ventilation air. Ladderways, power, air and water lines were easily installed from the top of the completed bored raise.

Successful application of raise boring for mine development, pioneering of flat-angle raise boring with accuracy, and the resulting low cost, drew the attention of the mining industry. In 1967, I presented a paper on Mineville raise boring to the American Mining Congress in Denver, Colorado. Following publication in the American Mining

Congress Journal, and an article in the London Mining Journal, engineers from mining companies in the United States, Canada, Europe and Australia came to Mineville to observe the raise boring operation.

While these mechanical improvements for driving rail haulage drifts and long raises were being installed, the 2100 Level mining plan was reviewed for application of trackless loaders and loader drifts to replace scram drift scraper operations. For details see, Appendix EE.

Trackless loaders, the first one purchased in January 1967, were used only for development of trackless loader mining areas in 1967 and 1968. From 1968 through 1971 these loaders handled both development and stope mining tons. By 1971 trackless loaders handled 44.5 percent of all crude ore tons hoisted. Funds were appropriated by Republic to purchase the two-drill jumbo, trackless drills and loaders, and the raise boring machine. However, development of the work areas and operation and maintenance of the equipment were charged directly to the mine cost. The trackless equipment made it possible to keep the mine in operation through July 1971.

25

The main objective at Mineville during all the 1960's was to keep the mine operating pending Republic's approval for sinking a 4,800-foot vertical shaft from surface. Underground mine development was scheduled to provide tons to keep the mine operating and to prepare mining areas for production from the new shaft. See Appendix FF for details.

During 1971 the plant operated 138 days from the first of the year through July 23. Mine production averaged 3,507 gross tons of crude ore per day, with a yield of 1,995 tons of concentrate at a ratio of 1.76. The plant then ceased operation for a one-month vacation period. At this time the ore market was depressed and we were apprehensive the vacation period might extend into a longer idle period. I thought of this as I watched the miners come up the hill to the change house at the end of the day shift on July 22; and again that night at home as I heard the locomotive whistle on the ore train from the mines to No. 7 Mill as it approached Sweeney's crossing on the Pilfershire road. That proved to be the final ore train from the Mineville Mines.

Bill Blomstran was informed in mid-August that the plant would not resume operation following the vacation period.

For the ten and one-half year period, 1961 through July 1971, production from Mineville mines was as follows:

Gross Tons Crude Ore Mined

Year	Old Bed	Harmony	Total
1961	64,341	39,200	103,541
1962	444,388	138,937	583,325
1963	586,890	183,208	770,098
1964	720,392	177,256	897,648
1965	Combined		922,046
1966	"		895,466
1967	"		840,909
1968	"		569,318
1969	"		767,118
1970	"		867,771
1971	"		484,002
Total			7,701,242

During this ten and one-half year period of mine operation, the following statistics were compiled, reflecting favorably on the skill, performance and cooperation of the work force.

Tons crude ore hoisted	7,701,242
Tons concentrate produced	4,250,423
Ratio - crude to concentrate	1.81
Hours worked - Mine	3,516,129
Tons crude ore mined per 8 hours worked	17.52
Lost time accidents	25
Fatal accidents	0
Miles of ringhole stope drilling	1,037.3
Tons crude ore per ringhole foot drilled	1.41

During 1970, 12,293 feet of development were completed and 6,426 feet completed in 1971. This footage included haulage drifts, trackless loader drifts and ramps, sublevels, scraper scram drifts, stope platform overbreaks, raises and bored raises. Explosives consumed for all mining and development averaged 0.96 pounds of powder per ton of crude ore produced.

During the ten and one-half years (1961-1971) of crude ore mining, 53.3 percent passed through minus 2100 pocket on No. 9 Slope. This meant that during those years more than half of all tons were handled several times and hauled over 12,000 feet from their source to surface. And yet, the mine remained cost competitive.

Safety statistics for the ten and one-half year period are noteworthy. There were no fatal accidents during those years. There were twenty-five lost time accidents while expending three and one-half million underground man hours producing 7,701,242 tons of crude ore. By comparison, during 1938 alone, Republic's first year of mining at Mineville, there were forty-five lost time accidents while producing 232,422 tons of crude ore. A lost time accident was a job-related injury that caused an employee to lose a day or more work. During 1968 there were no lost time accidents, the first such accident-free year in a century and one-half of Mineville mining.

During my years as superintendent of mines we held a safety meeting once a month with the entire mine force at the start of the day shift. At one time, when we had operated for a long period without a lost time accident but had had several "near misses," there was a serious accident in another mine operation similar to ours. The next day I had a special meeting in the portal house to discuss the accident and concluded by saying, "That mine just had your lost time accident. Remember, the longer we operate without a lost time accident, the nearer we are to the next one." As I finished one of the miners said, "You sure know how to say the right thing to make a man feel good at the start of the shift." A couple hours later one of the foremen called and said he was having a hard time getting ore moving as everyone was double checking for safety. I told him that was fine with me.

Cost estimates were maintained to predict the monthly shipping product cost. If costs looked bad about the third week of the month, we held a meeting with the mine force to tell them what was needed and why. One lesson I learned in my early years at Fisher Hill was to tell the work force about costs, production, safety and anything else that affected them. The mine was their livelihood as well as mine. We had a good source of ore, good working conditions, highly skilled workers, a good wage schedule and good labor relations. That is why we continued to operate long after many underground iron ore mines closed.

Production with safety had been the hallmark of Republic Steel Corporation Adirondack mining operations. However, mining is a hazardous occupation and despite a good safety program serious unforeseen accidents did occur. During 1951 there were five mining fatalities at Mineville in three separate accidents—the worst year of Republic Steel's long period of operations.

The worst single accident occurred in February 1951. Three men were fatally injured while waiting for the man cage at the end of the day shift on Don B Shaft 1035 Level platform. Don B Shaft is a decline of twenty-eight to thirty-six degrees. The roof was in solid ground and required little support. The forty-eight-man capacity cage was loaded at minus 1185 Level for the first trip to surface. A section of shaft roof fell at plus 200 Level and chunks rolled down the shaft, some landing on 1035 Level platform and one or more striking the back of the loaded cage at 1185 Level. Three of the men on 1035 Level platform were fatally injured. A couple of men on the loaded cage at 1185 Level received minor injuries. Following this accident a roof support system of steel posts, caps and cedar lagging was installed in the shaft. Gates were provided to keep men away from the shaft platforms until time to load the man cages.

From May 1, 1938 through July 1971 the downward trend of fatal accidents related to crude ore tons mined is shown as follows:

Time Period	Tons Crude Ore Mined	No. Fatal Accidents	Tons Per Fatal Accident
May '38 - Dec. '50	15,705,811	23	682,861
Jan. '51 - Dec. '60	13,636,254	12	1,136,355
Jan. '61 - July '71	7,701,242	No fatal accidents	
Total	37,043,307	35	1,058,380

Of the thirty-five fatalities, seven occurred in surface departments and twenty-eight in the mines. The last fatal accident at Mineville occurred in May 1959. From that time through July 1971, there were 8,844,912 tons mined without a fatal accident.

Total tons mined in the Town of Moriah during the one hundred fifty years from discovery through the end of Republic Steel operations in 1971, based on estimates of early years and available production records, were:

From discovery through Witherbee Sherman years	33,963,934
Republic Steel Corporation years	37,043,307
Total crude ore mined	71,007,241

Official announcement by Republic Steel in August 1971 that the mines and plant at Mineville would be idle indefinitely, but maintained on a standby basis, was a blow to the five hundred employees, local businesses and the surrounding area. The several million dollar annual payroll was a positive economic force in Essex County and the Adirondack Region. As long as the standby status remained, a future operation might be possible.

On August 31, 1972 Bill Blomstran retired and I became district superintendent. The force consisted of J. R. Brennan Jr., maintenance superintendent, two hoistmen, two maintenance men, one security officer, a mining engineer and a secretary. The maintenance force monitored mine pumping at Mineville and Fisher Hill, brought some of the mine equipment to surface, readied supplies and equipment for shipment to other Republic districts and kept the plant in general operating condition. The office force handled employee retirements, workers' compensation, insurance benefits, etc. Long range planning for possible future operations continued.

Iron ore tailings were an important consideration in future operations at Mineville. From the period back in 1850 when Dr. Ebenezer Emmons in association with the Hammonds of Crown Point acquired the rights to the "red sand" or apatite mineral in the Sanford and "21" ore beds, commercial recovery of the apatite mineral had been considered at various times. The last attempt was by Witherbee Sherman and Company in 1918 to produce apatite for fertilizer.

Iron ore tailings from Mineville had been used for decades in road building and construction. Tailings produced by the crushing and concentrating process ranged from fine sand to No. 3 size crushed stone. The stone, having a high compressive strength, was a durable highway material as it did not break down under heavy truck traffic. Over 200,000 tons of Mineville crushed rock were used in construction of the

Adirondack Northway through the North Country. For over thirty years, sales of crushed stone and sand to an on-site blacktop operation had benefited the iron ore product shipping cost.

In the early 1940's, the U.S. Geological Survey published a report listing the presence of rare earth minerals in the apatite found in Mineville Old Bed ore tailings. Molycorp, a producer of rare earth minerals, became interested in Mineville tailings and in July 1971 leased rights to tailings mineral recovery for three years. Molycorp tested the tailings areas by taking drill samples and bulk samples for laboratory analysis. Republic also secured independent analytical tests of tailings samples. In December 1974 Molycorp terminated its lease.

In 1974 the long range supply of iron ore for Republic's furnaces was cause for concern. Reserve Mining Company, one of Republic Steel's main sources of ore for the blast furnaces, was ordered to shut down on April 20, 1974 by U.S. District Court Judge, Miles Lord. See Appendix GG.

Other sources of iron ore for Republic at this time included an interest in the Iron Ore Company of Canada in Labrador; Liberia Mining Company in West Africa; a major interest in the Negaunee Mining Company operated by Cleveland Cliffs Iron Company in Northern Michigan; an interest in a large undeveloped ore body in South America; and full ownership of the idle Adirondack Mineville mine and mineral lands.

With Reserve Mining Company's future in litigation, its outlook for continued operation in 1974 appeared contingent on spending several hundred million dollars for an inland tailings disposal system. This would be in addition to the large capital debt the company carried for original and subsequent construction of facilities at Reserve.

In July 1974, Republic vice president of purchasing and raw materials, John Voyer, brought a group from Cleveland to Mineville to review the status of the mine and surface plant. Mr. Voyer expressed concern that Republic had become too dependent on Reserve, and other sources of ore should be developed. Some consideration was being given to abandoning Reserve Mining Company due to the high capital cost to construct on-land tailings disposal.

Mr. Voyer's group reviewed all aspects of the Mineville facilities. It was unlikely that Fisher Hill Mine could ever operate at an acceptable cost. Therefore, plans were discussed for taking up the Fisher Hill branch of the L. C. & M. Railroad, and dismantling Fisher Hill buildings except the hoist-compressor and crushing plant buildings which housed equipment that would be used in the proposed new vertical mine shaft project. The sinter plant at No. 7 Mill was to be razed as it would have to be replaced in a renewed operation.

Fisher Hill shops and storehouse and the change house and office buildings were of steel frame concrete curtain wall construction. I asked that these buildings be donated to Essex County for future industrial use. The buildings were eliminated from the dismantling contract and donated with nineteen acres of land to the Essex County Development Corporation.

In June 1975 a contract was awarded to Indeck Power and Equipment Company to dismantle plant facilities at Fisher Hill, No. 7 Sinter Plant and some structures at Mineville and Port Henry.

At this same time it was decided to dismantle and ship the four 3,200 c.f.m. Ingersoll-Rand air compressors at Fisher Hill to other Republic plants. This equipment was in A-one condition. Two complete units with aftercoolers, air receivers and fittings were shipped to Republic's Chicago district and two units to the Buffalo district.

Indeck Power assumed maintenance and pumping at Fisher Hill Mine during dismantling and salvage operations, and installed a small air compressor for their use. Sixty pound rails were removed from all mine levels and shipped to Republic's coal mining districts. Ninety-five tons of 112-pound ore track rails from Fisher Hill shaft were shipped to the coal mines. Mine pumps and air hoists, used in handling material, were removed from underground to surface.

On January 20, 1976, pumping from Fisher Hill Mine ended with removal of pumps from the 8th Level pump station. An average of 142,500 gallons of water per day had been pumped from the mine to a surface outfall with flow to the Lincoln Pond watershed and eventual discharge to Lake Champlain at Willsboro. A calculated mine flooding schedule projected Fisher Hill and Smith Mines would full flood to surface outlets during 1987.

As dismantling was a direct cost to Republic, the Cleveland general office determined that only mine rails and 4,500 feet of 500 MCM three conductor power cable would be removed from the mine for shipment to other Republic plants. Equipment left underground included eleven locomotives, fifty-three five cubic yard mine cars, forty-four Ingersoll-Rand slusher hoists, drill jumbos, numerous rock drills, and five installed transformers.

Underground salvage, abandonment of the mine and sealing of Fisher Hill Mine shaft were completed in November 1976. Razing Fisher Hill surface structures including portal house and headframe, sheave towers, primary crushing facilities, conveyors, crude and crushed ore bins was completed. During this same period rails on the Fisher Hill branch of the L. C. & M. Railroad and yard tracks at Fisher

Hill were salvaged. No. 7 sinter plant, Joker change house, Joker shaft house and bins at Mineville plant were razed. Several hundred tons of scrap metal from dismantling operations were shipped to Republic's blast furnaces at Buffalo.

At the July 1974 meeting at Mineville, Mr. Voyer asked what would be required to put the plant back in operation and produce a greater daily shipping product tonnage than when we ceased operation. I recommended the following:

1. Immediately proceed with the vertical mine shaft and conveyor to No. 7 Concentrating Mill.

2. Resume mine operations to finish mining developed ore on 2100 Level and above.

3. Concurrent with renewed mining, employ a development force large enough to finish developing ore areas remaining on 2100 Level and new areas on 2250 and 2400 Levels. This would prepare two new levels for mining when shaft sinking and connections to these levels were completed.

4. Immediately arrange for an independent geological study of the ore reserves by an outside consultant to resolve questions that had been raised concerning the district ore reserve estimates.

Mr. Voyer authorized the independent geological study of the Mineville ore reserves. Severn P. Brown of Dunn Geoscience Corporation, a geologist familiar with the Adirondack area, reviewed mine maps and geological data in the Mineville office files. On his recommendation an airborne geophysical study and report were completed. The completed work confirmed the continuation of the major Mineville ore structure, lending credibility to the ore reserve estimates previously calculated by the local mining engineering department.

S. R. (Russ) Crooks of the Raw Materials Department and formerly of Republic's Research Center, was appointed by Mr. Voyer to coordinate the mine development program. I worked with Russ on this program. The iron ore shipping product was to be determined whether sinter, as in the past, or a new product of pellets or briquettes.

During the period 1974-78, several meetings were held in Cleveland and Mineville to review and revise the Mineville shaft project. In May 1976 Republic's Purchasing and Raw Materials Departments were separated. John Voyer remained vice president of Purchasing and Russell Maier, Republic's chief industrial engineer, became vice president of Raw Materials. Thereafter, Adirondack District matters, including the Adirondack Shaft Project, were directed through Mr. Maier.

In June 1976 a top level meeting to review the Mineville project was held in Republic's Cleveland office. Attending were CEO William De-

Lancey, and vice presidents and executives from central engineering and raw materials. Consultant Severn Brown discussed the ore reserves. Projected capital, operating costs and other related matters were reviewed by Russ Crooks. I discussed production, ore handling and the available labor force.

I believed at that time we had more than a 50-50 chance of getting approval for the Mineville deep shaft project. Republic and Armco were still in litigation over Reserve Mining Company tailings disposal in Lake Superior. State agencies and environmental groups would not approve Reserve's proposed on-land tailings disposal plan which the company estimated would cost over $300 million.

In January 1976, Edward J. Devitt, chief federal judge in Minnesota, assigned himself to handle the Reserve Mining Company case in U.S. District Court in St. Paul, replacing Judge Miles Lord who had issued the original shutdown orders against Reserve. The appellate court removed Judge Lord because he showed "gross bias" against Reserve and seemed "to have shed the robe of the judge and to have assumed the mantle of the advocate." Even with the removal of Judge Lord in January 1976, it seemed the litigation over the Reserve tailings disposal plan would continue for some time. However, on January 31, 1977, a three-judge Minnesota District Court ordered the state agencies to grant Reserve the necessary permits to construct the proposed on-land tailings disposal site at Milepost 7. This was a big victory for Reserve and thereafter Republic and Armco committed the necessary funds.

Feasibility studies for the Mineville deep shaft project were continually revised and updated. A May 1977 review of the project included recovery of rare earth minerals. I realized that Republic's commitment of capital funds to Reserve Mining Company weakened our chances of receiving funding for the Mineville project.

At a meeting I attended in Cleveland in November 1977, a decision was made to generate some outside interest in the Mineville property. Possible courses to follow were joint venture, lease or sale of the property. Failing this, March 31, 1978 would be the decision date to terminate mine pumping at Mineville. It was also decided to focus attention on apatite recovery from surface tailings.

During the following months several companies were contacted for possible investment in the Mineville mining operations and apatite recovery. Several expressed serious interest. One company, primarily involved in tailings minerals, offered to fund a capital development program for mine development if Republic, or some other customer, would accept the iron ore. Republic did not pursue this. I assumed Cleveland office planners believed they had an adequate ore supply from Reserve

Mining Company and other long term commitments, and therefore were not interested.

On February 1, 1979 Republic Steel issued a news release stating that mine pumping would cease on June 1 and the mine permanently shut down. Without a commitment to put in the proposed mine shaft development program, there was no justification for continuing the more than $1,000,000 yearly expense for pumping, plant maintenance and other district idle expense costs.

Property taxes were a major item of expense. In 1973 the State Board of Equalization and Assessment had notified Republic that its Town of Moriah assessment was 100 percent above their estimated full value. Other property in the Town of Moriah was generally assessed at five to ten percent of full value. Republic had asked the town assessors to reduce its assessments each year but no major cuts were made. When the plant was operating taxes were a charge to product cost, but since the plant ceased operations they were a major item of idle expense. Republic filed suit to get the assessments reduced. The immediate response of the town assessors was to greatly increase the assessment on Republic property. This resulted in Republic paying a total tax increase in the Town of Moriah and school district from $375,315 for the tax year 1973-74 to $529,900 for the tax year 1974-75 and $572,816 for the tax year 1975-76.

The tax suit was brought to New York Supreme Court for trial on June 6-8, 1976. In a pre-trial discussion with the parties, Supreme Court Judge Harvey stated if the court found for the company, the town and school districts would have to pay back overpaid taxes from the time of filing the tax suit to final decision in court. The increased assessment imposed, resulting in a high tax payment for the tax years 1974-75 and 1975-76, was removed. Assessments on Republic plant facilities were to be reduced over a four-year period.

Republic chose to forgive payback of the tax overpayments. Payback would have been a severe burden for the town and school district to raise by taxes. Many of the taxpayers were former Republic employees. Judge Harvey praised the parties on reaching a settlement and complimented Republic Steel for showing concern for local residents in waiving payback of several hundred thousand dollars in past taxes overpaid. As we left the courthouse, the outside attorney representing Republic in the tax suit said that never in his experience in these matters had he known a company to be so generous.

Specifications were prepared for salvaging the Mineville mine and plant including demolishing buildings and structures, equipment and scrap recovery, sealing Don B Shaft and site cleanup with adherence to contract specifications and environmental regulations. For detail see Appendix HH.

At the south end of the village of Port Henry, between the highway and shore of Lake Champlain, Witherbee Sherman blast furnace foundations and abandoned yard rail tracks were an unattractive sight from the southern approach to the village. Republic contracted with A. P. Reale for $70,000 to demolish the foundations, level an elevated earth trestle approach and grade the area. This work was completed in early 1981.

The Harmony and New Bed Mine tailings piles at Mineville did not contain rare earth minerals worth recovery. These tailings piles included sand and a large amount of sized crushed stone valuable for highway construction and repair. Republic sold the Harmony tailings pile and its land parcel near Joyce Road to the Town of Moriah. Republic also sold the New Bed tailings pile with its twenty-acre land parcel to Essex County.

In 1981 Molycorp renewed its interest in Mineville rare earth minerals. They brought in diamond drill rigs to core drill the outcrop area in and contiguous to "21" open pit mine. Their geologist studied the area but Molycorp did not acquire the property.

Ed Fitzhugh, retired former Republic Steel chief geologist vacationing in the area, remarked to me that Republic should have put in the new vertical shaft at Mineville. It was ironic in view of the fact that he was the one person, who several times in twenty years, would not endorse our stated ore reserves when the project was being given serious consideration.

There were innumerable details involved in permanently closing this mining district that had operated for more than a century. Mine maps were filed as required by the New York State Industrial Code, and copies sent to the Federal Mine Map Depository in Pittsburgh, Pennsylvania. We sent to the Depository other mining property maps that were in the local files. Our Mineville office had been custodian of records for Chateaugay District at Lyon Mountain, New York and for Republic's former Northern Ore Mines in Michigan.

Records had been retained, dating back to 1870, of the Lake Champlain and Moriah Railroad. Employee work records, payroll, worker's compensation and medical, for both mines and railroad had been preserved. All of these, amounting to a trailer truck load, were transferred to Republic's Buffalo District for storage.

Arrangements were coordinated with the Town of Moriah for the elimination of the mine drinking water supply furnished to the hamlets of Mineville and Witherbee. The surface reservoir was conveyed to the town. Republic's fire equipment, firehouse and land parcel were donated to the newly formed Mineville-Witherbee Fire District. General overseeing of dismantling continued to its completion.

Reflecting back through the Republic operating years at Mineville, beginning November 15, 1937 through the end of ore production on July 23, 1971, the period was a prosperous era. Seventeen years of management by J. R. Linney, Robert J. Linney and William J. Linney before and during World War II and its aftermath, brought ore production from the Mineville Iron District to a record high. Promotions to supervisory positions were generally made from within the organization. Those men, with many years of varied mine and plant experience, contributed greatly to Republic's successful operations for nearly thirty-four years. See Appendix II.

Despite continued plans for renewed operations, final plant dismantling and sealing of mine shafts was completed in April 1980.

Epilogue

The town is quiet now. There is a new generation of adults who have never heard the whine of winding hoist ropes; the rumble of skips bringing ore to the surface; the thumping sound of the jaw crusher and ore striking the sides of metal storage bins. Nor have they heard the wailful sound of locomotive whistles signaling at road crossings as ore was brought down to the lake from the mines. Only photographs remain of the hundred-foot-high headframes outlined against the sky that identified the town.

The underground mine workings have been flooding. Fisher Hill Mine began flooding in late 1976 and was full flooded with 507 million gallons in 1987. The final flood level is the rock-overburden contact for Fisher Hill and Smith Mines below the first level of Fisher Hill Shaft. Old Bed-Harmony Mines have been flooding since September 1979 and are estimated to full flood to the rock-overburden contact during the year 2003. At that time these vast mine workings will impound about 4.2 billion gallons of water.

In April 1982 I retired, having completed forty-five years continuous service with Witherbee Sherman and Republic Steel Corporation at Mineville. I believe Republic Steel officials in Cleveland were fully aware of the benefits of a long-range Mineville operation. Locally we had explored every possibility for a continuing operation. We had demonstrated that Mineville high grade ore, with its blast furnace metallurgical advantage, could be produced from underground and delivered to consuming furnaces at a competitive price. However, the Mineville development project for continuous operations was doomed by other demands for Republic capital funds, readily available ore from other sources, and the low operating rate of the American steel industry.

Tailings minerals were attracting attention of several companies. In 1983 Williams Strategic Metals of Colorado purchased from Republic the No. 5 Mill tailings pile and land parcel; "21" Open Pit land area; part of the Mineville Plant Site land area; railroad right-of-way to No. 7 Plant and No. 7 Plant Site, including buildings and tailings areas. The Williams Company conducted extensive tests for mineral recovery from tailings, but in 1986 sold the property to Rhone-Poulenc, Inc., a large

French government-owned producer of rare earth minerals.

Republic Steel Corporation was purchased by LTV Corporation in 1984 and became a part of LTV Steel Company. Republic Adirondack properties were included in the LTV acquisition.

After retirement in 1982, I served as a consultant for Republic Steel on Adirondack matters; for the Williams Strategic Metals Corporation and Rhone-Poulenc, Inc. during their local mineral studies; and for LTV Steel Company through the final disposition of their interests in the area.

In the heyday years the Town of Moriah had six new car dealerships, seven gas stations, six barber shops, four ladies' clothing stores, four men's clothing stores, five shoe stores, thirteen groceries (with meat department), three movie theaters, nine churches, two parochial schools, three K-12 public schools, three K-8 elementary public schools, one hotel, six restaurants and several combination tavern-restaurants.

Today in the Town of Moriah, there is one grocery (with meat department), four small convenience groceries, one men's clothing store, one ladies' clothing store, one new car dealership, five gas stations, no parochial schools, one K-12 public school that centralized the former high schools and common school districts. At centralization there were about 1,450 students. Today there are less than nine hundred. There are four active churches, no hotel, two restaurants and several taverns.

The Yandon-Dillon Educational Center (BOCES), located in Mineville, provides Occupational and Special Education for public school students in southern Essex County. Essex Industries, a facility of the ARC, operates a wood products shop in a former parochial school at Grover Hills in Mineville. New York State acquired former Fisher Hill mine plant buildings and established the Moriah Shock Incarceration Facility, a minimum security prison.

During the last twenty-five years there have been additions to the Essex County complex in Elizabethtown and a new large addition is presently under construction. The county employs over 500 people.

In the Town of Moriah and other Essex County towns, "For Sale" signs abound, but, although property values are well below the assessed valuation, many new homes have been built. The real estate market has suffered from the area's high unemployment rate.

Attracting new business to the Town of Moriah and Essex County is a difficult problem. The county lies within the Adirondack Park and is hampered by the restrictive and time consuming regulations of the Adirondack Park Agency, and New York's reputation as a high tax state.

This story of the Mineville Iron District and its associated environs is an example of the pendulum-like swings of iron ore demand in one area during a century and one-half of high and low productivity.

I believe in future years there will be a rebirth of the American steel industry as a national necessity. Strong demand for the highest grade iron ore product, increased market for rare earth minerals, and new mining and metallurgical technology will focus renewed attention on the Mineville unmined ore reserves. However, the United States government policy in trade relations, with restrictions on unfair foreign government subsidized imports of iron ore, steel and products of steel, and equal access for American products abroad is necessary if the American iron and steel industries are to compete equally in the world marketplace.

—*P.F.F.*
1995

Patrick F. Farrell passed away
November 11, 1996

Guide to Appendices

Appendices

Colburn or East Moriah Furnace

The following description of the furnace by a Mr. Hodge appeared in an 1849 issue of *The American Railroad Journal*:

This furnace was built in 1848, four miles back from Port Henry. There being no water power in the place selected, a steam engine was provided of forty horse power. The stack is forty (40) feet three (3) inches high from bottom of hearth to the filling plate; its diameter across the boshes is ten (10) feet four (4) inches; across the tunnel head three (3) feet four (4) inches; and its capacity is twelve hundred and sixty bushels. The boshes slope, according to the usual plan of furnaces in this region, in three planes of sixty (60) degrees, fifty-five (55) degrees and fifty (50) degrees. The hearth, five and one-half (5½) feet high, is two (2) feet ten (10) inches square at the bottom, and three (3) feet ten (10) inches at the foot of the boshes; its length to the dam six (6) feet four (4) inches. The tuyeres, three in number, come in twenty-two inches above the bottom of the hearth.

The dam is five (5) inches below the tymp, and fifteen (15) inches high. There are two blowing cylinders four (4) feet in diameter and five (5) feet stroke, with a regulator eighteen (18) feet long and thirty-two (32) inches in diameter. The blast is introduced through nozzles of two (2) inches and three-eights (3/8) in diameter. The gases for the boiler and heating oven are taken out eleven (11) feet down by one pipe of twenty-two (22) inches diameter. The upright heating pipes are twenty-eight (28) in number, of circular form, six (6) inches diameter inside, arranged on two bed pieces and connected by an oxbow at top.

The ores are to come principally from the Sanford Ore Bed two miles distant; and according to a statement in my possession, they are estimated to cost at the furnace only $1.25 per ton. They must then be delivered as low as by the contract with Mr. Jackson (Westport Furnace). Other ores as the Hall ore, are estimated at $2.00 per ton. Charcoal at six (6) cents a bushel, about the usual cost in this section. Transportation to the lake fifty (50) cents per ton. Allowing 170 bushels of charcoal to the ton of iron, and a ton and two-thirds of ore at $2.00 per ton, we have the following estimate of cost of pig iron delivered at the lake:

Charcoal, 170 bushels at six cents	$10.20
Ore, 1-2/3 tons at $2.00	3.33
Flux, say fifty cents, other items $5.00	5.50
Transportation to the lake	.50
Total	$19.53

APPENDIX B

Fletcherville Furnace Detail by Thomas F. Witherbee

The Fletcherville Furnace stack was forty-two feet high, diameter of bosh eleven feet with an angle of about fifty-eight degrees; diameter of open tunnel head, forty-two inches; dam fifteen inches high; three tuyeres three inches in diameter, twenty-four inches high and tymp twenty-two and one half inches high. The steam engine was direct-acting horizontal non-condensing; steam cylinder twenty and one quarter inches; blast cylinder sixty-four inches; and stroke five feet. The furnace was built by Jerome B. Bailey of Plattsburgh who became its first manager. The furnace was first in blast from August to October 1865.

APPENDIX C

The Cedar Point Blast Furnace

"The Cedar Point Iron Company's Furnace No. 1 at Port Henry, Essex County, N.Y." by T. F. Witherbee, which appeared in *Transactions of The American Institute of Mining Engineers*, Volume 4, 1876 is quoted, verbatim, in part as follows:

The site selected for this furnace was, at the time of commencing work, October, 1872, entirely covered by the navigable waters of Lake Champlain. A coffer-dam was first built of cribs of round timber filled with stone, forming three sides, while the shore answered for the fourth. Considerable excavating was done with a steam dredge, a hole being left for it to pass out. The opening was then built up, and the cribbing banked up with blue clay from the bottom of the lake, to render it water-tight and the dam pumped out; the remainder of the excavating being done by hand. All of the foundations, with the exception of the elevator-tower, and fifteen feet of the east side of hot blast, rest on the Potsdam sandstone, which forms the shore line, dipping into the lake at an angle of fifteen degrees.

Owing to jogs in the formation, a much greater depth was found necessary than was at first anticipated, the foundation under the stack being 35 feet square at bottom, by 30 at top, and 40 feet high of solid cement stone masonry, with 5 feet of fire brick on top of that, making a total height of 45 feet.

The hot-blast foundation is 55 feet square by 35 feet high, of dry masonry, with the exception of 7 feet of the top, laid in cement, and containing the hot-blast gas and chimney flues.

The engine and boiler foundations are not so high, being nearer the shore. Altogether, nearly 40,000 perches of stone masonry were required in foundations. (Note: This would be 37,036 cu. yds.)

The stack is 70 feet high by 27 feet diameter at mantles, tapering from that point to 7 feet 3 inches from tunnel-head, where it is 33 ½ feet diameter, flaring from thence to top, to same diameter as at mantles. The boiler-plate shell rests on heavy cast-iron mantles, which are in turn supported by six cast-iron columns.

The weight in cast-iron foundations is as follows: 6 base plates, 12 tons; 6 columns, 18 tons; 6 caps, 9 tons; 6 mantles, 36 tons. Total 75 tons. Thickness of shell, first course, ½ inch, the remainder, 5/16th inches. The stack, as at present lined up, is 16 foot bosh; 13 ½ feet under bell at top; crucible, 5½ feet diameter, by 7 feet high, at commencement of bosh, incased with galvanized wrought-iron water-boxes, up to within 12 inches of tuyere arches, and 1 foot below bottom of hearth; angle of bosh, 71 degrees, closed hearth, with the lurmann cinder-block in two places, taking cinder out on the east side.

Cubic contents of stack as follows:

Shaft, 6,509 cubic feet; bosh, 1,764 cubic feet; crucible 166 cubic feet; total, 8,439 cubic feet.

Tunnel-head is closed by an ordinary bell and hopper, handled by a pneumatic cylinder. Diameter of bell, 7½ feet.

The casting-house is of brick, 112 feet long by 60 feet wide by 20 feet high at the eaves, covered with a galvanized corrugated iron roof. It extends past the stack to the first two stoves, which form the south end of it, leaving a space available for pig-beds of only 60 by 60 feet—too short by 30 feet at least. The gases are conveyed down by a firebrick lined wrought-iron flue 6 feet 3 inches in diameter, from which branches 4 feet in diameter lead to the boilers and hot-blast stoves. Each branch has a butterfly valve to shut off or regulate the flow of gas. As a precaution against explosions, the flues have four 30 inch safety valves and one safety cover, 38 inches square, besides boiler doors and explosion-valves on the stoves.

The boiler house is of brick, 66 feet long by 72 feet wide, with iron roof, and contains boiler capacity sufficient for two furnaces, consisting of eight boilers, each 55 feet long and 5 feet in diameter, connected together two and two by transverse mud drums 10½ feet long by 5 feet diameter, and also by steam-drums 9 feet long by 4 feet diameter.

Iron in shells 3/8 inches thick, and in heads ½ inch, of Bay State Co. No. 1. Each set has grate-surface 5 feet for direct firing; two, four, six, or eight can be used as required. By a system of air-passages in the walls, the gas is supplied with highly heated air for combustion.

A large brick flue runs across the west end of boilers, connecting them to a wrought-iron firebrick-lined chimney, 115 feet high by 8 feet 7 inches at bottom and 6 feet at top. The draft of each set is controlled by a butterfly damper. Each steam drum has one 6-inch Richardson safety valve, set to blow off at 60 pounds. A long copper 'goose neck' pipe connects each drum to an 18-inch wrought-iron steam pipe, 105 feet long, which conveys the steam to the blowing engine and pumps.

The blowing engine is a side condensing one, built by Henry G. Morris, Philadelphia, Pa., and is of the following dimensions: Steam-cylinder, 60 inches diameter; blast-cylinder, 100 inches diameter, each 8 feet stroke; capacity of blast-cylinder, 872 cubic feet per revolution. Two fly-wheels weigh 23 tons each. Two side levers 11 tons each. Two cross heads 2¼ tons each, of Bessemer steel. Diameter of main shaft and beam centre 18 inches. By means of an adjustable cut-off, steam can be made to follow to 7/8 or cut off at ¼ stroke. The condenser draws its water from a well in the basement of engine-room, which is supplied from the lake. The engine house is of brick, 66 feet long, by 60 feet wide, by 32 feet high at the eaves, and is covered by a slate roof, on top of which is a cupola for admission of air for the engine.

The engine-house is calculated for two engines; the place intended for the second one is now used as a machine-shop. The pumps are in the basement of the engine-room, and draw water from the lake through a 16-inch cast iron pipe, and also through a timber sluiceway 24 inches square in which the 16-inch pipe is laid. Two direct acting Knowles's pumps supply the tuyeres and hot-blast stoves with water. Steam-cylinders 24 inches, and water-cylinders 16 inches diameter by 24 inches stroke; capacity of water-cylinders, 20 gallons per stroke. The water is delivered direct to stoves and tuyeres by a 4-inch pipe, and also to a wrought-iron tank in the boiler-house, 51 feet 9 inches long by 8 feet diameter, with a standpipe 7 feet diameter by 24 feet 6 inches high. The whole holding about 25,000 gallons. From this tank water is also conveyed to stoves and tuyeres by a 4-inch pipe, connecting finally with the one mentioned as leading direct from the pumps, making a complete circuit. All of the pipes run uncovered in the open air, and are kept from freezing by pumping water from the hot well, when required. The speed of the pumps is controlled by a Fitts's governor-valve, worked by a tank and float placed on the second floor of the engine-room, and at the same height as overflow in main tank. Should the water fall below a certain point, an alarm whistle would be blown, and call the attention of the engineer to the fact. One of the pumps exhausts into the condenser of the blowing-engine, while the other has a Craig & Brevoort condenser. Both can be run non-condensing if required. The two feed-pumps are also in the basement, and consist of one letter A, and one 10 by 6 by 18 inches, Knowles's mining pumps. Water is taken from the hot well, and also from main water-pipe and tank. . . .

The Taws and Hartman pneumatic elevator was built by the Delamater Iron Works, New York. Cylinder 36 inches diameter by 74 feet 2 inches stroke, working a 4-barrow platform, two going up on either side of the cylinder at once. The usual safety devices are applied; four ¾-inch steel wire ropes connect the piston to the platform. The elevator also works a car on an inclined plane to bring up the coal and flux from the wharf to the level of the scale-house.

Blast for operating the hoist is usually taken from the main engine, but can be supplied by a Knowles's direct-acting blowing engine, with 14-inch steam and 30-inch air-cylinder by 36-inch stroke. This engine was put in principally to furnish cold, and consequently, dry air, in extremely cold weather, and thus prevent the hoist from freezing up.

Four Whitwell firebrick stoves heat the blast; each stove is 29½ feet high by 22 feet diameter, with about 11,000 square feet of heating surface. About 525 tons of firebricks were used in lining each stove, besides fire-clay mortar and packing (blast furnace cinder crushed up).

The blast is carried from the stoves to the furnace by a wrought-iron pipe 46 inches in diameter and 5/16 inch thick, lined with 14 inches of firebrick. This pipe connects with a continuous bustle wind-pipe inside the column, 30 inches in diameter, of wrought-iron 5/16 inches thick, and lined with 9 inches of firebricks. A wrought-iron chimney 115 feet high, lined with bricks, serves for the four stoves.

Connection is made with the Lake Champlain and Moriah Railroad, and also indirectly with the New York and Canada Railroad by 1,200 feet of trestle, built through the lake most of the way, and about 26 feet above the water. The Lake Champlain and Moriah Railroad delivers the ore and most of the flux used at the scale-house doors, direct from the mines and quarries. The coal so far has been delivered by canal boats on the wharf, but can be replaced directly from the Delaware and Hudson Canal Company, via the New York and Canada Railroad, whose track runs within 50 feet of the works on the west side. The latter road has freighted most of the iron so far. The dock on which coal is stored has a frontage of 500 feet, which will be rapidly extended by the enormous amount of cinder made. . . .

APPENDIX D

Bonanza and Joker Shafts, Witherbees Sherman and Company

The Bonanza Shaft is 300 feet south of the "21" Mine. It is vertical for 396 feet, then on a vertical curve down a 16 degree incline 325 feet, and around another curve and down vertically for 255 feet. The change in direction of the shaft was made to follow the footwall ore contact with the rock. There were two rail track skipways that followed the above course. In the 1880's the mine workings had extended about 150 feet beyond the bottom of the first vertical section of the shaft. The roof or hanging wall dipped about ten degrees to the southwest. The bottom or footwall of the ore had not been reached and the ore was stoped down from the roof. Pillars 40 to 50 feet in diameter were left to support the roof. The ore structure was a continuation of the massive "21" Mine ore, and therefore aptly named the Bonanza Mine.

The Joker Shaft, about 400 feet south of the Bonanza, was sunk in the 1880's at an angle of 78 degrees, passing through 90 feet of glacial fill, then through rock to a depth of over 500 feet below surface. Due to its unexpected depth to reach the ore, the shaft was named Joker. In the 1880's and '90's there were two skipways in the Joker Shaft; the east skipway descending with grade unchanged for 650 feet through ore and a rock fold to the lowest level; and the west skipway descending down to the top of the rock fold, then flattening through a curve to 26 degrees down along the top of the fold of rock for 300 feet, then through another curve continuing down vertically to the level below. In later years the Joker Shaft was realigned with both skipways descending at 78 degrees from surface for 1,100 feet.

APPENDIX E

1898 Description of Witherbees Sherman and Company Mine Operations

Charles Cady, general manager, described Joker-Bonanza mining operations as follows:

This is the only deposit that has of late been worked. It is an extension of "21" mine, Port Henry Iron Ore Co. It shows a development of some 1,050 feet in length, the greatest width being 400 feet, and a thickness at one point of 355 feet with 60 feet of rock intervening, forming the two principal veins now being worked in this ore body. At the point of greatest thickness there remains ore not mined about 170 feet in depth, as shown by diamond drill. If to the above we add the dimensions of the development in "21" mine, we have the ore developed for a distance of about 2,000 feet. On the latter property a thickness of 325 feet is shown by diamond drill, and a width corresponding to that noted in Bonanza-Joker. The Bonanza-Joker workings are entirely underground, the ore being attacked from two shafts sunk 400 and 450 feet respectively to cut the ore. The dip of the ore is to the Southeast. At the most southerly working, the vertical depth from surface is 550 feet. The roof of the mine is generally good. It is estimated that about 75% of the ore is won in the first mining operation, the balance being represented in pillar supports. Very little water has been encountered in this opening, which perhaps is best shown by the cost of fuel, which is for all purposes ($4.00 per gr. ton) $0.038 per ton of ore raised. With the present two shaft connections an annual production of about 200,000 tons can be made.

Estimate of ore in sight	1,921,959
Estimate of ore not in sight	4,528,000
Total gross tons available	6,449,959

Mr. Cady also described the new facilities constructed for efficient operation of Joker-Bonanza Mine as follows:

In 1896-7 the following improvements were made: A new plant was installed comprising brick power house with metal roof, two double hoisting plants with double corliss reversing engines - cylinders 16 x 26; hoisting drums 8 feet dia. 84 inches face to carry 1500 feet of 1¼ rope; two compressors; one compound condensing with steam cylinder 18 + 32 x 30, air cylinder 18 + 28 x 30; the other compressor 20 x 30 cylinder; Electric light plant, capacity 20 arc and 250 incandescent lights; Boilers - Babcock and Wilcox water tube 420 HP; sustaining steel plate chimney. This plant was equipped to operate Bonanza-Joker mine with a surplus boiler, compressor and electric capacity. Two new shaft houses, two new double skip roads from surface through mine laid with 30 lb. T rail. The entire cost of mine improvement made in 1896-7 was $92,044.15.

APPENDIX F

Harmony and Old Bed Mines and Mills, 1905

Harmony

Harmony Mines produced crude ore through "A" and "B" Shafts. Both shafts were rectangular, 17' by 8' in cross section, each with three compartments consisting of two skipways and a ladderway. They were timbered with 12" by 12" timber through the overburden into solid rock or ore. "A" Shaft was vertical from surface for 287 feet, then turned through a vertical curve into a decline on a sixteen degree slope. "B" Shaft was vertical for 376 feet, then turned on a vertical curve into a decline on a thirty degree slope. The shaft houses or headframes were constructed of heavy timber covered on the sides and roof with corrugated galvanized iron sheeting. Their height and canted style was typical of those found in the American mining industry during that period.

A seam of fresh water producing 200 gallons per minute was encountered in "B" Shaft requiring a storage reservoir and pumping station to be built 360 feet below surface. The main pump was a Knowles horizontal 6.5 by 8 inch triplex plunger pump driven by a 30 horse power electric motor and operated by a float switch. The reserve pump was a Knowles horizontal duplex steam driven pump. The storage reservoir, or sump, had a three hour storage capacity. This "B" Shaft water seam and storage sump is of particular interest as the water eventually proved to be the purest in the area. In later years the "B" Shaft water was pumped to a surface reservoir and from there supplied the communities of Mineville and Witherbee until 1980.

Hoisting equipment for "A" and "B" Shafts was located in A and B Power House and consisted of four Webster, Camp and Lane ten foot diameter hoisting drums with six foot face, each with a capacity of 1,500 feet of 1¼" dia. plow steel hoisting rope. Idler sheaves sliding on horizontal pipes and eight foot diameter turn and head sheaves at the headframe supported the hoisting rope from the hoisting drums to the ore skips. The hoisting equipment was driven by one 300 horsepower motor geared to the drums and arranged so that each drum could be operated independently or in any combination required. One and one-half ton capacity skip cars were hoisted at 600 feet per minute.

There was also in A and B Power House a Nordberg two-stage air compressor, belt driven by a 300 h.p. motor and capable of delivering 2,550 cubic feet of compressed air per minute to operate the underground drilling equipment. The drills were Ingersoll-Sergeant 2¾ inch diameter piston size, and drilled five to six eight-foot holes per driller in a ten-hour day. Drilled holes were loaded with 45% dynamite and fired with cap and fuse. Broken ore was hand shoveled into 1½ ton cars and pushed by hand on rail tracks to the shaft where the ore was dumped into the skip.

Skips hoisted in "B" Shaft dumped into a chute feeding a 30" x 18" Blake crusher through which the material was crushed to 1½" size, then moved on a 20" conveyor belt to a bin feeding a Ball & Norton single drum separator. Through the separator the cobbed ore, containing 61% iron, was raised on a 20" conveyor to a storage bin, then loaded into cars for rail shipment to the docks at Port Henry. This product was called Harmony Cobbed Ore and, because of its size, uniform high grade and handling ease, was a desirable product for furnace operators to mix with other lower grade ores. The tailings from the separator, being low grade ore, were raised by another 20" conveyor to a storage bin, then loaded into cars for rail transfer to No. 1 Mill. Crude ore hoisted in Harmony "A" Shaft was dumped into a bin, then fed through a chute into cars for rail transfer to No. 1 Mill.

The cars of crude ore from "A" Shaft and tailings from "B" Shaft were dumped, weighed and conveyed to a bin feeding a 30" x 18" Blake crusher at No. 1 Mill. Passing through the crusher, the ore was screened to ¾" mesh, with the fines going to a dryer and the oversize going to Gates secondary crushers, then to the dryer. The dryer was a tall brick stack with several horizontal rows of baffle bars followed by several more at right angles to the others. The ore was fed into the dryer at the top and was dispersed as it fell on the baffle bars, allowing a free flow of air through the ore as it descended. The dryer was built with a bridge wall and heated by an outside furnace. Gases from the furnace divided, passing over the bridge wall and up the chimney. The chimney was adjacent to the dryer shaft with openings in the walls to allow the gases to enter or exhaust from the dryer.

The dried ore was fed to a Ball and Norton single drum magnetic separator which recovered the rich particles of ore, as a coarse concentrate, for discharge directly to a shipping bin. The tails, or rejects, from this separator passed through a set of 40" x 15" Anaconda rolls, then elevated and passed over a 3/8" tower screen. From the screen the ore passed to two Ball and Norton belt separators. The recovered ore was conveyed directly to the shipping bin and the tails from the separators passed to two more Ball and Norton separators with higher magnetic intensity to make another separation; the recovered ore retained for further treatment and the tails going on a tailings conveyor to the tailings storage pile. The recovered ore was crushed finer by a pair of 36" x 14" Reliance rolls, then passed to two additional Ball and Norton belt-type separators for a final separation. The recovered ore was conveyed to the shipping bin and the tails deposited on the tailings conveyor to storage.

Four 50 horsepower Crocker-Wheeler direct current motors and one 75 horsepower General Electric motor furnished power to operate No. 1 Mill. The milling process, being dry and very dusty, required an enclosed motor room within the mill to protect the motors. Suitable belt drives from the motors transmitted power through line shafts and belts to the various pieces of equipment. This mill had been modified to treat the low phosphorous and sometimes leaner Harmony and New Bed ores.

Old Bed

Equipment for hoisting Old Bed high phosphorus ore through Joker and Bonanza Shafts was installed in the Old Bed (No. 1) Power House, located between the two shafts and just east of the concentrating mills. The power house was equipped with three Babcock and Wilcox steam boilers that carried 110 pounds pressure. Knowles and Worthington pumps supplied feed water to the boilers. A Reynolds corliss compound steam engine, producing 200 horse power, was belted to a Crocker-Wheeler 150 kw. direct current generator that produced 230 volts to the magnetic separators in both mills. A Southworth steam engine direct connected to a 30 kw. General Electric generator, and a General Electric motor-generator set, provided plant and mine lighting. There were also an Ingersoll-Sergeant two stage electric motor driven 1,200 c.f.m. air compressor and a steam driven modified Rand 1,750 c.f.m. air compressor.

The two compressors in No. 1 Power House and the Nordberg compressor in A and B Power House all delivered compressed air to a main air line system with branch lines to mine drills and pumps in the Joker, Bonanza and Harmony Mines, and to the machine shop and other surface areas requiring compressed air.

Joker and Bonanza hoisting machinery in No. 1 Power House was steam driven. Two Webster Camp and Lane double Corliss reversing engines, 16" x 36", drove two double eight-foot diameter drums, each capable of winding 1,200 feet of wire rope. Hoist rope arrangement from the engine room over sheaves to the headframes and attachment to the 1½ ton capacity skips was similar to that described for Harmony shafts. Mining and hand tramming to the shafts were also similar. Ore was hoisted at 600 feet per minute.

Old Bed ore, as mined, was generally uniform in grade, running about 60 percent iron but ranging from 1.35 to 2.25 percent phosphorus. The problem here was not a large amount of low grade iron as in the Harmony crude ore, but rather reducing the phosphorus or apatite crystals mechanically mixed with the ore and other gangue material in the crude ore mined. Crude ore hoisted was hand sorted or cobbed at the headframes with the rich pieces loaded to cars for shipment to Port Henry. The remainder was rail shipped to No. 2 Mill. Here the ore was weighed, dumped and conveyed to a storage bin.

No. 2 Mill structure was 232.5 feet long and featured three divisions consisting of a crushing plant, a separating plant and a retreating plant. Each division had independent power control for equipment and operation of the division. Surge bins with a capacity of two hours mill run were located between each division.

Crude ore entering the crushing section passed through a 30" x 18" Blake crusher to a ¾" screen. The oversize material passed through a 36" x 6" Blake double-jaw crusher and joined the undersize from the ¾" screen being fed to a 6 mesh screen. The 6 mesh screen oversize passed through 36" x 14" Reliance rolls and joined the 6 mesh undersize, ending in a minus 6 mesh product from the crushing section being fed to the dryer. The dryer was similar in construction to the dryer at No. 1 Mill.

Dried ore entering the separating division of the mill passed over Tower screens of 30, 16, 10 and 6 mesh. Oversize from the screens passed in closed circuit through 36" x 14" Reliance rolls and returned to the Tower screens. The 30, 16, and 6 mesh undersize passed to Ball & Norton belt separators and the 10 mesh undersize passed to Wetherill Type F separators. Iron concentrate recovered from the separators averaged about 65 percent iron and was conveyed directly to concentrate bins.

Tailings from the sized separations, containing apatite, hornblende, silica and iron entered the retreatment division of the mill. It first passed over a Ball and Norton belt separator where remaining particles of rich iron were recovered to the concentrate conveyor. The tailings from the separation then passed through 32" by 10" Traylor high speed finishing rolls for finer grinding. From the rolls the tailings passed to a Tower screen from which the material was divided into 10 and 16 mesh size and fed to Wetherill Type E Separators.

The Wetherill Type E Separators, capable of making a three part separation, featured high intensity magnets, suitable for recovering slightly magnetic material. The screened 10 and 16 mesh tailings were separated into three parts; iron recovered in the first stage; apatite containing 60 to 65 percent bone phosphate recovered in the second stage; and tailings containing 40 to 45 percent bone phosphate recovered in the final stage. Iron recovered in the first stage of the Type E separators passed to Ball and Norton separators where only the high grade particles were recovered to the concentrate bin, the remainder joining the tailings from the other separators on a conveyor to the tailings storage pile.

Continuous size screening in the process was to remove the high grade iron at each stage without grinding it finer than necessary, as the larger particles in the concentrate benefited blast furnace operation. Finer grinding and screening in the retreatment process broke down the attachment of slightly magnetic apatite crystals to small crystals of magnetic iron, permitting them to be recovered separately, thus reducing phosphorus in the final iron concentrate.

High grade apatite recovered by the Type E Wetherill separators was conveyed to a shipping bin and sold as first grade apatite for fertilizing purposes. The tailings from No. 2 Mill with the lower percent of apatite was sold as second grade apatite, although not in great demand. Most of this latter grade remained in tailings storage.

Shipping Products Produced During 1905

Iron Ore Products	Tons
Old Bed Concentrates - non-Bessemer grade	213,265
Harmony Concentrates - Bessemer grade	76,591
Direct shipping crude ore	107,574
Total	397,430

The figures show that 1.2 tons of crude ore were handled and processed to produce 1.0 ton of iron ore shipping product.

By-Products	Tons
Apatite - first grade	3,999
Apatite - second grade	5,684
Ore Tailings - rock and sand	1,795
Treating Commercial Ore	
Burden Iron Company concentrates	11,999
Carbon Iron and Steel Company concentrates	3,253

Apatite, some of the tailings, and commercial ore tons were processed in No. 2 Mill. Revenue from these products reduced the iron concentrate milling cost per ton by 21 percent.

Balance of the tailings sold was produced in No. 1 Mill. Revenue from these tailings sales reduced the iron concentrate milling cost per ton by 0.9 percent.

APPENDIX G

Mine Improvement, Development, and Joker Shaft Steel Headframe

Skip roads in mine shafts and skip loading and dumping arrangements were rebuilt with heavier material. A new steel headframe was erected at Joker Shaft including an 18" x 30" jaw crusher at a cost of $33,708. The Joker Shaft was idled from September 1 to November 23, while dismantling the old shaft house and erecting the new steel headframe.

Additional compressed air capacity was installed at A and B and No. 1 Power Houses. A tunnel was driven to consolidate the New Bed and Barton Hill mine workings for efficient operation. From the entrance timber it was driven 1,670 feet by December 31, 1908 at a cost of $36,199. For 510 feet the tunnel passed through the old mine workings of Lovers Hole, South Pit and North Pit. It was planned to continue on to Orchard Pit, with the tunnel area expected to develop substantial reserves of this very high grade ore.

APPENDIX H

Solomon LeFevre's 1908 Report on Cheever Mine

Solomon LeFevre, chief engineer for Witherbee Sherman and Company, visited the limited renewed Cheever Mine operation in December 1908 and commented in part as follows:

They are running one ten hour shift per day and shipping two cars of concentrates, say 75 tons per day, which is all they have orders for at present.

The gravity plane lowering concentrates to the railroad is working smoothly, operating two cars of 9,000 lbs. of ore or 18,000 lbs. per trip. It takes seven men to operate the plane, load and unload the concentrate.

The mill is doing good work. All the ore is ground fine. Judging from the appearance of the ore, it is rich enough to stand cobbing like our Harmony without running the concentrates below 60 percent iron. This would increase the capacity of the mill, but this is not very important at present as the mill capacity is more than the mine. The mill will now handle about 400 tons in ten hours and the mine is not equipped to do that much.

I went down in the Weldon Pit which is the only one from which ore is hoisted at present. The hoist will handle a car with one and one-half tons of ore, and they have hoisted 110 cars per shift which would make the capacity of the pit 165 tons per ten hours.

There is a good showing of ore in the Weldon Pit. The track starts from the surface toward the west, dipping about fifty degrees from horizontal. The angle becomes gradually flatter and the track curves until the direction is southwest at the bottom, which is 1,000 feet from dump. At the bottom of the track the ore is worked out about 75 feet wide and 6 to 10 feet thick. The working face continues about 300 feet in a southwest direction, and after going on a level about 75 feet, rises on a grade of about two feet in a hundred. In the heading the ore is quite flat, having no noticeable dip in any direction. The ore face shows 6 to 8 feet of good ore which I should judge would give 50 to 55 percent iron. In the old workings along the track before the bottom is reached, they are taking up about three feet of the footwall which is very good separating ore, running probably about 45 percent iron.

Between the Weldon Pit and the old workings on the north there is supposed to be about 400 feet of unmined ore which probably contains 200,000 to 300,000 tons of ore. On the south of the Weldon Pit there is another pit called the Tunnel Pit, worked about 1,000 feet on the slope and showing, I am told, about the same quality and quantity of ore in the bottom as the Weldon Pit. I have seen no map or survey to show how far apart these pits are or their relative levels, but I believe the Tunnel Pit is the lower.

If there is a roll dropping the ore to the south of the Weldon Pit toward the Tunnel Pit, a drift in the ore toward the south from the lowest part of the Weldon might work around the rise in the heading in line with the track. This would be on the supposition that there are two sets of rolls at approximately right angles, as is the case in Barton Hill. One set parallel to the track and making the division between the Weldon and Tunnel pits, and the other across the track, making the rise toward the heading. At the present time there is a chance to break more ore in the Weldon Pit than can be hoisted, and they have probably 5,000 or more tons broken now.

The difficulty when the demand for ore revives, will be to get enough ore broken and hoisted to run the mill at an economical rate. In what way it will be best to increase the mining capacity will require much careful consideration. If steam power is to be used, the compressor might be located at the lake to save hauling coal up the hill. If electric power is used, the compressor would be at the mine.

The formation is quite similar to Harmony and Barton Hill, and any of the pits are likely to be in squeezes part of the time when you would get little ore out of them. To insure a steady supply of ore, at least three pits should be equipped. To do this with suitable machinery and tools, storage bins, houses for men to produce 400 tons concentrates per ten hour day, might use up nearly $100,000 additional capital.

If the ore between the Weldon Pit and the old mine is to be attacked vigorously, it will probably be necessary to pump out the old mine. This would make available a considerable amount of lean ore reported as left in the old mine.

Power equipment at the Cheever Mine consisted of a boiler plant, one engine driven compressor, one double drum hoist, and one high speed slide valve engine for operating the mill. In addition to air operated pumps, the compressor supplied air to three drills. Engineers estimated $50,000 immediately required for equipment including a compressor building with 1,000 c.f.m. motor driven compressor with 200 HP motor and electrical control; air line piping; ten drills with fittings; two electric pumps; four surface headframes, each with a 150 ton storage bin; two 35 HP electric hoists with motors, hoisting cable, sheaves and track to equip 300 feet in each of these hoisting slopes to surface; tram cars and tracks underground; and surface cars and tracks.

APPENDIX I

Witherbee Sherman Interest in Minerals Outside Its Region

During 1909-10 Witherbee Sherman and Company acquired a large tract of land containing iron ore in Camaguey, Cuba. A considerable sum was spent in exploring the property to determine ore reserves, agricultural possibilities and rail and dock facilities for shipping. A holding company was formed named Cubitas Iron Ore Company. The property was not developed and the Cuban project was abandoned. Witherbee Sherman retained, at least on paper, the Cubitas Iron Ore Company.

To understand why Witherbee Sherman ventured into properties outside their own vast mineral lands we must view the company's position in the eastern iron ore trade, and the economic and competitive forces at work within and outside the region in 1910.

There were 2,000 square miles of iron bearing rocks in southeastern New York, New Jersey and Pennsylvania. Active magnetic iron mining had been carried on in these areas for over one hundred years. Ore reserves in these mines were known. Another area of concern at the time was the possible economic value of the Clinton hematite ores of New York which stretched in a practically unbroken line from St. Lawrence County about 200 miles to the Niagara River. Also, future conditions might justify exploring the known red and brown hematite iron ores of the several New England states.

Although magnetic iron ore was one of the first ores used in this country, it was the least developed, but of the mines developed, Mineville was the leader and no others compared favorably. It was recognized that magnetic iron ore would eventually become one of the main sources of ore supply. However, the major sources of iron ore for the fast growing American steel industry were the soft hematite ores mined in Michigan and Minnesota and shipped to Great Lakes ports. These hematite ores averaged 50 to 55 percent iron whereas magnetic ore concentrates averaged 62 to 68 percent iron.

Eastern furnaces in northern New York, along the Hudson River, in Massachusetts, New Jersey and Pennsylvania supplied pig iron to the Northeast. Mineville ore shipped to these furnaces had established a good reputation as furnace ore. With favorable shipping cost and high iron content versus Great Lakes ore, Mineville ore was delivered to the furnaces at an attractive price. A major source of concern was the rising trend of imports of iron ore and pig iron at east coast ports. These were a threat to both America's furnaces and iron ore mines.

APPENDIX J

Witherbee Sherman and Company Concentrating Mills, 1910-1916

No. 3 Concentrating Mill was built between Harmony A and B Shafts for greater productive capacity and to permit short conveyor transfer of crude ore from the shafts to the mill, thus eliminating the expensive rail haulage to No. 1 Mill. Construction was started in September 1909 and completed one year later at a cost of $179,000. The building was designed fireproof, with steel floor beams, concrete floors, block walls and metal roof.

At start-up in September 1910 it was decided to run New Bed ore through No. 3 Mill in order to make a thorough test of its quality. The mill was operated on this ore the rest of the year with satisfactory results. The ore was leaner than Harmony ore and required finer grinding. The tests showed that a mill built for New Bed ore would require more rolls for finer grinding to keep the iron in the tailings down to a minimum. No. 3 Mill began running Harmony ore in 1911 and in that year 174,540 tons of crude ore were processed from which 126,841 tons of concentrate and middlings were recovered at a ratio of 1.38 tons of crude ore per ton of finished product.

In May 1911 the company authorized $175,000 for construction of No. 4 Mill for treatment of New Bed-Barton Hill ore. No. 4 Mill was built about 300 feet from the tunnel entrance to New Bed Mine, and connected to it by a trestle over which electric mine locomotives delivered ore from within the mine to a storage bin. The mill building was of steel frame construction with metal sheeting on sides and roof. Steel floor beams were covered with wood flooring. The building was divided into two parts. The coarse crushing section, 36 feet wide by 100 feet long by 85 feet high, contained the crushers, dryer, coarse screens and bucket elevators. The concentrating section, 66 feet wide by 90 feet long by 90 feet high, contained the fine screens, separators and crushing rolls. The concentrate shipping bin was located on a rail siding north of the highway and east of Central Power House. In November 1912, ore was first put through the mill, and to the end of the year, 14,331 tons were processed from which 7,473 tons of New Bed concentrates were recovered at a ratio of 1.92. The concentrates ran over 66 percent iron and between .025 and .03 percent phosphorus. Production from the mine was 400 tons per day at the time, but the mill was capable of handling 1,400 tons per day.

On June 17, 1914, No. 1 and 2 Mills and Cobbing Plant were completely destroyed by fire. These facilities were insured for $150,000 and the company immediately began construction of No. 5 Mill. No. 2 Mill and Cobbing Plant were comparatively new and in good operating condition. No. 1 Mill was in poor condition and would have been replaced. No. 5 Mill was designed to combine the features of the Cobbing Plant and No. 2 Mill with capacity to replace all facilities destroyed in the fire. The site selected was the old No. 1 Mill site west of Joker Shaft. The building was of reinforced concrete with block curtain walls. For interior design, company engineers modified No. 4 Mill flow sheet for No. 5 Mill to handle Old Bed ore on one shift. Furnace or cobbed ore would be made at the head of the mill instead of in a separate plant as done previously. Construction cost, to be kept within $150,000 recovered from fire insurance, resulted in production design details being sacrificed for economy.

Following the fire and prior to completion of No. 5 Mill in 1915, Old Bed ore was transferred to No. 3 Mill. This particular time was a low production period in the iron trade and both Harmony and Old Bed ores were processed in No. 3 Mill on separate shifts. This was costly due to multiple inefficient handling to put Old Bed ore into the mill. The mill circuit had to be cleaned out at the end of each Old Bed ore shift to maintain the low phosphorus grade of Harmony ore through the mill.

Of associated interest with the operation of these mills was the processing of titaniferous ores from Tahawus. The MacIntyre Iron Company had been organized to reopen the mine and planned to build a railroad from Tahawus to Crown Point via Schroon River. In 1913 they erected a small mill and mined some ore for shipment from North Creek to Mineville for concentration followed by pig iron production tests at Port Henry. During 1914, before the mill fire, 2,989 tons of Tahawus ore was treated in No. 1 Mill. Following the fire, 3,179 tons of Tahawus ore was treated in No. 4 Mill. Subsequent furnace operation on this ore was not satisfactory due to the high titanium content. Market studies indicated these ores would not be acceptable in the iron trade and the MacIntyre Iron Company ended operations.

No. 5 Mill was designed to process high phosphorus ore whereas No. 3 and 4 Mills were designed to treat low phosphorus ores. All three mills featured a dry process, with crushers, a dryer, screens, secondary crushers, magnetic separators and crushing rolls. All utilized Ball and Norton separators as part of the process. Each mill flow sheet was a refinement of the operations of No. 1 and 2 Mills previously described in detail. The mills were very dusty and, with the silica content in the crude ore, constituted a severe health hazard by exposing employees to silicosis if they failed to wear protective respirators.

APPENDIX K

Mineville Miners Union Strike, 1912-1913

The Mineville Miners Union became active in a period of discord in 1912-13 and union officers were quoted in New York newspapers, leveling very serious charges against the company. The charges and reply by Witherbee Sherman & Company, quoted below, are taken from a statement by the company dated January 17, 1913 and published in area newspapers.

TO OUR EMPLOYEES
AND THE CITIZENS OF THE TOWN OF MORIAH

We herewith append extracts from articles which appeared in the *New York World, New York Globe* and *New York Journal* on Wednesday, January 15th and our reply thereto:

The World, N.Y., January 15th quotes as follows:

"We can produce affidavits," said Geo. Waldron, President of the Mineville Miners Union who was one of a delegation that waited on Senator Griffin, "that time and again men have been known to go down in the mines never to re-appear. They have been buried in cave-ins and no one has ever taken the trouble to dig their bodies out. The mine owners have a private cemetery at Mineville where other poor victims are buried hastily, their families knowing nothing of their fate and their graves unmarked.

"Gompers and Cannon assured Senator Griffin that if a committee were to visit Mineville it would be shown that the men are overworked, compelled to live in quarters unfit for habitation and made the subjects of what amounts to a rule of terrorism."

The Journal, N.Y., January 15th quotes as follows:

During the argument Senator Anthony J. Griffin was informed that at Mineville, ten miles from here, employees of Witherbee Sherman & Company are enduring penury, torture and starvation because of the rapacity and greed of their bosses.

The Globe, N.Y., January 15th quotes as follows:

Every house in the little town - and none of them is anything but a miserable shack - is owned by Witherbee Sherman and Co. and rented at a high rate to their employees. The income on this investment alone is enormous.

There is always a scarcity of houses. The company sees to this. To get a house an employee must pay a foreman or superintendent a bonus. Then he will discharge some other employee, order him out of the town, and his empty house is turned over to the man who paid the bonus.

It is a common practice to hurry the mangled body of the victims from a mine and rush it to the grave without even preparing it for burial. Within three hours after a man's life has been crushed out, his body will be in a rough box in a shallow grave in the mine Company's private cemetery.

The Witherbees don't want a Senate investigation. When threatened with one some time ago they declared they did not want a lot of senators "snooping" around up here, as all they would do would be to drink champagne at the public expense. They proposed a compromise with their workers at the time and agreed to investigate thoroughly all their complaints.

REPLY OF WITHERBEE SHERMAN & COMPANY

On reading these articles we communicated with Senator Wagner, leader of the Senate, asking for a full investigation of the actual conditions at Mineville. For that purpose also our Secretary, Mr.

Francis, went to Albany and urged the same action on other State Officials.

In answer to the above charges we quote an interview from us which appeared in *Essex County News* and *Ticonderoga Sentinel* this week:

The personnel of Witherbee Sherman & Company is sufficiently well known throughout this section to completely answer the attacks as made in New York and other papers of Jan. 15th and 16th at the investigation of certain labor agitators playing politics. The public, however, should be made acquainted with the facts as follows:

That this company has given for years, for the use of its employees, the Memorial Building at Mineville, costing about $70,000, in which meetings are regularly held by the employees. This building is equipped with clubrooms, billiard tables and meeting rooms.

The two companies have also erected at Mineville, at their own expense, a $70,000 school building. Another is to be erected, probably during the present year. A fully equipped hospital is maintained at the Company's expense where patients are treated free of charge.

In addition, all persons injured in the mines are given a benefit of $5 a week for a married man and $3 for a single man, during the time of disability, without charge of any kind being made.

Our homes are models of their kind, being built of concrete blocks, and everything is kept in the best possible sanitary condition. This work is in charge of a very competent man, who sees to the daily collection of garbage and refuse, and to the burning of the same in a recently installed incinerator.

And there is also employed a district nurse at the expense of the company, who makes daily visits among the families in Mineville and Witherbee to see that their houses are kept clean and sanitary, and that the people have proper medical attendance in case of sickness. This work is also free of charge to employees.

The company maintains a pension fund by which our old employees are taken care of during their life.

At a meeting held January 26th, 1912, with Messrs. Waldron, Wykes and Hughes, the following questions were asked:

"Is it not true that our employees have better houses, better facilities and convenience for living, than exist in any other mining town in the state?" Ans. Yes.

"Is it not true that we have in many ways improved the conditions of our employees, and of the people in the village of Mineville, for instance, in addition to giving the Memorial Building and school building, are we not lighting the streets of Mineville without additional charge or expense?" Ans. Yes.

"Do you not know that some years ago we voluntarily established a pension fund for persons injured while in our employment, whether that injury resulted from their own negligence or otherwise?" Ans. Yes.

"Do we not treat our employees better than any other company that you know of?" Ans. (by Wykes) I have never been treated by any company better than I have been by Witherbee Sherman & Company.

"Do you know of any similar mine or mines in the State of New York where the employees are better paid than our employees?" Ans. I don't know of any.

In addition to the above we might say that we have paid and are now paying the highest wages ruling in any Eastern Iron Ore District.

In regard to the charge about high rents, our rents are from $3.50 to $7.00 per month. The higher rent of $7.00 per month applies to a seven room concrete cottage.

Instead of an 'enormous income' from rents, we spent for maintenance last year $31,040.45 and received for rents $24,131.85, showing a deficiency of $6,908.60. Our 'shacks' consist of concrete houses with hardwood floors and electric lights. In regard to the scarcity of houses, we are building new houses as rapidly as possible and have now 18 tenements under construction, even in the Winter weather.

Our settlements in accident cases are based upon the New Jersey Compensation Law. The New Jersey Law was adopted by us because it yields a greater compensation than the Michigan or Ohio compensation laws. We advocate a similar law for New York State.

In reference to the charges regarding burials. We have never in the history of the Company had a man 'disappear' or 'unaccounted for' from any accident.

In all cases of fatalities the bodies have been put in the hands of a competent undertaker, provided with new clothes, a suitable casket, and a lot purchased in a regular public cemetery, all expense for the same being paid by the Company.

A year ago charges were made that a system of graft was in existence among our employees. A prompt investigation was made with the result that the abuse was stopped, and since that time there has been no evidence of any kind of its continuance, nor have any charges been made to us of this character. We notified our employees that any one receiving or giving money or 'presents' would be discharged.

We propose to materially extend our present welfare work. We have already started the establishment of change houses near the working places where men can change their clothes and bathe before going home, and will have established below ground before Winter is over comfortable convenient lunch rooms.

We regret that two of our employees, George Waldron and H. B. Wykes have so misrepresented conditions at Mineville and made false charges against us as shown in above extracts, that in justice to ourselves and the Mineville Community we have had to write them the following letter, discharging them from our employment:

"You are hereby discharged from employment by Witherbee Sherman & Company on account of disloyalty to the Company and your share in the publication of libelous articles published in the newspapers this week, whereby scandalous and untrue statements have been scattered broadcast over the Country to the detriment of the Company and the good name of the place where you have yourself made your home for many years.

"You are not discharged because of your activity in labor union matters, nor because you asked an investigation by the Senate of the State, as upon the publication of the articles referred to above, the Company urged upon the authorities in Albany an immediate and full investigation of the actual conditions in Mineville."

We have always prided ourselves in being foremost in providing for the welfare of our employees in every particular, and in endeavoring to keep their friendship and goodwill.

Witherbee Sherman & Company
Mineville, N.Y., January 17, 1913.

Labor relations had deteriorated despite a third wage increase in December 1912. Miners were difficult to secure and the efficiency of those working was decreased considerably. The company assumed both of these troubles were caused by agitation of outside labor leaders. The labor leaders demanded the company reinstate the two discharged employees and hire only union men. The company refused these two demands and a strike was declared.

The Witherbee Sherman & Company general superintendent's report for 1913 commented on the strike in part as follows:

There were in the employ of W. S. & Company and P. H. I. O. Company about 1,500 men. The union claimed a membership of 1,100, but it was afterwards shown there were fewer than 500 members in good standing. There were present at the meeting, when the strike was called, 219 men. Of this number 187 voted for the strike and 32 against it. These results show that the majority of our workmen were satisfied with wages and general conditions and did not want a strike; only 12% voting in favor of it.

As soon as the strike was called, the company posted their property and asked the sheriff to protect it, which he did by means of foot and horse deputies and every man who wanted to go to work was offered protection.

The first day of the strike 75 of W. S. & Company's men went underground and a few of the surface and mill men worked. The mines were operated one shift, and as soon as the men saw that they would be protected, they gradually came back to work.

On January 24th, W. S. & Company had 175 men underground and a total of 563 at work. The night shift at the mines was put on

February 3rd, and our reports show a total of 776 men at work, with 479 underground. On January 28th, notices were posted to the effect that former employees desiring work must apply before February 3rd. The result was that all our men except about 150 came back to work. Those who refused to work attempted to carry on the strike for a time, but as they got no results, finally gave it up and drifted away.

The company has always had an enviable reputation for fair dealing with their employees, and for this reason the good will of the County as a whole was with the company. No strike breakers were used and reliable deputies were easily obtained within the County.

Thirty day notices to vacate the company's houses were served on all former employees who refused to come back to work. No attention was paid to these notices and it was necessary to make several evictions before possession could be obtained.

There was no loss of life or property, strict order and discipline were maintained, and protection given to everyone who required it.

APPENDIX L

Witherbee Sherman & Company Recovery of Apatite, 1913-1919

Studies continued to improve the quality of apatite recovery. During 1913 samples of Old Bed tailings were screened and experiments conducted using Hooper Concentration Tables with a view of raising the phosphate content. Results were good and three Hooper Tables were installed in the lower end of No. 2 Mill. The output of these machines was shipped to a small fertilizer plant constructed at Port Henry.

The process at the planned phosphate plant, as described in the general superintendent's report for 1913, featured grinding the high grade heads from the Hooper machines to 95 -100 percent mesh and bagging them to be sold in competition with commercial ground phosphate rock. The middlings were mixed with barium sulphide to make barium-basic phosphate, to be sold in competition with acid phosphate. The barium sulphide was mixed with 50 percent by weight of gas coal and put through a reduction furnace. The reduced material was then mixed with nine parts of apatite middlings, ground to 95-100 percent mesh and marketed in that form.

Following the fire that destroyed No. 2 Mill in 1914 and the completion of No. 5 Mill in 1915, experiments to recover apatite by high intensity magnetic separation were continued in No. 5 Mill. Results were gratifying.

An arrangement was made in 1916 with Mr. Edmund Mortimer, formerly with one of the largest fertilizer houses in the country, to market the product. Extensive tests were made on farms throughout New England and New York State. A larger apatite plant was built at Mineville and expectations were high for securing a strong market. The product was successful, but being new, market penetration was slow. In 1919 the apatite plant at Mineville was destroyed by fire. Plans were made, but not carried out, to build a plant and warehouse in the Albany area. Fertilizer production and sales were discontinued.

APPENDIX M

Construction, Start-up and Operation of No. 2 Furnace, 1920-24

No. 2 Blast Furnace, the last blast furnace built in the Champlain Valley, was of the latest, most modern design. Height of the furnace was 87 feet; hearth 16' 3"; bosh 78 degrees 38 min. 48 sec.; angle of inwall .735 degrees and diameter of bell 11' 6". The furnace was filled by double skip, with the skip served by a larry car. The trestle was constructed of concrete columns and steel stringers. Bins were made of steel and V shaped with hand operated gates for discharging contents directly into the larry car. There were four stoves, each 22' x 100' with 4½" checkers. There were five 609 H.P. Sterling boilers rated at 250 pounds with steam pressure 125 degrees superheat. They were combination gas and coal fired and built to carry 100 percent overload.

A pump house was built at the lakeshore equipped with three Worthington centrifugal motor driven pumps with a capacity of 5,500 gallons per minute each. The pumps discharged into a stand pipe 20' dia. by 135' high.

In the main power house there was a 1,500 K.W. turbine generator; one 1,000 K.W. frequency changer; one motor generator set with switchboard; transformers and switchgear. Blowing equipment consisted of two Ingersoll-Rand turbo blowers with four stage, water cooled air end, direct connected to and driven by live steam condenser turbines. Capacity of each unit was 55,000 cubic feet per minute with 16 lb. pressure. The turbines were connected to a barometric condenser.

As noted earlier, Witherbee Sherman resumed control of the Cedar Point Furnace (No. 1) on April 1, 1919 and during the remainder of the year spent $154,663 repairing and upgrading the plant, raising its capacity to 225 tons per day. No. 1 Furnace began operations in 1920 and continued during construction and start-up of No. 2 Furnace in 1923. Below are shown blast furnace statistics for the five year period 1920-1924.

	No. 1 - Cedar Point		No. 2 - New Furnace		
Year	Days	Tons	Days	Tons	Total
1920	261	57,922			57,922
1921	179	39,368			39,368
1922	46	9,926			9,926
1923	308	55,861	138	36,285	92,146
1924	40	7,547	98	37,609	45,156
Total	834	170,624	236	73,894	244,518

For comparative purposes during those same years, Witherbee Sherman mine production of crude ore and shipping product (lump ore and concentrates) is shown in the following table. Year end inventory of shipping product and its value for those years is also shown.

	Mine Production - Tons		Year end Inventory	
Year	Crude Ore	Shipping Prod.	Tons	Value
1920	925,744	525,758	141,582	$ 511,554
1921	522,397	299,831	367,249	1,113,392
1922	444,518	245,012	536,430	1,532,263
1923	414,077	228,580	323,239	1,110,673
1924	174,966	107,923	343,992	1,091,619
Total	2,481,702	1,407,104		

New construction expenditures for the mine plant and for the blast furnace plants during those years were as follows:

Year	Mine Plant	Blast Furnace Plant	Total
1920	$179,305	$ 120,661	$ 299,966
1921	127,322	23,425	150,747
1922	41,397	1,206,324	1,247,721
1923	228,371	1,545,804	1,774,175
1924	92,805	93,317	186,122
Total	$669,200	$2,989,531	$3,658,731

APPENDIX N

No. 3 Concentrating Mill Fire and Ore Handling to No. 5 Mill

The destruction of No. 3 Concentrating Mill and Harmony "A" Shaft head-frame by fire required major changes in ore handling to keep Harmony Mine in operation. A connecting level on plus 200 Level between Harmony and Old Bed Mines was equipped for a haulage level to deliver Harmony ore through Joker Shaft to No. 5 Concentrating Mill. No. 3 and No. 5 Mills had been operating on a one shift basis due to reduced mine production. After the fire No. 5 Mill was operated on a two shift basis to treat both Old Bed and Harmony ore. In September, Old Bed Mine operations were discontinued and the mill ran Harmony ore only the remainder of the year and through February 1924. Harmony Mine remained idle the rest of 1924. Old Bed Mine operated from March 1 to May 17, 1924 when all mine operations ceased. Only mine pumping and equipment maintenance were continued. The mines remained idle during all of 1925.

No. 3 Concentrating Mill, built in 1910, was considered fireproof. Some wood platforms around machinery, conveyor belting, lubricants and electrical connections were potential sources of fire. In addition, the right mixture of fine dust and air within the mill building, once a fire started, provided an explosive atmosphere. The exact cause of the fire was not known. One man, who observed the fire from the bank in back of Memorial Hall, told me sheets of corrugated iron roofing from the mill building were lifted by the force of the fire a hundred feet in the air and resembled sheets of paper floating down. The mill was not rebuilt.

The timber frame, corrugated iron sheet covered headframe over "A" shaft, destroyed in the fire, was replaced with an all steel frame structure and the shaft house enclosed with corrugated iron sheeting. A crude ore bin at the headframe fed crude ore hoisted to an 8K Gates gyratory crusher which discharged via a short conveyor to railroad cars. The cars were hauled about one quarter mile to No. 5 Concentrating Mill. Transfer of Harmony ore to No. 4 Concentrating Mill at New Bed was tried but the excess handling proved too costly. Both Harmony and Old Bed ores were processed in No. 5 Mill until 1940.

APPENDIX O

H. A. Brassert & Co. Recommendations and Report

The Brassert Report, dated February 17, 1925, noted the financial position of Witherbee Sherman and Company by its balance sheet of November 30, 1924. Assets and liabilities were:

Assets		Liabilities	
Inventories	$1,875,248	Notes payable	$1,580,000
Notes & accts. receivable	194,640	Accts. payable	180,143
Cash	46,747	Accrued bond int.	19,000

Of the inventories, $1,198,226 was in iron ore, $111,213 in pig iron and $565,809 in supplies, stores, etc.

The Profit and Loss Statements showed a loss of $2,036,160 for 1923 and $818,553 for the first eleven months of 1924. The consulting engineers' report stated the company would be in the hands of its creditors unless this long period of loss could be immediately ended and profitable operations commenced.

A plan of immediate action was outlined in the report to ameliorate the situation. Features of the plan included operation of No. 2 Blast Furnace through the year 1925, producing 456 tons of pig iron per day. Ore inventories would be reduced by the furnace operation and a projected sale of 280,000 tons of ore on hand. Old Bed would resume operations in June and Harmony in August. If the pig iron and ore sales goals were met, 83,000 tons of Old Bed and Harmony concentrates would be carried in inventory into 1926. The projected plan would strengthen the working position of the company by reducing ore inventories by $845,239 and achieving an operating profit of $229,593.

Ore sales in volume were considered absolutely essential for the continued existence of the company. Operation of the furnace alone included a charge over operating cost of more then $4.00 per ton of pig iron for interest, sinking fund, taxes and idle expense. A successful sale of ore would reduce mining costs to favor the operation.

The consulting engineers' report examined the eastern ore market noting radical changes that had taken place in recent years. These were due in part to postwar causes leading to importation of European and African ore; the industrial depression and low exchange rates abroad; the oversupply of shipping and the expansion of Bethlehem Steel Corporation in the market area with fully integrated operations with respect to ore supply. In addition to these changes, there had been damaging competition since 1920 which had forced old established merchant plants into partial or complete inactivity. Potential sales of Witherbee Sherman ore to the remaining operating furnaces were estimated from a yearly minimum of 190,000 to a maximum of 563,500 tons, with no likelihood the maximum could be sold in 1925.

The Sinter Plant at Port Henry was a Greenawalt single pan plant with a daily capacity of 350 tons. It was originally designed to agglomerate blast furnace flue dust containing ore with fine concentrates for mixture in the blast furnace feed. Sinter was so successful in the blast furnace, particularly with Adirondack fine ore concentrates, that addition of two more units were recommended for immediate construction to provide a capacity of 1,050 tons of sinter per day. This would permit the Port Henry furnaces to operate at near full capacity with sinter feed and produce a superior pig iron product at lower cost.

The consulting engineers recommended Witherbee Sherman and Company push the sale of sinter to furnace customers, and the sale of concentrates to customers where sinter plants were installed. They correctly foresaw that much of the tonnage shipped from Port Henry in future years would be used in the blast furnaces as sinter. They stated that any failure on the part of the company to demonstrate the advantages of sinter, as applied to local ores, by full use in its own operation, by sale of sinter and by sale of ore for sintering in other plants, would be most lamentable.

In addition to competitive forces already mentioned, Port Henry furnaces were faced with competition in the near future by new furnace construction at Everett, Massachusetts, and rebuilding on an increased scale the furnace at Troy, New York. It was projected that these two furnaces would have an annual capacity of over 300,000 tons. This competition would require a strong competent sales effort if Witherbee Sherman was to acquire and hold a market share.

The H. A. Brassert & Company consulting engineers, in their report, recommended the following:

1. A contract be made with Pilling and Company of Philadelphia to handle the sales of ore and pig iron, with the services of George P. Pilling because of his technical expertise and knowledge of the market area.

2. Construction of the sintering plant addition, regretting that capital expenditures should be necessary at the time, but believing the company had no chance of successful operation with the current production of sintered ore.

3. The mines to be started as late in the year as possible, and that they operate at as high a rate of production as possible during the period of operation, avoiding the accumulation of inventories beyond the minimum necessary to carry on the business in sight, and definitely contemplating a winter shutdown in the absence of a

greater sale of the projected maximum considered possible.

4. The continued regulation of the idle expense at the mines was recommended with the expectation that many months would elapse before resumption of operations could be expected.

5. The extreme importance of economy in operation of the Lake Champlain and Moriah Railroad as a means of reducing the cost of ore for sale and for use in the manufacture of pig iron.

6. Finally, the report called attention to the fact that the competition in pig iron in the near future would call for greater economies than had yet been accomplished in the operation of the plants.

In conclusion the report stated, "Increased tonnage is a means to these economies, but still more truly, economies are a means of increased tonnage. Your company can only be extricated from its present position by a long period of favorable business, coupled with an intensive effort towards lower costs."

APPENDIX P

Mineville Ore Bodies and Mining Methods During the 1920's

The ore bodies of the Mineville District, mined through the Old Bed, Harmony and New Bed, are situated within the area of the Adirondack gneisses and Grenville limestone. This area is penetrated by small masses of intrusive gabro and the principal ore bodies are adjacent to one of these masses. The gneisses are pre-Cambrian and, from the associated presence of limestone, it is generally accepted that they are of sedimentary origin. The Country rock is thoroughly metamorphosed. Faulting is quite prominent with the fault planes cutting both gneissoid rocks and ore beds. The entire structure is folded and refolded, but the ore horizon is continuous.

The ore bodies dip to the southwest at an angle of from 20 to 30 degrees from the horizontal. They extend several thousand feet along the dip and the distance along the strike appeared to be increasing with depth during this period of operation and showed no signs of terminating. In thickness, the veins varied from six to one hundred feet, with the average being ten feet of mineable ore. The Lower Old Bed, mined through Joker Shaft and commonly called the Joker Mine, was high in phosphorus. Six hundred feet above and offset somewhat to the right looking down plunge was the Harmony vein, a medium phosphorus ore. Still further to the right was the New Bed vein, a low phosphorus ore.

The ore and footwall contact in all mines is very sharp. In Lower Old Bed the ore and hanging wall contact is also sharp. In Harmony and New Bed Mines, however, the ore gradually fades out into the gneiss forming the hanging wall. There was some martite, a crystalline hematite similar in appearance to magnetite, present in the Harmony vein. This could not be recovered by the magnetic milling process, and passed into mill tailings. The average grade of Lower Old Bed crude ore was 50 percent iron as mined; Harmony was 36 percent and New Bed 30 percent.

Due to the flatness of the ore bodies it was necessary to sink declined shafts, called slopes, along the footwall, and the main workings were turned off from them. The mining method was open stope with pillar support. In any mining area the hoisting slope was kept in advance of working faces. It was driven about seven feet in the footwall parallel with the ore. The distance was maintained to eliminate unnecessary mining in rock. Levels were driven on thirty foot intervals, leaving a shaft pillar thirty feet long. This practice was maintained in both main hoisting and auxiliary slopes. From the level driven from the hoisting slope a raise or inclined drift was driven to the level above.

As soon as a breakthrough was completed to form a pillar, slabbing operations by drilling and blasting were started; the broken ore falling to the lower level. One reason for the close spacing of levels was that the force of the blast would throw the ore down to the level where it was hand shoveled into a hand pushed tram car. The close level interval concentrated the work force for efficient supervision.

Slabbing operations were continued until the stope opening between the two levels was large enough to maintain a safe roof. The level was then advanced the width of another pillar and a second raise driven to the level above. The cycle of operations was then repeated. While the second pillar was being formed another level was started from the hoisting slope, and the shaft pillar was formed simultaneously with the second pillar of the level above. Each level opened lagged one cycle behind the next level above.

As these mining levels were advanced from the hoisting slope, light rails, generally thirty pounds per yard, were laid on hardwood ties and spaced three feet, the nominal gage of the car wheels. The drilling or slabbing operation was done by one drill operator, and it was required of him to blast enough ore for a two-man muck crew the next shift. The hand muckers kept their track in repair and laid rails as required. They used short handle round point shovels called in miners' jargon "muckstick," "banjo" or "Mexican dragline." The tram car, built in the company shops, was a one and one-half ton capacity end dump that was hand pushed by the muck crew to the hoisting slope and dumped directly into the hoisting skip, or in some cases into a small storage pocket. The muck crew then hand pushed the empty car back for reloading. Hand tramming distance occasionally exceeded three hundred feet. The track was slightly graded to favor pushing the loaded car.

Each hoisting slope had a slope boss in charge of the operation. He directed the drillers, usually marking the holes to be drilled with the flame of his carbide cap lamp. This left a black mark on the rock or ore wall. (Names and numbers marked on the wall in this manner and not blasted away were visible fifty years later.) The slope boss checked the hand mucking locations to insure that cars were fully loaded and production maintained. There was also a bell-ringer at the hoisting slope who tallied on a peg board cars dumped, and he made certain the hoisting skip was available when cars were ready to dump. Each slope also had a roofman to check the roof and take down loose ground in the work areas.

In well ventilated stopes drilling in the slabbing operation was done by one man with a tripod-mounted dry type air operated hammer drill. Hexagon 7/8" hollow drill steel was used with one end forged and hardened into a cross bit. Drill steel was forged and re-sharpened in a central underground drill shop at each mine. Each driller used several pieces of steel per shift and he brought his daily supply from and to the drill shop. Blasting was done with 40 percent gelatin dynamite in eight-inch cartridge form, and the blast initiated by a safety fuse and blasting cap in each drill hole. A hand-held jackhammer with a short drill steel was used to drill short holes in large chunks of ore or rock that were not broken fine enough in the slabbing operation. Smaller chunks, too heavy for the muckers to lift into the cars, were broken by them with twenty-pound sledge hammers.

I recall that in 1971 one of the maintenance men found an Ingersoll-Rand dry type jackhammer of 1920's vintage in the old mine workings on an upper level. He brought it to the underground repair shop where the drill repairman cleaned the caked dirt and corrosion off the exterior of the machine, then connected an air hose to the drill. It started and ran as if it had been used the day before. It had been well oiled when last used nearly fifty years earlier.

Each mine had a main hoisting slope that in cross section was usually twelve to fifteen feet high by twenty feet wide. This size permitted erection of station platforms over the slope, double tracks for balanced ore hoisting and room for a walkway, and main air and water lines. Numerous faults required driving auxiliary slopes within the fault blocks in order to eliminate frequent rock drifts. At intervals of 1,000 to 1,500 feet along the main hoisting slopes, main haulage levels were driven in the footwall. They were about ten feet high by fifteen feet wide in cross section. From these haulage levels crosscuts were driven to the ore body and storage pockets raised beneath the auxiliary slopes. These pockets were designed to hold from 500 to 1,000 tons of ore.

Haulage levels and rock crosscuts were driven by two-man drill crews. Heavy wet type air operated hammer drills were mounted on steel column bars which were wedged against the roof and floor of the drift. Round one and one-quarter-inch hollow drill steel, with cross bits forged on one end, was used in the drifts. A normal drift round required twenty-six holes to blast an advance of the drift heading six feet. The drift round was mucked up by a hand mucking crew, a small mechanical air shovel, or an electric shovel. A four-ton side dump car was used, with locomotive haulage over forty-five pound rail three foot gage track. These headings were gassy from powder smoke. Wetting down the roof, heading, walls and muck pile at the start of the muck shift, and exhaust or blow fan piping from a fresh air source helped. Otherwise, workers would develop a severe headache.

Trolley type electric locomotives were used in all the mines. Three ton and seven ton locomotives were each equipped with two General Electric direct current motors. There were also smaller trolley type locomotives, completely built in the company shops, that served for single car short distance haulage. The locomotives operated from an overhead trolley wire. The bare trolley wire was the source of a pretty good jolt to anyone carrying a drill steel or pipe over his shoulder if it happened to come in contact with the wire.

The main hoisting slopes in Lower Old Bed and Harmony Mines delivered ore to storage pockets at the foot of the surface hoisting shafts. New Bed Mine hoisting slopes delivered ore to storage pockets above the tunnel level from where it was hauled out of the mine by locomotive to the mill.

Loading ore with scrapers was developed at Mineville in the 1920's. Scraper loading was more productive and safer than hand mucking in open stopes. The scraper hoist used was designed by the company engineers and completely built in the local mine shops. It was a two drum clutch-type unit with planetary gearing mounted on a steel frame and driven by a 25 horsepower direct current motor. The scraper hoist motor could be operated by connecting it to the rail and trolley wire. The scraper drag was the hoe type, designed and built locally. Motors on the scrapers were later changed to operate on alternating current. One of these old units was still in operation in 1979 for scraping silt out of a remote water storage dam.

APPENDIX Q

Formation of Republic Steel Corporation, 1930

The formation of Republic Steel Corporation on April 9, 1930 was the result of long-range plans of industrial financier Cyrus Eaton to consolidate various mining and steel making facilities. Mr. Eaton had acquired the old Republic Iron and Steel Company as a nucleus for a new efficient profitable midwestern steel company. In putting the new company together he hired T. M. Girdler, president of Jones and Laughlin Steel Corporation, as chairman to effect the consolidation of other companies into Republic Steel. The task was a difficult one, for the company was launched at the beginning of the worst financial depression in American history.

Tom Girdler was a graduate mechanical engineer who, from the beginning of his career, had hands-on operating experience at all levels of operation and management in several steel companies. He possessed good organizational ability and could pick competent men and let them make decisions and run their operations. He brought Rufus J. Wysor and Charles M. White to Republic from Jones and Laughlin. Both of these men had broad plant operating experience that had elevated them to executive positions. Their immediate task under Girdler was to mold the various units and acquisitions of Republic into an efficient company, headquartered in Cleveland, Ohio. Despite the troubled economic depression of the early 1930's, their efforts were successful. I believe this was due largely to confidence of lending institutions in the record and capability of Republic's management team.

APPENDIX R

Crushing and Wet Concentrating Mill to Replace No. 5 Mill, 1940

The plan featured utilizing the existing primary crushers at Harmony and

Joker Shaft headframes with conveyors from the headframes to the new secondary dry crushing and screening plant to be located west of No. 5 Mill. An existing crude ore bin at Joker and a new 1,200-ton crude ore bin in the Harmony conveyor line would provide crude ore storage ahead of the crushing plant. Ore entering the plant would pass over and through vibrating screens and cone crushers to produce a minus 5/16" nominal size crushed ore, then conveyed to the existing No. 5 Mill rail shipping bin. Oversize material in the crushing plant screening process would pass over pulley-type single drum magnetic separators where rock in stone size No. 1 through 3 would be rejected to yard storage and the retained ore conveyed to the cone crushers for further grinding to crushed ore size. Crushed ore from the crushing plant shipping bin would be loaded directly into L. C. & M. Railroad cars and transferred to the new wet concentrating mill.

The wet concentrating mill was planned to be built on the company-owned lakeshore property at Port Henry. Here at Cedar Point the Witherbee Sherman blast furnaces had produced pig iron since 1875; the large sinter plant had converted No. 5 Mill concentrates to sinter; and the storage dock with ore bridge crane and rail lines furnished efficient rail car loading for year-round rail shipment or seasonal barge loading for water shipment to consuming plants.

Old Bed crude ore, hoisted to Joker shaft headframe, was passed over a slow moving Jeffrey Picking Table where several men hand picked the chunks of rich ore and put them in a chute that fed directly into a railroad car, or to a storage bin. This product was high in magnetic iron and made a suitable lump ore for direct feed into open hearth furnaces. The lump ore was about 25 percent of the crude ore mined. The remainder, or 75 percent of the Old Bed crude ore was conveyed to the new crushing plant or held in storage at Joker Shaft headframe.

The new crushing plant had a designed capacity of 300 tons per hour, operating two eight-hour shifts per day to handle production from both mines. An excellent dust collecting system, carefully monitored, reduced dust within the plant and outside atmosphere to acceptable standards.

The new wet concentrating mill at Port Henry, called No. 6 Mill, had a designed capacity of 200 tons per hour operating three eight-hour shifts per day. The mill featured two independent units. Crushed ore delivered from the Mineville crushing plant in railroad cars was gravity-dumped into either Harmony or Old Bed crushed ore bins.

With the general plan for the crushing plant and wet concentrating mill finalized, the local engineering group furnished the necessary survey work, maps and field work. Design and detail drafting was done in Republic's Buffalo district engineering office. Drawings were sent to the local engineering office for approval or necessary revisions. A couple of construction engineers came from Buffalo to assist in erecting the structures and equipment. However, the field work rested with the local group with Lowell Henry supervising engineering at the concentrating mill and John Jacka handling the Mineville engineering supervision.

From the bins the ore was fed by belt conveyor to high intensity wet magnetic rougher separators. There were two of these separators for each mill unit. The roughers removed as much free gangue, or waste tailings, as possible. The tailings flowed by gravity to an 8-inch pump and were discharged through a rubber-lined steel pipe to the tailings waste area. Iron-bearing material retained by the roughers was passed over 10 mesh vibrating screens. The screen oversize was fed to an 8 by 8-foot ball mill and ground to minus 10 mesh, and discharged to join the undersize from the 10 mesh vibrating screen flowing through launders to a second set of four high intensity wet magnetic separators called finishers. The finishers produced high grade magnetic iron concentrate and clean tailings. The tailings joined the rougher reject to waste disposal. The iron concentrate was dewatered by two 5 by 10-foot inside drum filters and elevated to storage bins for delivery to the sinter plant as required.

When processing 4,800 tons of crushed ore per day, the wet concentrating mill was estimated to produce 3,000 long tons of high grade iron concentrate, averaging 68 to 69 percent iron with a Harmony concentrate phosphorus content of 0.025 percent, and an Old Bed concentrate phosphorus content of 0.25 percent.

In the summer of 1940, when No. 6 Mill was ready to begin production, Republic Steel executives and several invited guests assembled at Port Henry to observe the operation. One of the invited guests was Dr. E. W. Davis, director of the University of Minnesota Mines Experiment Station. The demonstration was a success. The plant produced iron concentrate which was low in phosphorus and silica and contained over 70 percent iron.

Republic Steel vice president Donald B. Gillies, who was also present at the demonstration at No. 6 Mill, asked Dr. Davis to stop at Cleveland on his way back to Minnesota and describe the plant operation to other Republic officials. At the meeting in Cleveland Dr. Davis described the successful new wet concentration process. The success of the plant pleased Charles M. White, Vice President of Operations, and Dr. Davis told him he should go to Port Henry and see the plant in operation. He also remarked to Mr. White that he should visit Minnesota where there was a really big taconite magnetite property. Dr. Davis reported that Mr. White told him to go back to his laboratory and have a good time with that taconite, but not to expect him to have any interest "in that God-damned hard stuff or anything else in Minnesota until you get over the idea of taxing everything to death."

With the new crushing plant at Mineville and No. 6 wet concentrating mill at Port Henry in operation, No. 5 Mill at Mineville ended concentrate production. Hand sorting of Old Bed lump ore at Joker shaft was a costly operation with eight men per shift involved. It was decided to mechanize this operation by installing a lump ore plant in the idle No. 5 Mill building. The plant featured a double deck vibrating screen and two 30-inch-diameter by 36-inch face magnetic pulleys. Old Bed ore, primary crushed at Joker Shaft and conveyed to the lump ore plant, was fed onto the double deck screen. The top deck was covered with 3-inch screen and the bottom deck with 1½-inch screen. The 3-inch oversize ore from the top screen was fed by gravity to one magnetic pulley and the 3-inch undersize and the 1½-inch oversize ore from the bottom screen was fed to the other magnetic pulley. Lean ore rejected by the magnetic pulleys joined the 1½-inch screen undersize and was conveyed to the crushing plant. Lump ore retained was fed directlyinto railroad cars for shipment to consuming steel plants.

Concentrate produced at No. 6 Mill was conveyed from storage bins to the adjacent sintering plant built by Witherbee Sherman Corporation. Sintering is a process which results in partial fusion of iron ore particles. The purpose is to agglomerate the fine ore, giving the blast furnace operator a strong porous product charge for the furnace as contrasted to the dead, blanket-like charge of fine ore. With sinter the fine ore flue dust losses are lessened.

The sintering plant at Port Henry was a Greenawalt plant with five pans, each ten feet by twenty-four feet. The plant was divided into two parts for treating two grades of ore. Three pans sintered Old Bed and two pans sintered Harmony concentrate. Each part of the plant was a complete unit in itself, having its own conveying, elevating, mixing and charging equipment. Suction for the burning process was furnished by fans, one for each pan.

Ore from the concentrate bins and fine anthracite coal from storage bins were fed onto a common conveyor in the correct proportion by table feeders. The conveyor discharged onto a second conveyor which ran underneath the fines bins under the sintering pans. Approximately twenty percent sinter fines, ¾ inch or smaller size, were added to the incoming feed. The total mixture was elevated to the top floor of the sinter plant, then passed through a pug mill or mixer, where it was thoroughly mixed. Some water was added as a temporary binder. The pug mill discharged directly into a bin. A charge car, holding ten tons, which was loaded from beneath the bin, carried the mix to the pans and filled them to a depth of ten inches. One filling of the car was sufficient to charge one pan. After charging, an ignition car with low pressure fuel oil burners was placed over the pan. Suction was started and the top of the bed of ore ignited.

Burning continued for about seventeen to twenty minutes, depending on moisture, amount of return fines, porosity of the bed and amount of carbon present. At the completion of burning time, the pan was rotated on its trunions, and the sintered product was passed over screens to gondola railroad cars for shipment. The screened fines were returned to be included in the charge mix.

Republic Steel had made substantial improvements to the sinter plant by the time No. 6 Mill began operation. The five pans, handling minus ten mesh Old Bed and Harmony concentrates, had a capacity to handle the entire output of both Harmony and Old Bed Mines. Sinter had proved its value in the blast furnace, not only as a mix with other ores to improve grade, but sintered ore required less heat time in the blast furnace. This represented real savings to the furnace operator through lower fuel cost per ton of iron produced and increased tons per day of furnace operation. Republic Steel furnaces then had the capacity to use far more tons of sinter than its Adirondack district was developed to produce.

APPENDIX S

Ore Handling Plan for Single Shaft Hoisting

The Harmony and Old Bed Mines operated in two distinct ore beds, lying one above the other. The strike of both beds was southeast and northwest, dipping about thirty degrees to the southwest. The Harmony upper ore bed and Old Bed or Joker lower ore beds were connected underground at two elevations but were mined separately with the ore hoisted to surface through separate shafts. In the proposed new mining plan the existing mining method and ore handling system would be abandoned. Ore from both the Harmony and Old Bed ore beds would be handled through a single central hoisting shaft. As the new shaft was to be a decline located on the Harmony or upper ore bed, ore transfer drifts were planned at proper locations through the Harmony footwall to the Old Bed ore.

Following approval for sinking a new mine shaft to replace ore hoisting through Harmony "A" and Joker Shafts, extensive, precise survey work was begun. The shaft plan called for sinking an eight by twenty-foot declined shaft through 350 feet of overburden consisting of clay, quicksand and gravel containing many large boulders. This would connect with a raise to be driven from underground workings on line and grade with the shaft.

In Old Bed and Harmony Mines survey work had been carried underground from surface in each mine, starting from established survey stations on surface that had been used for Witherbee Sherman and Port Henry Iron Ore Company land surveys. Elevations were relative to the surface of Lake Champlain. Surface and underground mine locations were plus or minus the surface of the lake. The surface of the new shaft site was plus 1050 elevation.

Underground connection between the "21" and lower workings of Port Henry Iron Ore Company and Witherbee Sherman Old Bed Mine, or Joker workings, had been established in early years because both companies were mining parts of the same ore structure on their respective lands. Harmony Mine was first connected with the Old Bed workings by a crosscut drift on the plus 200 Level completed during the 1920's. In making the connection major survey errors, accumulated in the progressive mining in the two mines, were revealed. Check surveys were run and the errors corrected. The next connection was made on the minus 680 Level in 1937. A crosscut drift from Old Bed Mine intersected No. 3 and No. 8 Auxiliary Slopes sunk in Harmony Mine. I was working as a surveyor helper at the time these connections were made. Only minor survey closure errors were found at the breakthrough.

Connection of the new shaft from surface to the raise to be driven from the mine workings to meet it was critical. Repeated check surveys were run from main surface survey stations to underground stations to be used for continuing the shaft through and beyond existing mine workings. Our entire engineering group worked on this project running independent surveys. John Jacka, a mining engineer with shaft experience, was put in charge of survey work and engineering for the sinking operation. I was assigned to work with Mr. Jacka.

Harmony Mine "A" and "B" Shafts were vertical shafts from surface to the upper ore areas of Harmony Mine. To establish a precise survey for sinking the new shaft it was decided to plumb the two vertical shafts and survey the plumb lines from both surface and underground survey stations. To accomplish this a single wire was suspended in each shaft from surface to the underground level station in each shaft. Weights were hung on the end of the wires and each placed in a barrel of water to minimize movement of the wires. Multiple transit readings were taken from surface and underground survey stations to the wires. Independent readings were taken by Spencer LaMountain, Lowell Henry, Art Hughes and Ralph Mulholland. All of these surveys were balanced. The surveys were then carried from underground stations to the raise to surface, and from the surface stations to the sinking location of the new shaft.

A contract for sinking the shaft from surface through overburden to the mine workings was let to Dravo Corporation. Lloyd Fagley, superintendent for Dravo, and his crew of hand muckers were ready to begin excavation. After John Jacka and I staked out the sinking area, I handed a shovel to Jacka and, in an unofficial ground breaking ceremony, he took out the first shovel of dirt for the new shaft, handed the shovel to me, and I took out the second one. Thus began what later became known as the Don B Shaft in honor of Donald B. Gillies, vice president of Republic Steel Corporation.

Shaft sinking began in December, 1940. The grade angle was minus twenty-seven degrees and forty-four minutes. The line of the shaft passed under the electric shop and storehouse buildings. Steel shaft sets were erected every five feet as the heading advanced. Pneumatic spades were used to loosen the ground and the material was hand mucked into a small skip car. A single drum sinking hoist, set up on surface, raised and lowered men and material in the shaft. After the shaft had advanced fifty feet along the decline, the material over the shaft to surface was removed. Steel sets were installed and the area over the shaft backfilled. Thereafter for the next fifty feet along the decline the shaft passed through water-bearing free flowing ground.

In this quicksand area, spacing of shaft sets was reduced to two and one-half feet. We would set the grade for installing a steel set and within twenty-four hours it would settle three to four inches. We tried setting the steel high, but it could not be held to grade. The contractor and management considered putting in a caisson and driving the shaft under compressed air as was done with tunnels under the rivers in New York City. This would have been very expensive and time consuming. John Jacka suggested that as each shaft set was placed, the bottom sill be immediately concreted in place with quick-set cement, with the concrete extended to the sill on the previous steel set. This was tried and proved successful. We were able to place the sill pieces a little above grade, and within a few hours the grade was stabilized.

By March 10, 1941 the shaft heading was one hundred feet along the decline from surface. It had entered hard, dry consolidated ground strewn with many boulders that required blasting. Shaft sinking operations were on a three shift basis. That winter was extremely cold, with many days twenty-five degrees below zero or colder. I recall Jacka and I coming to surface after setting center lines and grades on those cold days. Our clothes, wet from working in the shaft, would freeze by the time we brought our instruments to the company garage, less than two hundred feet from the shaft.

By the end of March the shaft heading was one hundred ninety feet from surface. The heading was advanced one hundred twenty feet during April. At this point a seam of ground water was encountered and later piped to a mine reservoir. On May 22, 1941, five and one-half months after sinking began, the shaft holed through to the heading of the raise driven in rock from the Harmony Mine workings. When we set up the transit in the shaft and sighted to the center line string hanging in the mine raise, the transit vertical telescope line covered the string. The grade line was equally accurate. The shaft hole-through was dead on target.

While shaft sinking had been underway, surface facilities were under construction. A hoist building was built to house a 1,650 H.P. double drum Nordberg hoist that was formerly located at the Ironton Mine of McKinney Steel Company. Main switchboards and power control for the Mineville mines and surface plant were to be located in the hoist building. Foundations were poured for a second crude ore storage bin, portal house, headframe and 60" x 84" Traylor jaw crusher that had been purchased from the Ontario Power Commission.

Following breakthrough of the shaft from surface, the raise from mine workings to the shaft was enlarged to the eight by twenty-foot cross section size. The fully concrete-lined shaft through the overburden was continued with steel sets and concrete for fifty feet into the hard granitic gneiss country rock. The lined shaft was equipped with 110-pound rail double tracks and a manway.

To continue the shaft through old Harmony mine workings three large radius vertical curves were laid out along No. 3 Slope. The line of the old slope was not quite straight and it was necessary to remove some pillars and trim others to the planned shaft size. In grading the shaft bottom some graded material was put into the mined out areas. The roadbed of the shaft was provided with concrete piers at twenty-foot intervals to support four twelve by twelve-inch creosoted timber stringers. Six by eight-inch creosoted ties, fifteen feet long and spaced on thirty-inch centers, were bolted to the stringers to support the four 110-pound rails. Coarse reject rock from the crushing plant was used to ballast the track.

Level stations were constructed of concrete and steel at plus 200, plus 26, minus 550 and minus 680 Levels, with ore skip loading pockets below plus 200 Level and minus 680 Levels. As minus 680 Level was planned as an ore transfer level to bring Old Bed ore to the new shaft, two skip loading ore storage pockets were built at that level to segregate Harmony and Old Bed ore. This work was completed by 1943.

In later years the shaft was extended and level stations constructed at minus 850, minus 1035 and minus 1185 Levels, with ore skip loading pockets below minus 1035 and minus 1185 Levels. The final heading of the shaft was a little below the elevation of minus 1335 Level. The shaft grade from below 1185 Level to the heading was flattened to minus twenty degrees to assist the hoist in starting an overloaded ore skip. Hoisting loaded skips from 1185 pocket taxed the capacity of the hoisting equipment. Ore hoisting distances to surface were

2,500 feet from 200 pocket; 3,960 feet from 680 pockets; 4,500 feet from 1035 pocket and 4,900 feet from 1185 pocket. Don B Shaft ore skips weighed eleven net tons empty and carried an average ore load of fourteen gross tons for a total skip and ore load of 53,360 pounds.

The Don B Shaft and hoisting facilities were designed to serve the twenty-five-year term of the mining lease between Republic Steel Corporation and Witherbee Sherman Corporation. The lease would expire in May, 1963.

APPENDIX T

Old Bed Mine Plan to Deliver Ore to Don B Shaft

Improved ore handling underground in Old Bed Mine was concurrent with development of Don B Shaft from surface. Plans called for abandoning Joker Shaft and several underground main and auxiliary hoisting slopes. These would be replaced by one central underground hoisting slope with levels spaced at 300 feet along the slope. Studies indicated that slusher or scraper stope mining would efficiently operate at that level spacing. Larger locomotives and cars would transport each level production to the central underground slope. The hoisting slope would discharge to an ore pocket over a main haulage level crosscut drift to Don B Shaft.

There was some disagreement as to which underground slope would be redeveloped for the central Old Bed hoisting slope. No. 9 Slope was beneath and nearly in line with Don B Shaft. No. 10 Slope was east of No. 9 Slope and aimed more southerly. Some of the engineers believed the ore body would turn to the south but at the time there was no concrete evidence that would occur. No one offered a firm opinion in favor of No. 10 Slope. Based on the historical plunge of the Old Bed ore structure, and its logical projection, No. 9 Slope was selected by Bob Linney. No one argued against his choice. However, there was much second guessing in later years when further development revealed the ore structure swinging to the south.

The planned main haulage ore transfer drift for Old Bed ore to Don B Shaft utilized an existing drift on minus 680 Level connecting Harmony and Old Bed Mines. The drift was aligned and new track installed with overhead trolley wire for fast, safe train operation from a steel loading pocket beneath No. 9 Slope at Old Bed to the Old Bed car dumping station at Don B Shaft.

A 300 H.P. double-drum Nordberg hoist was relocated from another underground slope to a position in No. 9 Slope above the 680 Level ore transfer pocket. The hoist was equipped with the latest safety equipment. The drums were wound with one and one-eighth-inch diameter hemp center improved plow steel hoisting rope. The ropes were attached to seven-ton capacity ore skips for balanced hoisting. From 680 Level down, the slope was graded and double four foot gauge track installed on 13' 6" creosote treated ties. New mining level stations along No. 9 Slope were located at 300 foot intervals and constructed of steel and concrete. Steel skip loading pockets were installed below minus 1035 and 1335 Levels. The latter pocket served both 1185 and 1335 Levels. Skips loaded from these pockets dumped into the storage pocket above 680 Level from where ore was loaded by gravity into ore cars on 680 Level and transferred to the Old Bed ore pocket at Don B Shaft. The transfer haulage train consisted of a ten-ton trolley type locomotive and ten five-cubic-yard capacity side dump cars. Net load per car generally averaged ten long tons.

APPENDIX U

Changes in Underground Development and Mining Operations

Changes in development and mining methods were underway to coincide with completion of single shaft hoisting to surface through Don B Shaft.

All new mine levels were placed at a vertical interval of 150 feet. The general dip of the ore structure was 30 degrees, giving an inclined level interval of 300 feet which was the optimum distance for scraper stope operations. The vertical spacing was also ideal for gravity ore mining of the large folds in the Old Bed ore structure where a sublevel bench stoping method could be employed.

Compressed air at 100 pounds pressure for mining operations was furnished to Harmony "A" Shaft from compressors at A and B Power House, and to Clonan Shaft from a compressor in No. 1 Power House through twelve-inch lines to the shafts and underground. When Don B Shaft was constructed, a twelve-inch line was installed and continued as new mine levels were opened. A twelve-inch line was installed from Don B Shaft through 680 ore transfer level to Old Bed No. 9 Slope. At each level in both mines a six-inch air line was installed in drifts to the mine workings. Two-inch pipelines furnished compressed air from the drifts to the various stopes and work headings. Water for use in drilling and wetting down was similarly distributed to the work areas.

Electric power was furnished to the mine at 3,300 volts and stepped down for underground use to 440 and 110 volts. Underground ore hoists, pumps and scrapers operated at 440 volts. Power cables, suspended on messenger wire, were hung in the upper corner of drifts to carry power to stopes and other required locations. All equipment was carefully grounded.

The main mine levels from Don B Shaft and from No. 9 Slope were driven 9 feet high by 12 feet wide and on a plus ¾ of one percent grade to favor loaded trains from the work areas and for drainage of water. Drift tracks were 36-inch gauge with 60-pound rails laid on hardwood ties. The tracks were ballasted with material broken in the development operation. A drainage ditch was maintained on one side of the drift and air and water lines for drilling and development shovel operations were mounted on the side wall above the ditch. Drift curves were 50 foot diameter or more for good train operations.

Center and grade lines were put in by the mining engineers by precise survey. The direction line was set off center 18 inches on the gauge line of the left rail to aid in laying track. With a transit the engineers marked two points on line about eight feet apart on the roof of the drift. They then hand drilled a

5/8-inch hole about one inch deep at each point. A hardwood plug was driven into the drilled hole and a surveyor's spad driven into the wood plug on line. Strings were hung from the spads by the drill or track crews to sight the line. Grade lines were similarly installed with two spads eight feet apart on each side of the drift, four feet above the rail. Strings stretched across the drift furnished the line of sight for grade. In later years installing grade lines was simplified. Grade sticks with a hook on one end to engage the center line spad were cut to precise length and numbered 1 and 2. Number 1 stick was hung on the center line spad nearest the heading. Sighting along the bottom of the grade sticks maintained the ¾ of one percent grade. Sighting along the side of the sticks established direction.

In the nominally flat-lying ore areas, drifting generally followed the hanging wall of the ore. Overbreaks for scraper stope locations were shot 9 feet into the roof of the drift at 75-foot intervals. Two 8' x 12' rounds were driven back on each side of the overbreak above the drift. A loading platform was constructed over the haulage drift. Four 10" x 10" timbers were laid across the drift at the bottom of the overbreak. The timbers were covered with 3-inch hardwood plank and steel plate. A loading hole for dropping broken ore into cars was cut in the center of the platform over the track. In the side rounds on the hanging wall side of the overbreak, a 50 H.P. Ingersoll-Rand double drum slusher hoist was anchored in place. A five-foot wide hoe type scraper drag was provided to pull the ore or development material from the stope to the loading platform. The pull drum of the slusher hoist was wound with 350 feet of ¾" steel wire rope and the pull back drum was wound with 700 feet of 5/8" wire rope.

In the side rounds on the mining side of the overbreak a 6' x 8' raise was started to be driven up along the ore hanging wall to the level above. Air and water lines for drilling were carried forward as the raise was advanced. After blasting, a 10" sheave block was anchored at the heading to hold the pull back rope for the scraping operation. Following hole-through of the raise to the level above, air and water lines in the raise were connected to the lines on the level above. The lines were disconnected at the bottom of the raise. Stope mining was begun twenty-five feet from the platform and the raise widened twenty-five feet on each side to mine the ore along the hanging wall. As the heading advanced, ore in the bottom of the stope was mined by drilling down from a bench at the heading. Twenty-five-foot diameter pillars were fashioned between the stopes as the headings were advanced.

Mining from the raise and a bench from the raise along the hanging wall provided good ventilation and safe access to the stope after blasting. The goal in stope drilling and blasting was to break the ore sufficiently for the scraper to drag the ore to the scraper platform. Here, chunks too large to pass through the 30-inch-square loading hole were broken by a sledge. Larger chunks were blasted by a short drilled hole loaded with a minimum amount of explosive.

In the big folds of the ore structure in Old Bed Mine a major part of the ore was steep enough for gravity mining. The axis of the folds pitch downward about thirty degrees. In these areas an overbreak with loading platform and slusher hoist was installed as described above. On the stope side of the overbreak an 8' x 12' wide scram drift was driven along the strike of the ore body on a slight grade for drainage to the platform. From this scram drift fifty degree steep raises were driven on 45-foot centers up into the ore. At one end of the scram drift a raise was driven through to the level above. From this raise two 5' x 7' subdrifts were driven in the ore above and parallel to the scram drift. The subdrifts were spaced to leave a 30-foot floor pillar to support the haulage level above. A small two-drum air-operated slusher mounted at the raise and a 3-foot hoe type scraper pulled the broken ore from the sublevels to the raise. After the sublevels were completed the raise was equipped with a ladderway, air and water lines, and served as a manway for mining operations. At the opposite end of the scram drift a raise was driven up to connect with the sublevels. The opening was then enlarged and mining operations started.

Mounted jackhammers were used for slashing the ore from foot to hanging and hand-held jackhammers were used for drilling the benches. Explosives used in the mining operations were 40 percent gelatin dynamite in one-inch by eight-inch cartridges. Blasting was initiated by capped safety fuse. Blasted ore dropped by gravity through the raises to the scram drift. The ore was scraped and loaded as earlier described. As mining progressed in the sublevels, the drillers retreated toward the manway raise, mining the benches down and breaking into successive short raises which had been driven from the scram drift. By this mining method the miners were less exposed to the hazards of large open stope areas with high roofs.

Sublevel stope mining in large folds of ore as described above was a modification of the mining method applied at Lyon Mountain. At that mine instead of a scram drift for scraper loading from the raises, the raises were driven from the haulage drift and a timber chute with cut-off gate was installed for loading ore from each raise directly into ore cars. This method was tried at Mineville; however, Mineville ore was much heavier than the low-grade Lyon Mountain crude ore and broken ore falling to the chutes fractured the supporting timbers.

Prior to the introduction of sublevel stope mining in the big ore folds at Mineville, only occasional steep raises were driven for ore pockets or some other special purpose. In these instances the drilling method featured column mounted drills set up on a staging after each blast. This was back-breaking work. At Lyon Mountain the R-91 Gardner-Denver stoper drill was used for one-man steep raise drilling.

Victor and Walter Lashway were transferred from Lyon Mountain to instruct in sublevel stope mining and in use of the stoper drill for steep raises. Thereafter the stoper drill became a favorite tool for development miners. The Lashway brothers became section foremen at Mineville and remained until their retirement.

Ore trains for handling development and stope tons on the new levels featured five or more ten-ton capacity side dump cars hauled by Goodman or General Electric thirteen-ton locomotives powered by 54-cell, 108-volt Philco or Exide storage batteries. Each level was equipped with battery charging equipment. Development tons from drift headings or overbreaks were loaded by air-operated Eimco Model 21 shovel loaders. Stope tons were loaded by scrapers.

Development drillers and shovel operators were paid a bonus based on footage advance of development headings during a pay period. Stope miners were paid on the basis of tons mined, trammed and dumped into the level ore pocket in a pay period.

APPENDIX V

Crushing and Milling Facilities for Treating Fisher Hill Ore

The primary jaw crusher at Fisher Hill Mine was 48" x 60". The secondary crushing plant featured seven-foot Nordberg Symons standard and short head cone crushers and Tyler Ty-Rock 5' x 12' screens. The plant was equipped to handle 3,000 gross tons of crude ore per shift.

Permanent buildings at Fisher Hill and No. 7 Plant sites were constructed for large production and long life. At Fisher Hill the shaft portal house and headframe, ore bins, conveyors and secondary crushing plant were steel frame on concrete foundations and covered with corrugated iron sheeting. The hoist-compressor, storehouse-shops and change house-office buildings were of steel frame construction with concrete block curtain walls and metal doors and window sash. These facilities were built for a capacity of 800 employees but in peak production years only about one-third that number were employed at Fisher Hill. At No. 7 Plant the five-story mill, hydro-separator and pump houses were of steel frame concrete block curtain wall construction. The sinter plant building and conveyors were steel frame covered with corrugated iron.

Topography at No. 7 Concentrating Mill, sloping to the east, was downhill and favored product flow. Crushed ore, from the time it entered the mill until it ended in a finished iron concentrate, flowed by gravity from one section to the next. This was a wet magnetic separation process. Water was pumped from a storage dam on Bartlett Brook to a retaining pond at the mill. Seventy-five percent of the water used in the milling process was recovered by means of a hydro-separator, rake classifier and a 200-foot diameter thickener.

A sixteen-inch diameter steel pipeline was installed from a pump station at Lake Champlain to the mill as a backup if dry seasons reduced available water from Bartlett Brook. The water supply never failed and the lake pump station and three-mile pipeline to the mill were never used during the thirty-eight-year period of No. 7 Mill operations. However, twice during those years the lake pumps were started and the line to the mill checked for leaks.

The mill flowsheet, other then utilizing the advantage of gravity product flow, was similar in design to No. 6 Mill at Port Henry. No. 7 Mill, however, featured three independent units to mill Harmony, Old Bed and Fisher Hill ores separately. There was flexibility in design so any ore could be milled on any one or all three units. Each unit was capable of producing 100 tons of concentrate per hour. The milling equipment for each unit consisted of vibrating screens, a rod mill for grinding, magnetic separators and filters. The improved wet magnetic separators at No. 7 Mill were designed and patented by Bob Linney. In a series of tests on production these machines had produced over 71 percent magnetic iron concentrate, close to the 72.4 percent pure.

Northeast of No. 7 Concentrating Mill on the downslope of the terrain, the sintering plant was built to agglomerate the iron concentrate. The plant differed in design from the pan type plant at Port Henry. It featured two Dwight Lloyd 72" wide by 90' long, 14 windbox, continuous sintering machines. The plant layout provided space for a third sintering strand but it was never built. Support equipment for the sintering machines included a 100,000 cu. ft. per minute suction fan, pug mills, conveyors, feeders and ignition furnaces. Total sinter plant capacity was 3,000 long tons per twenty-four hours.

Although the mechanical features of the sinter plant at No. 7 Mill were of different design from the sinter plant at No. 6 Mill in Port Henry, the process for sintering concentrate was about the same. At No. 7 Plant, as at Port Henry, fine anthracite coal was mixed with concentrate, spread on a grate, the top of the bed ignited and air sucked down through the bed. The burning action of the coal mixed with the concentrate fused the iron particles in a porous mass that was discharged directly into railroad cars. At No. 7 Plant, however, the continuous traveling grate sintering machines, with the mixed coal and concentrate, ignited at one end of the sintering machine by a stationary ignition hood, completed the burning process in the travel distance of the moving sinter bed. Loading and discharge were continuous versus the intermittent charge car and ignition car loading and ignition of the sintering pans at the Port Henry plant.

With construction of Fisher Hill and No. 7 Plants, increased electric power was a necessity. A joint substation was built by Niagara Mohawk Power Corporation and Republic Steel in Mineville east of Plank Road. A 115 KV transmission line was run by Niagara Mohawk to the substation. Here six main transformers with switchgear reduced the 115,000 voltage to 34,500 for distribution to secondary substations at Fisher Hill, the Mineville Plant, and No. 7 Plant. The line to Fisher Hill ran north from the substation directly to the Fisher Hill substation; the line to the Mineville Plant ran westerly to a substation near Don B Shaft, then southerly to Moriah Center, continuing easterly to the No. 7 Plant substation. The 34,500 primary power at Don B substation was reduced to 3,300 volts. At Fisher Hill and No. 7 Plants it was reduced from 34,500 to 2,300 volts. Smaller substations provided further voltage reductions as required.

APPENDIX W

Railroad Equipment and Transfer of Milling to No. 7 Plant

Prior to plant expansion at Mineville and construction of Fisher Hill and No. 7 Plants, haulage equipment on the L. C. & M. Railroad was operating at capacity. Rolling stock included four steam locomotives and 100 thirty-cubic-yard, two-hopper, 50-ton capacity cars. Engines 16 and 17 were 85-ton main line locomotives. Engines 15 and 18 were 65-ton switch engines. All of this equipment, while having been well maintained, had been in service many years and was costly to operate. The main line locomotives could only haul fourteen empty cars up the steep grades from Port Henry to the mines. However, on the return trip twenty loaded cars could be brought down from Mineville to Port Henry. The ore cars were equipped with air brakes and brakemen rode the cars to assist the braking manually for reduced speed on curves and the steepest grades. The brakeman's job was hazardous, particularly during rainy or icy weather.

Producing concentrates from crushed ore through No. 6 Mill at Port Henry, and increased production from the mines, exceeded capacity of the railroad equipment. A new 1,000-horsepower, 125-ton diesel-electric locomotive and fifty new 35-cubic yard, 60-ton capacity ore cars were purchased in 1940. Within a year the four steam locomotives were removed from service and the diesel-electric engine handled all main line and yard switching requirements. The new equipment included improved braking features which greatly reduced the accident risk to brakemen. About one and one-quarter million tons of crushed ore per year were hauled from the mines to Port Henry at reduced operating and maintenance costs.

For handling the additional crushed ore produced at Fisher Hill, a second diesel-electric locomotive and fifty additional ore cars were purchased. All ore car wheels were changed from chilled cast iron to solid steel. This eliminated chipping of the treads and provided more protection to trains on the sharp curves. The new equipment and improvements did not reduce the trip time per train but tons per trip were nearly doubled.

Completion of new facilities shifted concentrate and sinter production from No. 6 Mill at Port Henry to No. 7 Plant in 1944. Concentrate production through Mills 5, 6 and 7 from May 1, 1938 through 1944 is shown below.

	No. 5 Mill	No. 6 Mill	No. 7 Mill
1938	132,926		
1939	398,294		
1940	117,896	312,050	
1941		542,523	
1942		555,150	
1943		545,270	
1944		39,380	711,551

The tabulation illustrates the shift of a major plant operation during a seven-year period with normal start-up and shut-down problems. No. 6 Mill was shut down during 1944 and only reopened for a few weeks in 1946 while negotiations between Republic Steel Corporation and Defense Plant Corporation were underway concerning lease and royalty for use of the facilities. In those few weeks, 64,672 tons of concentrate were produced through No. 6 Mill and the plant was then finally shut down. In its time, No. 6 Mill produced 2,058,045 gross tons of very high grade magnetic iron ore concentrate. Operating on a full production schedule with the fine grinding wet magnetic separation process, No. 6 Mill became a pilot plant for the North American magnetic iron ore industry.

Fisher Hill Mine began producing ore to the mill in December 1943 with 2,851 tons. Fisher Hill concentrates were first produced at No. 7 Mill in 1944, and in that year 88,891 tons were produced from 255,218 tons of Fisher Hill crude ore hoisted. The ratio was 3.10 tons of crude ore per ton of concentrate. The Fisher Hill concentrate was very high grade, over 68 percent iron and 0.009 percent phosphorus. This was the lowest phosphorus ore in the Mineville Iron District, comparable to the famous Chateaugay low phosphorus ore mined at Lyon Mountain.

APPENDIX X

Port Henry Iron Ore Co. Mining Method from "21" and Clonan Shafts in Late 1800's to 1924 and Republic Steel Mining Method from 1941

Underground mining from "21" Mine required sinking a decline shaft from the bottom of the open pit continuing the existing skipway from the tipple at surface down to the underground workings. The room and pillar mining method had been used to some extent underground in the massive ore above the bottom of "21" open pit and massive pillars of solid ore left to support the roof.

Underground from the decline "21" Shaft, the heading and bluff system of mining was used in early years wherein a heading was advanced beyond the shaft pillar on each level forming a room with a roof about 20 feet below the floor of the level above. The room was advanced around planned pillar locations by driving a heading about seven feet high along the roof of the room and following with an inclined bluff, mined by drilling lifters. Broken ore was hand loaded and trammed to the shaft.

Working near the shaft station in those early years, men used wheelbarrows to haul the ore and dump it directly into the skip. In going through the Welch mine workings many years ago we found one of the old wheelbarrows. It had a small box near the wheel, and very long handles which provided leverage for the mucker. They used to tell that one day in the early 1900's, a mucker in "21" Mine wheeled a load of ore to the shaft and, dumping it into the skip, hung onto the long handles and both he and the wheelbarrow went down the shaft. When the accident was reported, the mine foreman said, "Damn, that was a new wheelbarrow."

The mining method in "21" Mine was changed around 1900 wherein a vertical winze was sunk behind the shaft pillar on each level to the level below. Glory-holing was done around the winze until the broken ore reached its natural angle of repose. The bluff was then mined from the next level below by drilling lifters and advancing the bluff around regularly spaced symmetrical pillars. At planned elevations, floors were left between pillars to serve as braces to support the very high pillars of ore. On each lower level, pillars were located by careful survey directly below pillars on the level above. This provided a safe mine but left very high solid ore pillars standing with connecting floors.

Sinking of Clonan Shaft by Port Henry Iron Ore Company in 1909 improved ore hoisting to surface in "21" Mine. Electric shovels and locomotive haulage were introduced in 1916 to further improve the mining system and reduce costs. However, these measures did not forestall final shut-down of Port Henry Iron Ore Company operations in 1924.

In 1941 the refurbished Clonan Shaft provided access to the unmined Port Henry Iron Ore Company ore reserves for mining by Republic Steel during a period of high ore demand.

Inspections revealed the stable condition of pillars and connecting floors of solid ore. This indicated many could be safely mined. Pillars below and above the "horse" of rock were to be left for structural support. Those on either side of the "horse" with their floor braces were considered safe for removal. Pillars to be removed were cut away from the roof at the top, then mined down their full length.

To begin mining a pillar, long ladder sections were joined and raised from a sidewall bench or floor to the top of the pillar and anchored there with steel pins. Working from the ladder, a slash was drilled and blasted 8 feet high and 4 feet wide. For this first slash, a bar mount for the drill was securely clamped to the ladder. After the first slash was completed drillers were able to drill additional slashes from a column bar mounted drill jacked against the pillar and roof. In this manner the pillar was cut free from the roof.

Local shop-made steel eye pins were securely anchored to the roof above the pillar. From these pins long safety ropes were attached to each man working on the pillar. Down holes were then drilled with hand-held jackhammers and blasted to bench mine the pillar to the floor below. Ore from the mined pillars fell to the 430 Level. Here the broken ore was scraper loaded into mine cars using Ingersoll-Rand 50 H.P. slushers with local shop-built five-foot scrapers. Cars were locomotive hauled to the 430 Clonan Shaft pocket to be hoisted to surface. Three pillars were mined in this manner, furnishing about 60,000 gross tons of rich magnetite ore.

Pillar reclamation continued in several sections of the "21"-Joker- Bonanza ore body. Height of pillars varied between 100 and 400 feet. Those over 150 feet high had floor pillars and braces connecting to other pillars and the side walls. To mine some of these it was necessary to break through the floors before cutting off the top of the pillar to permit broken ore to fall through to the scrapers below. Access to the floors and braces was accomplished by raising ladders or driving short raises.

Time lost in maintenance of ladders led to the use of catwalks, suspended from the roof, for access to the pillars. These catwalks were projected from another pillar or from the sidewall to the pillar to be reclaimed. The suspended catwalks also furnished a means for inspection of the roof. Drilling a pillar following cut away from the roof was improved over the hand-held jackhammer method. Diamond drill equipment was hoisted to the top of the pillar and set up for down hole drilling. Vertical holes were drilled the full length of the pillar, loaded with dynamite and blasted with the blast detonated by Primacord. Thirteen vertical holes blasted in one of these pillars yielded over 16,000 gross tons of ore.

Pillars drilled and blasted by the long hole diamond drill method was a safer operation. All primary drilling was done under a low roof at the top of the pillar, versus the former benching method. Broken ore from the long hole blast laid in a pile beneath the catwalk. Required secondary blasting of large chunks and scraper loading operations were made safer by continuous daily roof inspections from the suspended catwalk.

APPENDIX Y

Drifting and Shaft Sinking in Fisher Hill and Smith Mines

Republic appropriated funds to sink the Fisher Hill Shaft from the sixth to below the twelfth level. This would provide six additional mine production levels and mine the ore structure to the limit of its hoisting facilities. Crosscuts were planned from two of these levels back through the footwall to ore projected from Smith Mine.

The sixth level drill crew consistently advanced the drift heading nine feet or better per drill cycle. Fisher Hill Mine ground, when properly drilled, broke well. The shovel operator on the sixth level always managed to have the heading cleaned and ready for the drillers on day shift. Sixth level development muck was locomotive hauled to the shaft station and dumped directly into the ore skip.

Fisher Hill Shaft, declined at thirty-three and one-half degrees, was 10' by 30' in cross section and featured three tracks of 5' 4" track gauge. Rails were supported on creosote treated ties fastened to 12" x 12" creosoted timbers supported every twenty feet on concrete piers. The south track was for man and material cage operation and was served by a single drum 500 H.P. Nordberg hoist operating at 800 feet per minute and winding one and one-eighth-inch diameter wire rope. The man cage was forty-eight man capacity, and long material was lowered on a flat car attached to the lower end of the cage. The north and center tracks were for ore hoisting by means of a double drum 2,000 H.P. Nordberg hoist winding one and three-quarter-inch wire rope. Ore hoisting could operate at 2,800 feet per minute but we cut down the speed to 2,100 feet per minute to conserve power and reduce risk of derailment at the higher speed.

Smith Mine ore body was Old Bed type ore that had last been mined prior to 1920 through Cook Shaft, with additional access through O'Neil Shaft. The ore dipped to the southwest and its continuation, proved by diamond drilling, lay beneath Fisher Hill ore. The vertical distance between the two ores was several hundred feet and similar to the relationship of Harmony and Lower Old Bed ores at Mineville. Studies indicated Smith Mine ore should be handled to surface through Fisher Hill facilities.

In the wartime development of Fisher Hill Mine a 3,000-foot crosscut drift was driven back through the footwall from the Fisher Hill third level to Smith Mine. Smith Mine had been full flooded since the 1920's and the flood water level was several hundred feet above the elevation of the third level drift. The crosscut drift was planned to pass close to O'Neil Shaft. When the heading was within a few hundred feet, a diamond drill hole was drilled to the shaft to drain mine flood water above the level of the drift. The water flowed through the crosscut drift to a Fisher Hill Mine pump station and was pumped to surface.

After draining Smith Mine through O'Neil Shaft, the crosscut drift was continued. At O'Neil Shaft a side round from the drift was opened to the shaft to furnish surface fresh air ventilation through the drift to Fisher Hill Mine. The crosscut drift was continued until it intersected the area that had been mined through Cook Shaft. The crosscut had been driven at a slight upgrade for drainage and when it intersected the mine workings, the Smith Mine flood water level was several feet below the floor of the drift. The drift was continued along the footwall of Smith Mine to the north bounds of the mine workings. No further development at Smith Mine was done at that time.

With the reopening of Fisher Hill in 1947, Smith Mine was to be drained and developed for mining. The depth of Smith Mine workings was at the same elevation as the sixth level of Fisher Hill Mine. The crosscut driven from Fisher Hill third level to a mined out area of Smith Mine in 1943-44 should have been driven from the fifth or sixth level. The lower flooded workings of Smith Mine had been developed but not mined by Witherbee Sherman and Company.

A power line was run through the crosscut, a substation installed, and a single drum hoist set up at an old hoisting slope. Pumping began on a twenty-four hour basis. As the mine water level receded, track was installed in the slope for about seven hundred feet. Two lower levels showed about eight feet of good Old Bed ore. On the south side of Smith Mine, Witherbee Sherman had developed a double track slope for several hundred feet that would have been a main hoisting slope. This slope heading also ended in ore and was planned for the major development of Smith Mine by Republic. A hoist location for the slope was excavated at the crosscut and the crosscut drift extended into the footwall of Smith Mine for a hoisting storage pocket.

Ed Winning, Republic's assistant vice president for mining operations, visited Fisher Hill Mine. He emphasized the urgency of getting Smith Mine development and Fisher Hill Shaft sinking underway with the recently appropriated funds.

For extending the shaft below the sixth level, we laid out a drill pattern that would permit slusher scraping to clean the heading. I designed a wheel mounted scraper slide with an Ingersoll-Rand 50 H.P. slusher hoist for the mucking operation. The standard box type scraper drag digging angle was modified to suit the scraping condition. Two men operated the scraper slide on the mucking shift, loading the small skip on the center track which replaced the center track ore skip for the shaft cleaning operation.

Fisher Hill Shaft was sunk at a thirty-three and one-half degree decline to just above the planned ninth level station, but far enough to build a shaft loading pocket that would serve the sixth, seventh and eighth levels.

APPENDIX Z

Republic Steel Ore Interest in Liberia and Minnesota

Republic Steel acquired a major interest in Liberia Mining Company which owned a large iron ore deposit in Liberia, West Africa. The Bomi Hills ore deposit was forty-five miles inland from the Liberian seaport of Monrovia. Ore from the mine was to be shipped by ocean freighter from the port at Monrovia to Baltimore, Maryland from where it would be rail shipped to Republic plants at Youngstown and Cleveland, Ohio. Charles Dewey, who had been involved in the initial development of Fisher Hill Mine and later transferred to Republic's Southern Ore Mines, was sent to Liberia Mining Company and placed in charge of the start-up and operations of the Bomi Hills Mine. An immediate problem facing Dewey was constructing and equipping a railroad from Monrovia to the mine.

In June 1950, Edward Greenwood, superintendent of the L. C. & M. Railroad, was sent from Port Henry to Africa to build the railroad. In July he started construction of the 42-inch narrow gauge railroad inland over the Liberian swampland northward to Bomi Hills. With a native force of 278 men, working in 95-degree heat, the forty-five-mile railroad, including nine steel bridges, was completed in 274 days. Ed returned home from Liberia May 4, 1951 and resumed charge of the L. C. & M. Railroad.

Domestically, Dr. E. W. Davis of the University of Minnesota Mines Experiment Station had been impressed with the No. 6 Mill fine grinding wet magnetic separation process he observed at Port Henry in 1940. He believed that process was the answer for developing the immense low grade Minnesota taconite ore reserves that had been known but undeveloped for decades. Dr. Davis recalled his 1940 discussion of taconite with Charlie White in which Mr. White told him not to expect him to have any interest in taconite or anything else in Minnesota until they got over taxing everything to death. Mr. White's strong statement undoubtedly reflected the opinions of other steel company executives.

Dr. Davis realized that taconite development was a dead issue unless the unfair Minnesota *ad valorem* tax on unmined ore was reduced or repealed. The law required that a mine property be taxed, usually 50 percent of full value, from the time of discovery until the ore was all mined out. Towns and cities had extended their corporate limits wherever possible to include ore properties and take advantage of the lucrative tax benefit. The mining companies' huge tax revenues available to the communities often resulted in excess civic expenditures for which there was no justifiable reason except that the money was there, supplied at little or no cost to voting homeowners and small businesses.

Attempts by mining companies and the Minnesota Legislature to control excess spending were strongly resisted until a report by a Legislative Commission on iron ore taxation was released in 1939. It clearly showed the high spending of communities with mining company tax income versus those without such income. The report was an education for many legislators. Some knew there were mines in the northern part of the state supplying ore to the steel industry, but had no knowledge of mining or its problems. Dr. Davis summed up the general public's attitude toward a mining venture as how much tax it would pay, rather than how large its payroll would be. The mining industry as a whole was partially to blame for failing to spend the time and funds to inform legislators and the general public of its problems and benefits.

In 1941 the Minnesota Legislature passed and Governor Stassen signed the Taconite Tax Law exempting taconite ore deposits from the formerly pro-hibitive *ad valorem* tax on mining lands. Two measures were included. One was a very small *ad valorem* tax retained for taconite, as its complete removal would have required a state constitutional amendment. In addition, a sliding scale tax of five to six cents per ton tied to grade of iron concentrate shipped was in-cluded.

Dr. Davis had been the moving force in getting legislators, chambers of commerce, news publishers, legal experts and others together to support tax laws that might get taconite mining started. He made countless speeches throughout the state to business and civic groups. There had been no organized opposition to the proposed law, as many people did not think the taconite indus-try would amount to anything. At one tax committee hearing on the bill, Dr. Davis spoke at length on the declining mining industry and the importance of taconite. One committee member was overhead remarking, "I think the old boy actually believes that stuff." The effect passage of the tax law would have on developing taconite mining remained to be seen. With its passage Dr. Davis sent copies of the new law to Charles White of Republic Steel.

Reserve Mining Company, formed in 1939 by Oglebay Norton, owned the old Mesabi Iron Company with a plant at Babbitt. Armco Steel Company was associated with Oglebay Norton in efforts to develop taconite mining. Erie Min-ing Company, formed in 1940 and owned by four steel companies, was man-aged by Pickands Mather. These two companies, Erie and Reserve, spent large sums and worked separately to develop the necessary technology for producing taconite iron pellets as a blast furnace feed.

By 1950, Reserve Mining Company was owned jointly by Armco and Republic Steel. Initially $185,000,000 was committed to build a mine plant at Babbitt, concentrating and pelletizing plants at a site on Lake Superior named Silver Bay, and a fifty-mile connecting railroad. The plans included complete townsites at Babbitt and Silver Bay, with harbor and ship loading facilities at Silver Bay for lake shipping to the two steel companies' consuming furnaces. Republic Steel was depending on a large annual tonnage of Reserve pellets when the plant achieved full production.

APPENDIX AA

Underground Development in Fisher Hill and Old Bed Mines in the 1950's

Mine development at Fisher Hill was expedited to provide replacement stopes for mining areas depleted on the upper levels. The shaft heading had been developed to near the ninth level location. This furnished sufficient room for a skip loading pocket that would handle ore from the sixth, seventh and eighth levels. The sixth level was nearly ready for production. Prior plans called for a shaft pocket to serve the sixth and seventh levels. However, due to the shaft heading location, the loading pocket plan was changed to serve levels six, seven and eight. Shaft stations were completed on levels seven and eight and drifts on these levels advanced to permit ore pass transfer raises to be driven from the eighth to seventh and seventh to sixth levels. The ore pocket below the eighth level was excavated and a steel loading pocket structure erected about forty feet from the shaft heading.

On the eighth level, excavations for a transformer substation, locomotive battery charging station, pump station and storage dam were completed and equipment installed. Main mine pumps were relocated from the fifth level to the eighth level pump station. Control gates were built at the ore passes on the seventh and eighth levels to control flow of ore as needed from the sixth and seventh levels. With these facilities in place, the Fisher Hill ore handling system was capable of handling full production to final mining through the eighth level.

Old Bed Mine was the major district ore producer. By 1950, as production shifted to lower mine levels, No. 9 Hoisting Slope became a production bottleneck. As hoisting distance increased from new producing levels to the 680 ore transfer drift, tons per hour hoisted decreased. The 1185 Level crosscut drift from Don B Shaft to Old Bed replaced 680 Level for Old Bed ore transfer. To reduce No. 9 Slope hoisting distance, an ore pocket was excavated and a skip dump erected in No. 9 Slope above 1185 Level for car loading on 1185 Level. A hoist room was excavated on 1185 Level and a rope raise driven from the hoist room to a skip dump in No. 9 Slope above 1185 Level. A double drum hoist, formerly at Harmony "A" Shaft, was rebuilt and installed in the hoist room with head sheaves at the top of the rope raise. A trolley type locomotive pulling a ten-car train hauled one hundred tons per trip 1,400 feet to the Old Bed pocket at Don B Shaft. The 680 hoist and ore transfer system were abandoned.

When No. 9 Slope was sunk to 1185 Level in the early 1940's, an auxiliary slope, east of and parallel to the double track ore hoisting slope, was begun. This slope would handle men and material and would be used to develop access to new levels. A skip dump and hoist room, with a shop-rebuilt single drum hoist, were provided on 1185 Level for the auxiliary slope. When the auxiliary slope began operating, it was used for development and moving men and material below 1185 Level. The decline of the slope was thirty degrees which permitted development muck to be scraper loaded into a small skip. As the auxiliary slope reached each level location, the level station was excavated and a loading chute built for passing development muck to the skip. From the level station a short drift was driven west to No. 9 Hoisting Slope. A raise was then driven to the bottom of the hoisting slope with only a small hole opened for ventilation. This left a temporary protective rock wall between the bottom of the slope and the new section being developed. This permitted enlarging the slope raise to the full hoisting slope size with new track work without interfering with ore hoisting on No. 9 Slope above. Broken muck from raising and enlarging the slope was scraper hauled and loaded at the auxiliary slope. Permanent air, water and pump lines to serve new levels were installed in the auxiliary slope.

No. 9 Auxiliary Slope was eventually completed to minus 2650 elevation. Level stations were built at minus 1500, 1650, 1800, 1950, 2100, 2250 and 2400 elevations. No. 9 Hoisting Slope was extended to minus 2250 Level. Skip loading pockets were constructed below Levels 1335, 1650, 1800 and 2100. Ore transfer pocket raises were installed from 1335 to 1185 Level, 1650 to 1500 Level, and 2100 to 1950 Level. These facilities served Old Bed Mine to final shutdown of the mines.

APPENDIX BB

Increased Ore Handling Problems, 1962

By 1962, seventy-five percent of ore mined was from Old Bed Levels 1500, 1800 and 1950. The remainder came from Harmony 1185 Level. This meant that three-quarters of crude tons mined had to be scraper loaded into cars at the stopes, locomotive hauled nearly 3,000 feet to No. 9 Slope storage pocket, loaded into No. 9 Slope skips and hoisted 2,180 feet through No. 9 Slope to 1185 transfer storage pocket, loaded into ore transfer cars, and locomotive hauled fourteen hundred feet to Don B Shaft 1185 storage pocket, and finally loaded into Don B Shaft skips and hoisted 4,825 feet through Don B Shaft to surface.

No. 9 Slope was the ore handling bottleneck. Haulage cars of ten-ton capacity delivered ore to No. 9 hoisting slope; 9 Slope ore skips held only six tons; 1185 ore transfer haulage cars held ten tons; and Don B Shaft ore skips had a capacity of thirteen tons. As production shifted more to the lower levels, No. 9 Slope hoisting became an around-the-clock operation. Frequently to supply ore for a five-day surface plant operation, it was necessary for No. 9 hoisting slope to operate twenty shifts to keep ahead of a five-day-week stope production and furnish enough ore to Don B Shaft for a daily two-shift hoisting schedule.

Development of 2100 Level was speeded up to ready replacement stopes for those nearing completion on upper levels. In prior years long crosscut drifts had been driven in rock from No. 9 Slope to the ore. Slusher drifts, raises and sublevels for ringhole stope drilling were scheduled to complete mining of available ore above 2100 Level. Sublevels and raises were normally driven in ore. Ore recovered from development work benefited the ratio of crude to concentrate. No funds were appropriated for the required development, thus the work was done as a part of mine cost.

The Old Bed ore structure down plunge had been cut by two major geological faults which raised the ore on the south side of the faults. This condition thus increased mining areas available on 2100 Level. Development of 2100 Level passed through these fault zones. Ground conditions were good, and roof support in drifts was maintained with roof bolts where required. However, steel support with cedar lagging was installed where development drifts, sublevels and scraper drifts encountered faults.

More ore was available on 2100 Level than on either 1800 or 1950 Levels. It was obvious this level would be the major and final producer from the mines if a new mine shaft development was not soon started. Our studies indicated that an operating hoisting shaft and surface plant facility would require a minimum of three years' time following completion of plans and contract award for construction. We planned to develop from underground one or two mining levels that would be ready for mining when the shaft was completed. Existing mine facilities would continue in use and only be abandoned when production was achieved through the new hoisting shaft. Failing this, it would take an additional two or three years for the new facilities to achieve full production.

APPENDIX CC

Development and Mining Methods, 1962

Initial development followed the slusher or scraper scram drift method with scraper hoists mounted on car loading platforms above the haulage level. For many years a locally built three-drill jumbo, with a three-man crew, was used for driving haulage drifts. For drilling a ten-foot hole, one and one quarter-inch round drill rods three, six, nine and ten and one-half foot long were used. Thirty-one holes were drilled per drift round to advance the heading nine to ten feet.

Scram drifts were driven from platforms on a slight grade for drainage. A raise was driven about fifty feet inside each scram drift to 1950 Level, a vertical distance of 150 feet. The raise followed the ore wherever possible. Long raises, six by eight feet in cross section, were usually forty-five to fifty-five degrees from horizontal and approximately two hundred feet long. Raise drilling was a tough job physically. It was a single shift operation, and a long raise usually required four to six weeks to complete. Our development drillers in the 1960's averaged over thirty-five years in age and very few were willing to drive long raises.

Heading advance in a raise was about eight feet per blast. The driller had to climb up the raise to the heading, attach a rope to his safety belt, scale down loose rock or ore, wash down and examine the heading for misfired holes, prepare a setup for his stoper drill, and add air and water piping as needed. He then drilled nineteen nine-foot holes, removed equipment to a side round, carried blasting powder and fuse up the raise to the heading, loaded and blasted the round at the end of the shift.

From the completed raise at fifty and one hundred feet above the scram drift, sublevels were driven 9' x 9' along the footwall of the ore by two-man drill crews using column mounted Ingersoll-Rand three-inch bore drifter drills with power feed. To advance the heading nine feet per day, twenty-six holes were drilled and loaded with 250 pounds of 40 percent gelatin dynamite. Cap and fuse initiated the blast.

For cleaning sublevels a slusher hoist was mounted at the raise and a scraper drag pulled the broken ore to the raise where it fell to the scram drift below. Cleanup was done on the night shift by a two-man crew who ordinarily cleaned more than one heading. They scaled loose material from the roof and sidewalls and fired any misfired holes. Access to sublevels was usually from the level above by a ladderway. Compressed air, water and power lines were installed in the raise from the level above. Sublevel development crews were paid above the guaranteed rate on the basis of footage advance during the weekly pay period.

The length of a scram drift for loading ore to cars was normally two hundred feet. From the scram drift six or seven short 6' by 8' raises were driven along the footwall at fifty degrees to about twenty-five feet above the scram drift toward the first or lower sublevel. These were widened or belled out above the opening to a funnel shape. The last 6' x 8' raise, near the heading of the scram drift, was driven to the lower or undercut sublevel and continued up to the upper mining sublevel. This raise became a stope starting raise for mining.

From the stope starting raise at the undercut sublevel, long holes were drilled according to a sketch pattern provided by the mining engineers. The pattern consisted of parallel rings spaced four feet apart. They were drilled fanlike from the sublevel to the limit of the ore from horizontal down to complete the belling that was started in the short raises. As this drilling was blasted and retreated along the undercut sublevel, the area below the undercut sublevel was opened so that ore mined from the mining sublevel would fall to the scram drift through the short raises.

After long hole mining on the undercut sublevel had retreated about fifty feet, mining was started at the stope starting raise on the upper or mining sublevel. Here parallel rings of holes spaced at four feet were drilled in ore to the stope ore-rock contact, or to a length determined by the mining engineers. The stope starting raise was opened up to a slot the width of the ore. As each ring was blasted, a slice of the ore fell to the belled out raises feeding the scram drift. Ring drilling on both sublevels was kept well in advance of blasting so that blasting could be done as required without removing drilling equipment.

For long hole stope mining we used Gardner-Denver DH-99 and D-123 drills with four-foot power feed shells. Four-foot sectional drill rods, couplings, shanks and tungsten carbide cross bits supplied by Ingersoll-Rand were used with the long hole drills. The bits were sharpened daily in the surface drill shop. Drilling with this equipment was most efficient if holes in ring drill patterns were fifty feet long or less. Within the ring the ends of the holes were spaced four feet. In some instances holes one hundred feet long were drilled with the D-123 drill.

Long holes in ringhole stope mining were loaded with 1½" x 24" sticks of 40 percent gelatin dynamite with primacord running the full length of each hole. Primer cartridge with a millisecond delay electric blasting cap was placed eight to ten feet from the collar of each hole. The explosive primacord would carry the detonating force the full length of the hole. The blast was wired for proper detonation sequence and all circuits carefully tested before connecting to the power source. Magnetite iron ore is conductive, and extreme care was taken to test for stray currents. All electrical equipment was continuously checked for proper grounding. Large blasts in long hole drill stopes were usually fired on weekends.

Blasted ore, properly fragmented, fell to the finger raises and flowed to the scram drifts without serious problems. Large chunks blocking the flow at the mouth of the finger raises were either drilled at the finger raises or blasted by an explosive charge fastened to a long pole and placed against the hang-up. Occasionally, large hang-ups of ore or rock that had peeled from the stope walls with the blast could not be broken in this manner. After examination by the miners and foremen, a ladder would be put up in the finger raise and the chunks drilled up in the stope and blasted down. This was extremely dangerous and the work was done by highly skilled roofmen.

We were fortunate to have available technical expertise and service from equipment and explosive suppliers. Mineville was a proving ground for mining equipment and Republic was willing to try anything that would improve production and cost.

We had one hundred fifty Ingersoll-Rand slusher hoists for underground and surface scraper loading operations. At the time the mine ceased operation many of these units had been in service over twenty-five years. In later years we tried some new larger units from manufacturers including Ingersoll-Rand, but found that none performed as well as the fifty H.P. units we had in service.

The stoper drill was a feed leg type drill ideal for driving steep raises. The Gardner-Denver R-91 model had been used at Lyon Mountain and later at Mineville. Over a period of time, following trials in the hard rock raises at Mineville, Gardner-Denver designed the greatly improved Model R-94 stoper drill.

At the start of long hole stope drilling at Mineville in the 1940's, Chicago Pneumatic diamond drills were used. However, for increased long hole drilling efficiency, Models DH-99 and D-123 percussion drills, developed by Gardner-Denver, became the choice over other drills for ringhole drilling. The drill was mounted on a column bar and operated by a driller and helper. The two-man crew drilled between 200 and 300 feet per shift. In the late 1950's and early 1960's we had as many as thirty-six long hole drillers, each with a helper, in Harmony and Old Bed Mines.

Air-operated shovel loaders for cleaning development drift headings were purchased from the Eimco Corporation. The Eimco Model 21 shovel used back in the 1940's to clean drifts at Mineville featured a bucket with rocker arms attached that rocked back and forth on a flat deck to throw the muck back over the shovel to an attached mine car. The operator stood on a stand at the side of the machine and from there controlled the forward and back travel, and digging, raising and dumping of the bucket. The hose, furnishing compressed air to operate the shovel, was connected from an air line on the side of the drift to the operating side of the shovel. The hose was long enough to permit the shovel, with a coupled mine car, to move forward and backward. A shovel helper tended the hose and changed the loaded car for an empty car as needed. Operating an Eimco 21 shovel was somewhat like riding a bucking bronco and required considerable skill. The Model 21 shovel was not manufactured beyond the mid-1950's, but used machines were in demand by some small mines, even in the 1970's. In the late 1940's Eimco, using the same concept, developed the Model 40 with a larger bucket and an attached conveyor for better car loading.

I understand the Eimco shovel rocker arm concept was originally conceived by a hoistman at one of the Michigan mines. He had been a hand mucker for some years before becoming a hoistman and remembered the hard physical labor, using a short handle shovel to load the required number of cars for a day's pay.

APPENDIX DD

Introduction and Successful Operation of Raise Boring

We observed two new prototype raise boring machines operating in northern Michigan mines. One machine, more suitable to our operation, was designed to bore an 8-5/8" diameter pilot hole down from the machine to a lower level. The bit was then removed, and a 40" diameter reamer attached to the drill string for reaming the bore hole back up to the machine. Tungsten carbide insert roller cone bits were used for boring the pilot hole, and tungsten carbide insert roller cutters were installed on the reamer for reaming the pilot hole to a 40" diameter size.

Both raise boring machines observed were designed to bore and ream steep raises in the range of seventy-five to ninety degrees from horizontal. Flatter angle raises thirty-five degrees and above from horizontal were required for the Mineville mining layout. Additionally, rock bored in the Michigan mines was of lower compressive strength than the hard granite Mineville rock. Feasibility studies were done, with laboratory compressive strength and boring tests on Mineville rock and ore samples. Machine capability for boring fairly flat raises was reviewed with the James Robbins Company. Pilot bit and reamer cutter performance was projected by Hughes Tool Company and Dresser Industries.

In 1965 six raises were bored in Old Bed-Harmony Mines using a Model 41-R Robbins raise boring machine on a contract basis by Bowden-Cannon Company of Hibbing, Minnesota. The raises were drilled down and reamed up, and were from 157 to 173 feet in length for a total of 1,030 feet. Boring angle of the raises ranged from 45 to 70 degrees from horizontal. The pilot holes were 8-5/8" in diameter and all six raises were reamed to 48" diameter.

Evaluation of the raises bored resulted in Republic purchasing a Robbins raise boring machine and accessories in 1966. From November 1966 through July 1971, twenty-two four and five-foot-diameter raises were bored in varying lengths for a total of 4,990 feet. Boring angle of the twenty-two raises ranged from 26 to 84 degrees from horizontal. This was the first time raises flatter than

75 degrees from horizontal had ever been bored. The pilot hole penetration rate averaged 9.18 feet per hour and the reaming rate 2.35 feet per hour.

APPENDIX EE

Introduction of Trackless Mining to Replace Scraper Scram Drifts to Improve Explosives Practice

While mechanical improvements for driving drifts and long raises were being installed, the 2100 Level mining plan was reviewed for application of trackless loaders to replace scram drift scraper operations. A large, undeveloped section of 2100 Level was selected for trackless mining. If successful, this method would be adopted for future mine levels.

Trackless mining was successful in many domestic and foreign underground metal mines. The coal mining industry had been years ahead of metal mines applying trackless mining with special equipment designed for their operations. In the 1960's mining equipment companies developed load-haul-dump machines particularly suited to underground metal mines. All featured rubber tire traction, diesel water or air cooled engines, short turning radius, and were capable of picking up and transporting a large load several hundred feet to a dumping point. Republic purchased an Eimco 916 load-haul-dump machine, the first of that model placed in a producing mine. Molten Engineering Company designed and built for Republic a diesel-driven rubber-tired jumbo, equipped with Ingersoll-Rand D-475 drills, hydraulic booms and controls as on the rail jumbo.

Trackless haulage drifts, nine feet high by thirteen feet wide, were started at three locations where rail haulage crosscut drifts reached the undeveloped ore. Unlike scraper scram drifts driven eight feet above the track level, trackless drifts were driven at rail track level in the hanging wall rock. Short stub drifts, spaced about forty feet, were angled thirty to forty degrees from the trackless drift and driven to the ore. Finger raises and undercut and mining sublevels above the stub drift draw points were as described for conventional scram drift mining. However, the openings at the draw points were designed larger for free flow of ore with less hang-ups.

To speed up development in the trackless mining section of 2100 Level a second Eimco 916 loader, an improved Eimco 915 loader and a smaller Eimco 912 loader were purchased. Molten Engineering Company designed and built a trackless single boom drill jumbo with an extendable boom, an air compressor for the drill and a water tank for wet drilling. This unit was for drilling to blast large chunks at the draw points or, with the extendable boom, drilling chunks that blocked the opening above. This self-contained unit required no air or water lines along the loader drifts. The operator ran the drill from the roof-protected cab. This was a great safety feature for drilling chunks and hang-ups.

To install and service the jumbos and loaders, two large shops were built on 2100 Level, one near No. 9 Slope and the other in the trackless equipment operating area. The five-cubic-yard loaders and the jumbos had to be dismantled on surface and reassembled on 2100 Level. They were assembled in the service shop near No. 9 Slope, then driven through the rail haulage drift to the trackless area. A diesel oil storage tank station with a containment wall was built near the loader operating area. Special tanks were fabricated for transporting diesel oil from surface to 2100 Level.

Development drift and stope tonnage in the trackless mining areas was hauled to the rail drift crosscuts and dumped into ten-ton capacity mine cars. The cars were coupled to an electric trolley locomotive as a ten-car train and hauled 4,000 feet through 2100 Level to No. 9 ore hoisting slope storage pocket.

Trackless drilling and loader occupations were non-incentive. The equipment operators filed grievances, contending that these jobs should be paid an incentive as were scraper loading and other drilling occupations. The company denied the grievances as the equipment and its use was a new revised mining method at Mineville. The grievances were processed through the various steps of the labor agreement to arbitration. Following arbitration hearings held in Syracuse, the arbitrator came to Mineville and visited the underground operations accompanied by union and company personnel. In the arbitration decision the company position was sustained. These incentive grievances were the first in many years that were taken to arbitration. All other grievances were amicably settled at the local level.

Long hole stope drilling, with parallel rings spaced at four feet and the ends of holes within each ring spaced at four feet, gave good fragmentation when blasted. Ingersoll-Rand tungsten-carbide-tipped two-inch-diameter cross bits, used for several years in long hole stope drilling, were replaced by two-inch button bits. These bits featured six tungsten-carbide buttons on the face of the bit. With thirty to thirty-six ring hole drills operating, cross bits were returned each day to the surface shop for re-sharpening. Button bits did not require re-sharpening. Introduction of button bits in ring hole and development drilling reduced drill shop labor cost. For the operating period 1961 through 1971 there were 1,037.3 miles of ring hole drilling completed. This produced 1.41 gross tons of crude ore per foot of hole drilled. For each drill bit expended, 917 feet were drilled.

Local design and fabrication of a two-drill skid-mounted ring hole jumbo permitted the elimination of the majority of ring hole drill helpers. Mounted drills on the jumbo were spaced so that each driller could complete a ring pattern. A single movement of the jumbo positioned the two drills for drilling two new parallel rings.

Explosives practice was updated for improved safety and cost. Electric blasting was discontinued at Mineville primarily due to possible stray electric currents in the conductive iron ore body. Non-electric fast delay Ledcore blasting caps, developed by DuPont Company, became a replacement for fast delay electric caps in ring hole blasting. Introduction of ammonium nitrate pre-mixed prills (ANFO) in stope blasting sharply reduced use of the higher cost dynamite.

For loading long drill holes, primacord was used the full length of the hole with one stick of dynamite placed at the bottom of the hole. As the hole was loaded with ammonium nitrate prills, a stick of dynamite was placed at every twenty feet of the hole. A Ledcore cap in a primer cartridge was placed several feet below the collar of the drill hole. All Ledcore caps were connected to primacord trunk lines and each series so connected was fired by a No. 6 blasting cap and fuse.

Long hole blasting using ammonium nitrate and non-electric blasting caps was immediately successful. The first large single blast using those materials included a section in 1185-28 stope and a floor pillar on 1035 Level in Harmony Mine. The blast consisted of 330 holes with Ledcore millisecond delays, 11,000 pounds of ANFO prills, 3,750 pounds of gelatin dynamite and 8,000 feet of primacord. Fragmentation was good with no missed or cut off holes.

Ammonium nitrate (ANFO) was tried in all blasting locations. ANFO, placed in a plastic bag with a small stick of dynamite fastened to primacord, and all tied to a long pole, was successful in blasting down hang-ups in finger raises. After the charge was placed, a capped fuse was attached to the end of the primacord at a safe position away from the finger raise.

Trials of ANFO in development drifts, sublevels and raises were not efficient. Although fragmentation in development headings was good, loading holes with ANFO required more time than using twenty-four-inch-long sticks of gelatin dynamite. A development heading had to be blasted at the end of each drill shift. Travel time to and from development sections consumed about 25 percent of the work shift, leaving no extra time for loading ANFO explosives.

In secondary blasting of stope and development chunks too large for a scraper or a loader bucket to handle, a short block hole was drilled in the chunk. Blasting was with a partial stick of dynamite, initiated by cap and fuse.

Total explosives used for all development and stope mining averaged 0.96 pounds per ton of crude ore hoisted. Ammonium nitrate was far less costly than dynamite and by 1971 was 26 percent of total explosives used.

APPENDIX FF

Underground Development Including Tunnel Boring, 1967

Underground development at Mineville during the 1960's was to keep the mine operating pending Republic's approval for sinking a 4,800-foot vertical shaft from surface with overland conveyor ore haulage to No. 7 Concentrating Mill. This proposed installation would permit economic mining of the main Old Bed ore structure to its known limits. Concurrent underground development of new mining areas below 2100 Level would place the new hoisting and conveyor system in full production when completed. For some distance below and south of 2100 Level ore had been definitely proved and its configuration known. There were no facilities for handling ore from below 2100 Level. Extending No. 9 Slope with long crosscut drifting to the ore was not feasible as it would increase hoisting distance and further reduce productive capacity.

The plan for immediate development below 2100 Level was to sink a decline slope or winze at the ore-rock contact of the anticline thick fold of ore which had been exposed by 2100 Level development drifting. The completed winze would furnish access for geological study and for beginning development of minus 2250 and 2400 mine levels. These two mine levels could then be fully developed for mining during the two to three years required for completion of the shaft sinking program.

The down plunge of the ore was under thirty degrees. Rather than conventional drilling and blasting, a ten-foot-diameter slope would be bored, using a tunnel boring machine. Selecting this method was based on the proven success of raise boring at Mineville, and our observation of a Jarva machine boring an eight-foot-diameter tunnel for the Mississippi Pollution Abatement Project at St. Louis, Missouri. However, the St. Louis tunnel was bored slightly above level grade. The structure bored was a thin-bedded limestone with chert strata and occasional zones of heavy lamination. Compressive strength of the rock ranged from 12,000 to 15,000 pounds per square inch.

A decline slope had never been bored with a tunnel boring machine and the structure to be bored at Mineville might have rock intrusions in the ore. Compressive strength of ore and lean ore ranged from 6,500 to 26,400 pounds per square inch. Horneblende biotite and granitic gneiss rocks ranged from 12,600 to 43,000 pounds per square inch. Boring capabilities were discussed with engineers from Reed International of Houston, Texas. The ten-foot-diameter decline slope was to be twenty-six and one-half degrees below horizontal.

A Jarva ten-foot-diameter tunnel boring machine built by S. & M. Constructors of Cleveland, Ohio was leased by Republic. The machine had a thrust or push force of 693,000 pounds, drive power by four 100 H.P. motors, 21 cutters on the 9 r.p.m. boring head, and a hydraulic system with a 40 H.P., 32 g.p.m. pump set at 2,000 pounds maximum pressure. Power supply was 3-phase, 440-volt.

Prior to arrival of the tunnel borer, hoist room and skip dump areas were prepared, and a single drum hoist installed. At the collar area of the bored slope a ten and one-half foot diameter circular section, sixteen feet long, declined to the grade of the winze, was excavated by the drill and blast method to provide a uniform circular section for starting the boring operation. The machine arrived disassembled in four tractor trailer trucks; was assembled without the cutter head in the main underground shop on 2100 Level; and transported on dollies to the bored slope location. Here the cutter head was installed and the machine maneuvered into boring position.

Boring was started on April 25, 1967 and advanced 28 feet to make room for installing track, a skip dump, a muck skip and a trailing conveyor attached to the borer for loading the skip. With these muck handling facilities in place, boring was resumed on May 25, and through June 30 the slope heading was advanced 227 feet completely in ore. Steel-tooth cutters were used for boring in a full heading of ore. Penetration rate averaged 2.38 feet per machine operating hour. The work force for boring on each operating shift included one foreman, two machine operators, one supplyman and one hoistman.

The mine was idle for employee vacations during July. Boring was resumed August 1 and the heading remained in ore to 290 feet of bored distance. For the remaining distance bored the machine encountered horneblende biotite gneiss and granitic gneiss with intermittent contacts and streaks of ore adjacent to the major ore structure. With the appearance of rock at the heading, steel tooth cutters were no longer effective. Roller cutters with tungsten carbide inserts, which had proved successful in the raise boring program, were best suited for tunnel boring in the hard rocks.

From August 1 through November 20 the slope was advanced 512 feet through headings of ore, ore and rock, and rock. The penetration rate varied from 1.04 to 2.04 and averaged 1.38 feet per hour. In this area of the slope, rock intrusions generated loose ground at the rock contacts in the roof. Screen plate was roof bolted in the arch to stabilize the roof. If the slope had been driven conventionally by drill and blast, the ground would have been fractured by blasting and costly heavy steel and timber support would have been required.

The angle of the bored slope was minus twenty-six and one-half degrees, with the heading face sixty-three and one-half degrees. This caused fine bored cuttings to adhere to the face and impede boring. Spring-loaded belt scrapers were installed ahead of the cutter rotation which greatly improved cutter performance. Dust generated by boring was controlled by forced fan ventilation and sprays of water with detergent.

Following the end of boring on November 20 the machine cutter head was disconnected from the machine at the heading and the borer backed up the slope to 2100 Level. The cutter head was disassembled at the heading and brought to 2100 Level. The boring machine was transported on dollies to the main shop near No. 9 Auxiliary Slope where it was disassembled and brought to surface for return to S. & M. Constructors. Removing the machine from the slope was hazardous and the work was accomplished without injury. For the entire winze boring operation there were no personal injury lost time accidents. Boring statistics were as follows:

Feet bored	767.8
Penetration hours	495.1
Penetration rate - ft./hr.	1.55
Cutters expended	137
Ft. bored per expended cutter	5.60

The winze had been bored to the minus 2,450 elevation and would furnish access to begin development of two additional mine levels. Following removal of the tunnel borer, a ring of diamond drill holes was drilled from the heading of the winze to confirm geological projections of the ore structure.

Four years earlier, in September 1963, Republic's chairman and chief executive officer, T. F. Patton, Charles Dewey and Bill Coghill toured Old Bed Mine with Bill Blomstran and me. Mr. Patton seemed impressed with the mining operations, and we were confident our project would be approved. During the early 1960's Harry Allen, Republic's vice president, visited the district on several occasions and supported our plans for new facilities. However, during these years Republic's chief geologist, E. Fitzhugh, would not agree with the ore reserve figures calculated by our local mining engineers. This was a major stumbling block in getting approval for a new shaft.

Following completion of the bored slope an engineering group from Republic's Cleveland office came to Mineville to review the proposed shaft project. Alternative plans to a new shaft from surface were discussed. One plan featured a long decline slope from the bottom of minus 1185 Level southward to eliminate No. 9 hoisting slope and 1185 ore transfer. The proposed slope would service new lower mine levels. Another plan would extend minus 1185 Harmony haulage drift to the south and from there sink a vertical hoisting shaft to the proposed new mine levels. We made force studies and cost estimates for the various plans but, in final analysis, all agreed our original plan for a new shaft from surface with ore conveyor transportation to the concentrating mill was the most productive and cost effective.

As Harmony mining was depleted on levels 1185 and above, Harmony ore was mined on 1335 and lower levels with the ore handled through No. 9 hoisting slope, and mixed with Old Bed ore. After 1964, the mixed crude ore was milled and the shipping product called Port Henry Concentrates and Port Henry Sinter. Maintaining good crude ore costs became difficult due to the limited hoisting capacity of No. 9 Slope.

After completing the bored slope, and with no commitment for a new shaft from surface, it was vital we develop mining areas below 2100 Level and haul the ore through 2100 Level to No. 9 slope if the mine was to remain in production. A trackless spiral decline ramp was started from the loader drift area down to develop the mining and undercut sublevels in ore for 2250 Level. A skip loading station platform was built on 2250 Level at the bored slope. Drift headings were started and a raise was bored from 2100 Level to 2250 Level for ventilation. An ore hoisting plan for balanced hoisting from 2250 and 2400 Levels to 2100 Level through two bored raises was designed. These measures were to provide increased development ore tonnage to augment the dwindling supply of crude ore as upper levels were mined out.

APPENDIX GG

Reserve Mining Company Ordered Shutdown, April 20, 1974

One of Republic Steel's main sources of iron ore for its blast furnaces was its fifty percent ownership of Reserve Mining Company which produced taconite iron ore pellets at Silver Bay, Minnesota. Taconite iron ore, mined and primary crushed inland at Babbitt, Minnesota, was rail hauled forty-seven miles to the concentrating and pelletizing facilities at Silver Bay on the shore of Lake Superior. Waste tailings from the concentrating process were dumped into a very deep trench in the lake. Design of the system for discharging tailings into the lake had been approved by federal and state agencies. Placed in operation in 1950, the Silver Bay Plant had furnished several million tons of iron ore pellets per year to Republic Steel and Armco Steel Company blast furnaces. In producing these iron ore pellets, about 67,000 tons of waste concentrate tailings were dumped into Lake Superior each day.

In response to actions through the legal process by environmentalists and others against dumping tailings in the lake, U.S. District Court Judge Miles Lord ordered Reserve Mining's plant at Silver Bay shut down on April 20, 1974. The Eighth U. S. Circuit Court two days later granted Reserve a stay of Judge Lord's order. The stay order was further extended to allow Reserve to continue to operate while developing a suitable on-land plan for tailings disposal. The major claim against Reserve cited "asbestos like" fibers were polluting lake water which was a source of drinking water for populated areas contiguous to the lake. Soon, however, the word "like" was dropped by supporters of Judge Lord's decision. Extensive laboratory tests and studies by several sources could not validate existence of a health hazard due to the Reserve tailings.

APPENDIX HH

Dismantlement of Mineville Plant and Equipment

Without a plan for new development at Mineville, the Fisher Hill equipment retained for possible use was no longer required. Mesaba Service and Supply Company purchased the double drum Nordberg ore hoist for $300,000. The Nordberg single drum man and material hoist was sold for $75,000. Mesaba also purchased for $200,000 the 48 x 60-inch primary jaw crusher and the equipment in the Fisher Hill crushing plant building. Republic sold the raise boring equipment at Mineville for $90,000. Trackless loaders and drilling equipment were sold or transferred to other Republic Steel plants or mines.

Mesaba Service and Supply Company, the successful bidder, purchased for $518,000 the plant structures to be demolished; surface and underground supplies and equipment; surface yard rail tracks at Mineville; railroad cars at Mineville and No. 7 Plant; and the main line railroad track material from the Mineville Plant to the dumping trestle at No. 7 Plant. Mesaba also purchased from Republic the Fisher Hill hoist and crushing plant buildings with their land parcel to be used as a storage area for salvaged equipment and supplies. Control of the mine plant and pumping passed from Republic to Mesaba on June 1, 1979.

In July 1979 a $212,000 contract for sealing Republic's idle land mine openings was awarded to A. P. Reale and Sons. These openings included Cook, O'Neil, Welch, Brinsmade, Clonan, Harmony "B" and Thoman Shafts; also other surface openings to Miller Pit, New Bed and Pilfershire Mines. In Clonan and O'Neil vertical shafts, steel and reinforced concrete bulkheads were built in the shafts and the area backfilled to surface grade. Several openings were filled with rubble, some were covered with steel beam and plate bulkheads and covered with sand. Bonanza Shaft, located adjacent to the Mineville-Witherbee highway and bulkheaded and filled many years earlier, was covered at surface with a reinforced concrete pad. At a cost of $40,000 a chain-link fence, with steel posts set in concrete and the fence topped with three strands of barbed wire, was built around the "21" Open Pit. Razing Clonan Shaft headframe was part of the Mesaba contract. However, as Reale was to seal this 1,132-foot vertical shaft, Mesaba sublet dismantling the headframe to Reale.

Clonan Shaft headframe stood one hundred feet high near a bend in the highway between Mineville and Witherbee. Erected in 1909, it was steel framed, covered with corrugated sheeting and had the dramatic canted architectural style of turn of the century Iron Country headframes. Of all the plant buildings to be demolished, I regretted the destruction of Clonan Shaft headframe as it symbolized the town. However, for reasons of safety and maintenance costs, it could not remain.

The timbered Clonan Shaft sunk from surface, reached bedrock at 90 feet, and from bedrock to surface it was lined with concrete. No drawings of the concrete lining were available, but test drill holes showed the walls three to four feet thick. The concrete was extremely hard. Twenty-five to thirty feet below surface Reale's crew cut a slot in the two opposite long concrete walls. Heavy steel beams were placed across the shaft in the slots, then covered with steel plate. This steel bulkhead was covered with one foot of concrete with rebars, the concrete extending around the beam ends in the sidewall slots. The shaft was backfilled with sand and rubble to level grade at surface.

By the end of December 1979 Mesaba had completed recovery of material and equipment from mine levels below 1185 Level. The lower levels were being flooded and the flood water was above the entrance to 2100 Level. No. 9 Slope ore hoist and No. 9 Auxiliary Slope man hoist on 1185 Level were dismantled and removed to surface. Republic had Mesaba recover Don B shaft rails from surface down to plus 26 Level for shipment to Republic's Buffalo Plant. In Don B Shaft 10,000 feet of rails were left in place from plus 26 Level down to the shaft heading. Pumps on plus 200 and No. 7 Levels were removed and all power to underground was disconnected in April 1980. In that same month Don B Shaft was sealed with a steel bulkhead, built in the concrete-lined section thirty feet below surface, and the shaft backfilled with sand and rubble to surface grade.

Mesaba removed the Don B Shaft Nordberg double drum surface hoist and razed the hoist building. Crushing plant, storehouse, No. 5 Mill, ore bins, garage, and other surface structures were demolished, and the area graded. The only plant structure remaining was Harmony Change House building. That building and plot of land were donated by Republic Steel to the Essex County Chapter of the New York State Association for Retarded Children, Inc. The A.R.C. later sold the property to a private individual.

APPENDIX II

Operating Personnel, Republic Steel Mineville Operations, 1938-1971

District Managers: T.F. Myners, J.R. Linney, R.J. Linney, W.J. Linney, F.J. Myers, W.A. Blomstran

Assistant District Managers: A.C. Hansen, R.J. Linney, F.J. Myers

Chief Engineers: J.J. Jacka, A.H. Engel, L.C. Henry, A.K. McClennan, Jr., E. Knox

Chief Mining Engineer: W.A. Blomstran

Mining Engineers: F.S. LaMountain, R.E. Mulholland, A.F. Hughes, J.T. Finkbeiner, L. Pullen, E. Sullivan, C.M. Baker, P.F. Farrell, W.A. Gray, G. Bushey, H. Butterfield

Geologist: F. Blackwell

Industrial Engineers: W.H. Coghill, J.R. Scott, T.E. Kirch, F. Robinson, W.A. Gray

Mine Superintendents: F. Kane, J.R. Brennan, Sr., J.R. Murphy, P.F. Farrell

Assistant Mine Superintendents: C.H. Dewey, H.S. Berube, P.F. Farrell, F.W. Robinson

Crushing Plant Superintendents: T. Catanzarita, W. Hunt

Concentrating Mill and Sinter Plant Superintendents: F.J. Myers, L. Dufrane, T. Catanzarita, J.R. Scott, P.W. Gebo, J. Tolosky, Jr.

Laboratory Chief Chemists: H. Gehret, R. Tindula, J.J. Jacka, B.B. Vetter, F.T. Corbo

Hospital Physicians and Surgeons: Doctors T.J. Cummins, J. Glavin, O. Greene, C. Moisan

L.C. and M. Railroad Superintendents: E.J. Greenwood, J.R. Murphy

Surface Labor and Mobile Equipment: F.W. Waite, L. Burhart

Maintenance Superintendents: M.L. Dezendorf, J.R. Brennan, Jr.

Machine and Electric Shops: L.C. Bouchard, C.A. Carlson, L. Dufrane, J.R. Brennan, Jr., W. MacDonough, C. Pattison

District Accountants or Controllers: A.K. McClellan, Sr., G.V. Slater, R.A. Sirrine

Purchasing and Stores: F. Wissing, B. Matrow, A.J. Meacham, E.T. McClellan, P. Stacavich

Industrial Relations and Safety: P.R. Steffe, J.L. Shea, R.F. Munson, W. J. Thiesen, F. Parsons, W. Myers

Glossary

ADIT - A passageway or opening driven into the side of a hill, open on one end to the atmosphere. Similar to a tunnel that is open to the atmosphere on both ends.

ANTICLINE - An arch or fold in the layers of rock shaped like the crest of a wave.

APATITE - A granular mineral, calcium flurophosphate, in varied colors of white, blue, green, brown, etc.

BALL MILL - A piece of milling equipment used to grind ore into small particles. It is a cylindrical-shaped steel container filled with steel balls into which crushed ore is fed. The ball mill is rotated, causing the balls to tumble, thereby grinding the ore.

BEDROCK - Solid rock forming the earth's crust, may be covered with water or over-burden.

BIT - The cutting end of a boring instrument. In rock drilling, it may be forged and sharpened, but is more frequently made with extra-hard material such as tungsten carbide or diamond inserts.

BLACK ROCK - An Adirondack iron miner's term for horneblende biotite gneiss.

BLAST FURNACE - A metallurgical furnace in which mixed charges of iron ore, flux (generally limestone), and fuel are blown with a continuous blast of hot air for the chemical reduction of iron ore into a metallic state.

BONANZA - Very rich ore or situation, as was the Bonanza Mine of Witherbee Sherman Corporation.

BOSH - That part of one of the sloping sides of a blast furnace extending from the belly to the hearth.

BOX HOLE - A short raise or opening driven above a drift for drawing ore from a stope. Also called finger raise.

CAGE - A conveyance to transport men, material and equipment in a mine shaft.

CHANGE HOUSE - A building constructed at a mine where miners change to their working clothes. Also called a dry house.

CHUTE - An inclined opening constructed of steel or timber, covered with steel plate and equipped with a gate through which ore is drawn from a stope into a mine car, or from a shaft storage pocket into a skip.

COFFEE MILL - In this use, a hand mill for grinding minerals to a rather fine, uniform size.

CONCENTRATE - An ore product containing the valuable minerals from which most of the waste material in the ore has been removed.

CONCENTRATING MILL - A plant that produces a concentrate of the valuable minerals in ore. Also called a concentrator.

CROSSCUT - A horizontal opening driven from a mine shaft or winze to an ore structure.

CRUSHER - A machine for crushing ore or rock, as a jaw crusher, gyratory crusher, cone crusher, etc.

CUPOLA FURNACE - A shaft furnace used for melting iron.

DEVELOPMENT - In underground mining, the work involved in opening a mineral deposit or additional mining area. It can include shaft sinking, crosscutting, drifting or raising.

DIAMOND DRILL - A rotary type of drill with the bit set with diamonds and attached to the end of long hollow rods. The bit cuts a core of rock or ore an inch or more in diameter, which is recovered.

DIP - The angle at which an ore or rock structure is declined from the horizontal, as measured at right angle to the strike.

DRIFT - A horizontal, or nearly horizontal passage driven in a mine.

DRUM FILTER - A revolving drum which removes water from fine ground ore in the milling process.

FAULT - A break in the earth's crust caused by forces which moved the rock on one side with respect to the other side.

FEEDER - A machine or device to regulate the flow of material, as ore to a crusher or from a storage bin to a conveyor.

FINGER RAISE - A small opening beneath a stope through which mined ore passes.

FLUX - A substance used in a furnace to react with gangue minerals and liberate them and form slags that float on the molten bath of metal.

FOOTWALL - The wall or rock underneath an ore vein or structure.

GABBRO - A dark, coarse-grained igneous rock.

GANGUE - Worthless minerals associated with valuable minerals in an ore deposit.

GEOPHYSICAL SURVEY - A scientific method of prospecting for minerals, utilizing their physical properties to detect their presence.

GLORY HOLING - Mining around a vertical or steep raise to permit passage of broken ore to a level below.

GNEISS - A metamorphic rock consisting generally of the same components as granite, and many rocks containing feldspar.

GREENAWALT SINTER PLANT - An agglomeration plant for producing iron ore sinter. A mixture of fine iron concentrate and a small amount of fine coal is placed on a pan-type bed and the top ignited. Suction fans draw air down through the mixture, burning off the coal and forming the iron concentrate in a porous mass that makes an iron ore sinter that is an excellent blast furnace feed.

HAND MUCKERS - Miners using hand shovels to load mined ore into a mine car or skip.

HANGING WALL - The wall or rock on the upper side of an ore vein or structure.

HEADFRAME - A structure directly over a mine shaft through which ore mined underground is hoisted to surface.

HEARTH - The lowest part in a blast furnace through which the melted metal flows.

HEMATITE - An iron oxide mineral, a common ore of iron (Fe_2O_3).

HOIST - The machine used for raising or lowering the cage in a mine shaft or winze.

HORSE - A mass of waste rock lying within an ore body.

IGNEOUS ROCKS - Rocks formed from molten material that originated within the earth and became solidified.

ILMENITE - A titanium ore; an iron oxide containing iron and titanium.

JAW CRUSHER - A machine through which ore or rock is broken by the movement of steel jaws. It is usually a primary crusher.

JUMBO - A track or trackless conveyance equipped with rock drill equipment for drilling holes to advance a mining access heading.

LAUNDERS - Chutes or pipes for conveying mixed ore and water to screens or separators in a milling process.

LENTICULAR - A lens-shaped ore structure having the shape of a double convex lens.

LIGHT HOLE - The surface opening through which daylight can be seen from underground in a mine.

LODESTONE - A variety of magnetite that shows polarity and acts like a magnet when freely suspended.

MAGNETIC SEPARATION - A process in which a mineral is separated from gangue material by the attraction of magnets; used to recover iron ore and some other minerals.

MAGNETITE - Magnetic iron ore, a black iron oxide containing 72.4 percent metallic iron when pure.

MARTITE - A crystalline form of hematite iron ore.

MUCK - Ore broken by blasting.

ORE RESERVES - The measured assets of a mine as to grade and tonnage. Usually classified as proven, probable and possible.

ORE TRANSFER DRIFT - A mine haulage drift used for moving mined ore from one section of a mine to another.

OUTCROP - An exposure of rock or a mineral deposit that can be seen on surface, and not covered by overburden or water.

OVERBURDEN - Surface material such as earth, sand or boulders covering the rock surface.

PELLET - A marble-sized ball of iron concentrate roasted in a furnace for hardness.

PERCH - A measure of stone: 1.5' wide by 1.0' high, by 16.5' long = 24.75 cubic feet.

PIG IRON - The molten iron produced in a blast furnace and cast into ingots called pigs.

PILLAR - A block of solid rock or ore left in place to support the roof or sides of a mine.

PLUNGE - Referring to the downward direction of an ore structure.

POCKETS - Excavations above a haulage drift or shaft for holding mined ore to be loaded for transfer or hoisted to surface.

PORTAL HOUSE - A building area adjoining or part of the headframe structure of a mine.

POWDERMAN - A miner assigned to transfer explosives for use in a mine, or to load and blast drilled holes.

PUDDLING - The operation of making wrought iron from pig iron.

PUDDLING FURNACE - A reverberatory furnace for puddling pig iron.

PUG MILL - A device for mixing materials such as sinter fines, iron concentrates and coal for sinter machine feed.

QUICKSILVER - Metallic mercury, widely used in metallurgy, industry and the arts.

RAISE - A vertical or inclined mine working that has been excavated from a lower level upward.

RAISE BORING - Excavating a raise by using a mechanical boring machine rather than by drilling and blasting.

ROD MILL - A rotating cylindrical mill which utilizes steel rods to grind crushed ore fine.

ROOF BOLTING - Anchoring and applying tension to steel bolts in holes drilled for the purpose of supporting or consolidating the roof or walls in a mine.

ROUGHER - In the milling process rougher separators remove some ore from the mill feed, with the remaining passing to finisher separators.

SCRAM DRIFT - A drift driven on or above a haulage level to finger raises beneath a stope.

SCRAPER - A bucket or slusher used to drag mined ore through a scram drift to a loading point.

SCRAPER SCRAM DRIFT METHOD - A means of moving mined ore from finger raises using a double drum electric powered slusher or scraper hoist with wire ropes attached to a scraper bucket to load ore cars for haulage to a storage pocket.

SCREENING - Passing mined or milled ore over screens of varied mesh openings to segregate the ore by size.

SEDIMENTARY ROCKS - Secondary rocks, generally a layered structure formed from rock particles which were laid down under water.

SHAFT - A narrow, vertical or declined excavation into a mine.

SHEAVE WHEEL - A large grooved wheel set in the top of a shaft headframe, over which the hoist rope passes from the hoist to the cage or skip.

SHEAVE TOWERS - Structures, usually steel, with sheave wheels to support the hoisting rope between the hoist and the head sheave in the headframe.

SINTER - Fine iron ore particles heat treated to produce larger porous pieces for blast furnace feed.

SKIP - A self-dumping bucket or car used in a shaft for hoisting ore or rock.

SLAG - A basic iron silicate that floats on the surface of molten iron.

SLASH - Rock or ore blasted from the side of a drift or stope to widen the opening or mine the ore.

SLUSHER HOIST MOTOR - Electric or air powered motors that drive slusher or scraper hoists.

SPAD - A surveyor's pointed nail with a hook or eye on one end for hanging a plumb line.

STOPE - An excavation in a mine from which ore is being or has been mined.

STOPER DRILL - A rock drill powered by compressed air. It has a feed leg that maintains pressure, moving the drill forward as the hole is drilled.

STRIKE - The direction that is the bearing of an ore structure measured on a level surface.

SUB-LEVEL - An intermediate working level in a mine.

SUMP - An underground excavation used to catch water, as at the bottom of a shaft, to be pumped to surface.

SYNCLINE - A down-arched fold or trough in bedded rocks.

TACONITE - A term for a siliceous iron formation, containing iron ores that have to be concentrated to an acceptable grade.

TAILINGS - Reject material from a mill after recovering valuable minerals from the ore.

TIPPLE - An apparatus for dumping loaded ore cars.

TRACKLESS MINING - Using rubber-tired diesel-powered jumbos and load-haul-dump bucket loaders to mine and move ore to transfer trains or loading pockets.

TROMPE - An apparatus that supplies a blast of air, as to a forge, by the action of a thin column of water falling through a large, long tube, and thus carrying air by entanglement.

TUYERE - The pipe through which air is forced into a furnace or forge. Also spelled *twyere.*

TYMP - The stone or the water-cooled iron casting protecting the top of the opening through which molten iron and slag continually pass into the forehearth in an old type open-front blast furnace.

VEIN - A fissure, fault or crack in rock filled by minerals that have traveled upwards from some deep source.

WHIM - An old form of mine hoist, run by horsepower.

WINZE - A vertical or declined opening, similar to a shaft, sunk from a place inside a mine.